IEG | **WORLD BANK GROUP**
INDEPENDENT
EVALUATION GROUP
World Bank • IFC • MIGA

Investment Climate Reforms

AN INDEPENDENT EVALUATION OF WORLD BANK GROUP SUPPORT TO REFORMS OF BUSINESS REGULATIONS

ISBN (paper): 978-1-4648-0628-5
ISBN (electronic): 978-1-4648-0629-2
DOI: 10.1596/978-1-4648-0628-5

Design: Crabtree + Company www.crabtreecompany.com
Cover: © Jorgen McLeman. Used with permission of Jorgen McLeman/Shutterstock. Further permission required for reuse.

Library of Congress Cataloging-in-Publication Data.

Investment climate reforms : an independent evaluation of World Bank Group support to reforms of business regulations.

    pages cm
  Includes bibliographical references and index.
  ISBN 978-1-4648-0628-5 (alk. paper) – ISBN 978-1-4648-0629-2 (alk. paper)

1. Investments, Foreign—Developing countries. 2. Trade regulation—Developing countries. 3. Industrial policy—Developing countries. 4. Economic development—Developing countries. 5. World Bank—Developing countries. I. World Bank, issuing body.
  HG5993.I5945 2015
  332.64'3091724—dc23

                                    2015026850

Contents

Figures

Tables

Abbreviations

ADR	Alternative Dispute Resolution
BICF	Bangladesh Investment Climate Facility
CAS	Country Assistance Strategy
CASCR	Country Assistance Strategy Completion Report
CIC	Investment Climate Practice
DPL	development policy loan
FCS	fragile and conflict-affected situations
FDI	foreign direct investment
FIAS	Foreign Investment Climate Advisory Services
FPD	Finance and Private Sector Development
ICR	Implementation Completion and Results Report
IEG	Independent Evaluation Group
IFC	International Finance Corporation
M&E	monitoring and evaluation
MIGA	Multilateral Investment Guarantee Agency
OPCS	Operations Policy and Country Services
PCR	Project Completion Report
PREM	Poverty Reduction and Economic Management Network
PSD	private sector development
RIA	Regulatory Impact Assessment (Kenya)
SCM	standard cost model
SDN	Social Development Network
SEZ	special economic zone
T&C	Trade and Competitiveness (Global Practice)
WEF	World Economic Forum

Acknowledgments

This evaluation was prepared by an Independent Evaluation Group team led by Giuseppe Iarossi in collaboration with Izlem Yenice. It was carried out under the direction of Marvin Taylor-Dormond (Director) and Stoyan Tenev (Manager) and the overall guidance of Caroline Heider (Director General, Evaluation).

The portfolio analysis was conducted by Jacqueline Andrieu, Samia Ausaf, Francesco Bolognesi, Adrienne Carey, Jose Martin Frech Frech, Houqi Hong, Edna Kallon, Maria Kopyta, Helena Kwang, Laura Moens, Rebecca Riso, Alexandra Solano Rocha, Abishek Saurav, Zhan Shi, Srinath Sinha, Monica Vidili, Khaliun Yadamsuren, and Izlem Yenice.

The country field studies were conducted by Amitava Banerjee, Sidney Edelmann, Giuseppe Iarossi, and Izlem Yenice.

The background papers were written by Elena Bardasi, Joseph Battat, Rebecca Chamberlain-Creanga, George Clarke, Mark Hart, John Kitching, Anders Olofsgard, Andrew Stone, Nickolas Wilson, and Izlem Yenice.

The peer reviewers were M'Hammed Cherif (BizClim), James Habyarimana (Georgetown University), and Dileep Wagle (former World Bank Lead Private Sector Specialist). Additional guidance was provided by Kelly Andrews Johnson, Ana Belen Barbeito, Ann Flanagan, Beata Lenard, Andrew H.W. Stone, and Robert Yin. Finally, useful comments were received by a number of colleagues in the Private Sector, Public Sector, Country and Corporate, and Communication and Strategy units of the Independent Evaluation Group.

Heather Dittbrenner edited the report and Emelda Cudilla provided administrative support and formatted the report. Marylou Kam-Cheong and Rosemarie Pena provided resource management support.

Overview | SUMMARY

Private firms are at the forefront of the development process, providing more than 90percent of jobs, supplying goods and services, and representing a significant source of tax revenues. Their ability to grow, create jobs, and reduce poverty depends critically on a well-functioning investment climate, defined as the policy, legal, and institutional arrangements underpinning the functioning of markets and the level of transaction costs and risks associated with starting, operating, and closing a business. The World Bank Group has been providing extensive support to investment climate reforms—having supported over the period FY07–13 819 projects with investment climate interventions in 119 countries for a total estimated value of $3.7 billion. This evaluation is designed to assess the relevance, effectiveness, and social value as they relate to concerns for inclusion and shared prosperity of World Bank Group support to investment climate reforms.

In this evaluation, the Independent Evaluation Group (IEG) finds that the World Bank Group has supported a comprehensive menu of investment climate reforms. These reforms were generally supported in the right countries and generally addressed the right areas of the regulatory environment. In providing its support, the Bank Group relies on a variety of investment climate diagnostic tools, but their coverage is incomplete.

Intervention and country case analysis shows that, within the limits of the available measures of investment climate indicators, the Bank Group has been successful in improving investment climate in client countries, as measured by number of laws enacted, streamlining of processes and time, or simple cost savings for private firms. However, the impact on investment, jobs, business formation, and growth is not straightforward, and the social value of regulatory reforms—that is, their implications for inclusion and shared prosperity as reflected in effects on a range of stakeholders—has not been properly included in the design of reforms and assessment of their impact. While regulatory reforms need to be designed and implemented with both economic and social costs and benefits in mind, in practice, World Bank Group support focuses predominantly on reducing costs to businesses.

Simplicity of design and good risk assessment play a special role in achieving satisfactory outcomes. Political instability and lack of political commitment remain major problems, limiting the effectiveness of investment climate reforms.

In supporting investment climate reforms, the World Bank and the International Finance Corporation (IFC) use two distinct but complementary business models. Coordination within the World Bank Group on investment climate reforms is higher than in the rest of the Bank Group; but despite the fact that investment climate is the most integrated business unit in the World Bank Group, coordination is mostly informal, relying mainly on personal contacts.

IEG has the following recommendations to the World Bank Group:

Recommendation 1: Expand the coverage of current diagnostic tools and integrate them to produce comparable indicators so that these can capture the areas of the business environment not yet covered by existing tools.

Recommendation 2: Develop a differentiated approach to identify the social effects of regulatory reforms on all groups expected to be affected by them beyond the business community.

Recommendation 3: Ensure that the World Bank Group takes advantage of the complementarity and strengths of the World Bank and IFC business models when designing the new T&C Global Practice. Exploit synergies by ensuring that World Bank and IFC staff improve their understanding of each other's work and business models. Maintain the richness of the two delivery models while addressing factors that discourage collaboration.

Introduction

World Bank Group support to investment climate reforms is an integral part of Bank Group efforts to eliminate extreme poverty and boost shared prosperity. There is a good understanding that broad-based private investment, which is key for inclusive growth and job creation, will only occur when the business environment is favorable. If private firms believe that their investment is not secure, that regulation is too burdensome or unpredictable, or that infrastructure is poor, they will not invest. A good business environment affects firm productivity, which is the foundation for sustained improvements in living standards. Many firm-level studies show that total factor productivity is higher in countries and regions within countries where the business environment is more hospitable.

This evaluation is part of a programmatic series of assessments by IEG of critical aspects of the World Bank Group's support for financial and private sector development (PSD). It aims to assess the extent to which the Bank Group has achieved the goal of helping its client countries improve the investment climate in which firms operate. The evaluation coincides with the establishment of the global practice on trade and competitiveness, which will be the focal point of World Bank Group work on investment climate reforms. The findings and conclusions of this evaluation are thus intended to offer insights into this aspect of the Bank Group change process.

Definition of Investment Climate Interventions

In line with the World Bank Group operations, in this evaluation IEG adopts the definition of investment climate interventions as support for policy, legal, and institutional reforms intended to improve the functioning of markets and reduce transaction costs and risks associated with starting, operating, and closing a business. Within this context, the evaluation covers World Bank Group efforts aiming to promote regulatory reforms to improve the conditions for firms to enter, operate, and exit in both domestic and international markets as well as in key sectors.

Evaluation Design and Methodology

The conceptual framework of the evaluation derives from a combination of theoretical literature and the World Bank Group's strategic priorities and objectives. It starts with the strategic priorities of fostering business creation and growth while taking into account the broad social interests of all stakeholders in society, beyond just businesses. It connects specific areas of intervention—entry, operation, and exit—and, within them, specific topics such as registration, commercial law, and bankruptcy, which represent a good practice standard in business regulations. These interventions are then examined in light of specific indicators of output and outcomes that are directly attributable to them. Finally, these outcomes should be related to a number of economic development goals—including productivity, investment, and employment growth, and greater socioeconomic inclusion. However, because of the complexity and multiplicity of determinants, some well outside the scope of this study, IEG does not quantify this level of impact.

Regulatory reforms affect a wide set of stakeholders in society, not just businesses. Furthermore, not all stakeholders are impacted evenly. Therefore, the framework takes into account the social and distributional aspects of investment climate reforms.

This evaluation includes two units of analysis: interventions (such as regulations for entry, bankruptcy law, and so forth) and client countries. Reforms produce results at the country level and are not implemented in isolation—rather they are the consequence of a sustained and prolonged engagement with the client country. With respect to interventions, this report covers the period FY07–13 and includes in the analysis of performance projects that have been evaluated by IEG. With respect to countries, the report is based on 25 country cases with regulatory reforms within the period FY07–13, as well country visits for a subset of 5 case studies.

World Bank Group Business Models in Investment Climate

In supporting investment climate reforms, the World Bank Group has adopted two distinct business models. IFC's business model is implemented through stand-alone advisory services. They are structured under a set of defined products and tend to form focused, concrete, short-term, and rapid interventions. They are mostly funded through internal budget and trust funds, with some client contribution.

In contrast, the World Bank business model is implemented not only through analytic and advisory activities, but also through lending and budget support. When not funded through loans, advisory services are generally funded through trust funds or reimbursable advisory services.

The World Bank is involved in upstream policy dialogue on PSD and overall economic reforms and supports interventions that tend to have a wider and deeper scope and to be of longer tenure, whereas IFC supports interventions that tend to be standardized and narrowly focused.

The Latin America and the Caribbean Region is an example where investment climate work is jointly managed by the Bank and IFC. This collaboration fostered better client management and more collaborative project development, though at a high administrative cost.

Each business model has its own strengths and weaknesses. A staff survey conducted for the evaluation shows that a small share of staff (6 percent) perceived the difference between the IFC model and the World Bank model only as a positive factor in fostering collaboration. A significant share—30 percent—saw the existence of the two models only as discouraging collaboration. However, the majority of staff—almost 50 percent—saw the differences in the two models as a factor both fostering and hampering collaboration. Hence, if properly understood and taken into account in the change process, these differences might represent an opportunity for collaboration and impact in investment climate work.

Investment Climate Good Practice Standard

IEG developed a good practice standard of regulatory areas. A list of regulatory areas was created based on the top five regulatory environments, according to the World Economic Forum (2013) and Doing Business (2013). This list is taken as a good practice standard of the set of regulatory areas a typical country with the best regulatory environment would have. The list includes 18 regulatory areas.

Further, IEG reviewed evidence of the extent to which the main World Bank Group diagnostic tools cover the good practice areas. About half of the regulatory areas are covered by these diagnostic tools. Interestingly, the areas covered by Doing Business and Enterprise Surveys are those where the Bank Group supports client countries heavily, such as business registration, taxation, and trade. The evidence implies that these two diagnostic tools are only partially relevant in helping the Bank Group identify appropriate areas of intervention.

Investment Climate Portfolio

IEG classified the World Bank Group portfolio by various characteristics, with a special focus on areas identified as priorities in the Bank Group investment climate strategy, such as gender, fragile and conflict affected situations (FCS), and key industries.

PROJECTS AND INTERVENTIONS

Over the period FY07–13, the Bank Group supported 819 projects with multiple investment climate *interventions* (a project may contain several interventions). Of the 819 projects, 476 were from the World Bank and 343 from IFC, for a total estimated value of investment climate interventions of $3.7 billion. Of this, $350 million was from IFC and $3.35 billion from the World Bank. Between 2007 and 2013, the World Bank Group has supported regulatory reforms in 119 countries through nearly 15 types of interventions.

In terms of share of projects, the Poverty Reduction and Economic Management Network, the Sustainable Development Network and Finance and Private Sector Development represent the main networks with investment climate projects. In absolute terms, the Poverty Reduction and Economic Management Network has the highest number of projects with investment climate interventions—often in the context of development policy lending. However, within networks, the Finance and Private Sector Development Network has the highest proportion of network operations with investment climate interventions.

IFC investment climate projects are only advisory, whereas the World Bank includes investment climate components in both lending and budget support operations in approximately equal proportions. In terms of share, one in three development policy operations include investment climate components, while only one in ten lending operations does so.

The Bank Group activities in investment climate can be grouped in three main areas of the business environment: entry, operation, and exit. Within each of these areas, the Bank Group implements a number of different interventions. These interventions aim to simplify and streamline regulatory procedures, remove sector-specific administrative constraints, revise the legal framework and institutions, establish effective dialogue systems between private and public sectors, and harmonize procedures and systems.

It is important to note, however, that although both institutions operate in the same space, the scope of their investment climate interventions is generally different, with some overlap. The World Bank focuses more on higher-level reforms, such as revising and harmonizing laws and codes, reforming institutions, developing strategies, and coordinating government agencies and ministries. IFC, in contrast, mostly focuses on streamlining and simplifying procedures and processes, providing technical assistance, and automating systems.

In formulating solutions, the Bank Group has focused mostly on business operations and business entry, and the solutions varied from specific or limited interventions to comprehensive packages and programmatic approaches covering many different aspects of the investment climate. For example, in the Republic of Yemen and Vietnam the Bank Group focused on business entry and operations and provided a comprehensive solution package. In contrast, in Cambodia the investment climate interventions focused on specific areas such as trade promotion.

Across interventions, licensing, permits, and administrative barriers; trade; and investment promotion account for almost half. There is a "division of labor" among the two institutions. The World Bank does interventions in trade and property rights almost exclusively (over 80 percent of all), as well as the majority of interventions on investment promotion. IFC, in contrast, undertakes more (60 percent) licensing and registration efforts. Both institutions operate equally in licensing/permits/administrative barriers and public-private dialogue.

In terms of value, investment climate interventions are small, particularly for IFC. The average value of one intervention is less than $1 million for IFC and less than $6 million for the World Bank.

On average, investment climate interventions are implemented in less than 3 years (32 months). However, as part of World Bank lending operations, the average length is substantially higher—more than six years. The distribution of investment climate interventions across regions and income levels shows that both the World Bank and IFC intervene mostly in Sub-Saharan Africa (37 percent of all interventions for both institutions) and Europe and Central Asia (24 percent for the World Bank and 17 percent for IFC), followed by the Latin America and the Caribbean Region for the World Bank (17 percent) and the East Asia and Pacific Region for IFC (15 percent).

GENDER AND INCLUSION

Regulations may affect various subgroups differently, and this needs to be taken into account to achieve a level playing field.

The disadvantageous position of women in entrepreneurship has been widely documented. Gender-specific obstacles make it harder for women than for men to start and grow enterprises, and fewer women than men own and manage businesses worldwide.

In the investment climate portfolio, explicit targeting—either based on the entrepreneur or the firm characteristics—is not common. Only 8 percent of all projects specifically targeted women, and a similar percentage targeted firms based on their industry and formality status. Targeting based on proprietor age, geographical area, or export status is even rarer. A review of the investment climate portfolio shows that in 10 percent of cases, no targeting is done when there are legal constraints in the countries that would make investment climate reforms not "gender neutral."

INVESTMENT CLIMATE IN FRAGILE AND CONFLICT-AFFECTED SITUATIONS

Support to PSD in FCS only started to gain attention from policy makers, donors, and nongovernmental organizations in the last decade. Despite this, there is general agreement that building competitive, inclusive markets and businesses is crucial for post-conflict recovery, just as fragile situations present special challenges and opportunities for PSD. There is no clear consensus over the most effective starting point to PSD in FCS. The debate is essentially about sequencing, whether "doing reforms" to improve the investment climate or "doing deals" with targeted enterprises and sectors should come first in a fragile environment.

Experience with and research on PSD in FCS inside and outside the World Bank Group suggest that regulatory and "doing deals" approaches should not be viewed as mutually exclusive, but as complementary in encouraging growth in fragile environments. The 2011 World Development Report also highlights that investment climate reforms and direct interventions are equally important for fragile states.

Overall, 15 percent of investment climate projects are implemented in FCS situations. IFC shows a slightly higher share of such projects than the World Bank. Over time, the number of investment climate projects in FCS has held steady at around 12 per year, with both institutions having seen a fall in the number of projects over the last few years. In terms of intervention, the most common interventions in FCS (accounting for over 50 percent of all) are represented by licensing/permits/administrative barriers, investment promotion, trade, and public-private dialogue.

INVESTMENT CLIMATE FOR SPECIFIC INDUSTRIES

Although some aspects of the investment climate apply to all firms participating in the economy, others are far more specific and can create a "micro" investment climate for firms with particular characteristics, or those in a particular region or sector.

Agribusiness and tourism sectors can be engines for inclusive growth in developing countries and have been identified as key priority sectors in the World Bank Group investment climate strategy (World Bank 2011). In 17 country case studies where sectoral priorities were identified, all included agribusiness or the agriculture sector as key, and 10 included tourism. In 13 of these countries, agriculture and/or tourism growth are identified as priority or strategic objectives, and 9 country strategies connect growth of these sectors with overall economic growth and poverty alleviation.

Investment climate projects with components that focused on agribusiness and/or tourism constitute 18 percent of World Bank and 16 percent of IFC investment climate projects. Whereas the number and value of investment projects in the World Bank does not show a clear trend since the creation of a practice group, the IFC advisory portfolio has expanded in recent years.

Relevance of World Bank Group Operations

IEG assesses the relevance of World Bank Group operations in investment climate at three levels: (i) the strategic level—do corporate and country strategies identify investment climate reforms as a priority? (ii) the intervention level—is the Bank Group offering the right set of investment climate reforms in the right countries? and (iii) the analytical level—do diagnostic tools adequately inform investment climate reforms supported by the World Bank Group?

The World Bank Group strategies related to investment climate reforms intend to enhance competition, foster enterprise creation and growth, facilitate international trade and investment, and unlock sustainable investment opportunities in key sectors, such as agribusiness and tourism.

These strategies aim to reduce time, cost, and procedures and to simplify regulations. In general, the strategies focus on creating favorable market conditions for enterprises and do not take into account their impact on stakeholders in society beyond businesses. In other words, they don't verify or assure that broader social objectives will be protected or enhanced through the reform.

RELEVANCE AT THE STRATEGIC LEVEL

At the corporate level, the most recent Bank Group Strategy (World Bank 2013) acknowledges improving business climate as key to stimulate private sector investment and jobs and to achieve the twin goals of ending extreme poverty and promoting shared prosperity. Similarly, earlier World Bank and IFC corporate strategies made improving the investment climate a strategic pillar of PSD.

At the network level, a number of sectors have identified improving the regulatory environment as a key aspect of their strategy. The 2002 World Bank Group PSD Strategy has the most emphasis on investment climate activities. Other networks' strategies have devoted attention to the policy and regulatory environment. For example, one of the priorities of the World Bank trade strategy is to support regulatory reform and cooperation. The most recent agriculture strategy envisages the expansion of its role in regulatory reforms. Similarly, the most recent energy (2013), environment sector (2012–22), and infrastructure sector (FY12–15) strategies emphasize the importance of strong institutions, legislation, regulation, and enforcement.

In parallel to corporate and sector strategies, regional strategies identify improving the regulatory environment as an area to support. IEG's 25 country case studies show that nearly all Bank Group country partnerships see a lack of competition, barriers to establishing and operating businesses, the cost of doing business, and regulatory burdens as the main business environment constraints. In sum, improving and supporting investment climate reforms is viewed as a priority in Bank Group strategies at various levels. However, it is worth noting that in very few of the countries' own development strategies—such as in Cambodia, Georgia,

Kenya, Liberia, Rwanda, and the Republic of Yemen—were regulatory reforms specifically identified as an important part of the country development strategy.

The World Bank Group offers a broad menu of interventions. Virtually all regulatory areas for a business-friendly regulatory environment are covered by Bank Group interventions.

But is the Bank Group using the right interventions in the right countries? A comparison between the severity of what firms see as obstacles and the intensity of Bank Group interventions shows a high and significant correlation, suggesting that priorities perceived by enterprise managers are broadly in line with interventions by the Bank Group. Furthermore, for each area of the business environment, IEG compared how problematic they were in countries with Bank Group interventions and without interventions. The results indicate that the Bank Group targets the right countries (those with worse initial conditions) in its support of regulatory reforms.

The World Bank Group identifies the regulatory reforms it supports on the basis of stakeholder consultations and diagnostic analysis. IEG's review of 25 country strategies indicates that, at the level of Country Assistance Strategies, the Bank Group generally has a sound consultation process. In India, in fact, notwithstanding the multiplicity and geographical distribution of the stakeholders, the consultation process included client surveys, online consultations, workshops, and targeted meetings. At the diagnostic level, IEG conducted a mapping exercise of the areas covered in the two most commonly used diagnostic tools for regulatory reforms—Doing Business and Enterprise Survey data.

This mapping showed that the use of diagnostic tools was more common in World Bank projects (68 percent). IFC advisory projects relied on diagnostic tools in 47 percent of the projects; IFC relied more on government requests or stakeholder consultations when designing investment climate projects. Historically, IFC's investment climate projects have relied on the Facility for Investment Climate Advisory Services' administrative barriers diagnostic reports. Over time, Doing Business started to become a de facto diagnostic tool for IFC. Among the projects that used a diagnostic tool, the Doing Business report has been used 62 percent of the time in IFC and 20 percent of the time in the design of World Bank investment climate projects.

In sum, the World Bank Group has supported a comprehensive menu of investment climate reforms. IEG analysis indicates that improving and supporting investment climate reforms is viewed as a priority in World Bank Group strategies at various levels. For the interventions with available data, reforms were generally supported in the right countries and generally addressed the right areas of the regulatory environment. Finally, the Bank Group relies on a variety of investment climate diagnostic tools, but the coverage of these tools is incomplete.

Effectiveness of World Bank Group Support to Investment Climate Reforms

Have regulatory reforms supported by the World Bank Group improved the regulatory environment in which businesses operate?

PROJECT AND INTERVENTION OUTCOMES

With respect to project ratings, both World Bank and IFC investment climate projects are as successful as the rest of the portfolio. In the World Bank Group the majority of investment climate projects achieve their development objective (75 percent in the World Bank and 55 percent in IFC). There is a significant degree of variability in the success rate of different interventions.

Beyond ratings, to determine the impact of investment climate interventions, IEG identified 39 investment climate outcome indicators and utilized three approaches to measure results: before and after, propensity score matching, and difference in difference. According to the before and after method, seven of the eight World Bank Group interventions analyzed— with the only exception of investment promotion—show a positive and statistically significant outcome. However, the results of the other two methods are significantly different. While with before and after almost 80 percent of the impact indicators reflected significant and positive changes, this share drops to 30 percent and 60 percent with propensity score and difference in difference methods, respectively. Hence the method of analysis used influences the extent of effectiveness recorded. Simplistic methods such as before and after show a much wider impact than more sophisticated approaches. Using difference in difference, IEG is able to find evidence that—within the limits of available data—all but one intervention—investment promotion—produce positive outcomes.

This conclusion, nevertheless, is qualified by at least four important considerations. First, the great majority of indicators used in the analysis are from Doing Business and present methodological problems that might compromise their reliability. Second, the literature on the impact of regulatory reforms on growth, investment, entry, and jobs is extensive but presents mixed and qualified results. Third, case studies conducted by IEG confirmed that simply achieving improvements in outcome indicators of regulatory indicators does not guarantee an impact on investments. This is the case, for example, of Rwanda compared to Cambodia.

And fourth, a proper assessment of the impact of investment climate interventions must take into account that regulatory reforms should improve outcomes for society as a whole, not only for businesses.

Overall evidence indicates that many regulatory reforms succeeded in simplifying procedures and reducing time and cost; however, the overall impact of these solutions on investments, jobs, and entry at the country level is not straightforward, as the case of Rwanda suggests.

Gender

IEG identified and classified 19 investment climate projects as "gender focused," that is, as having the potential to address constraints that are especially binding for female entrepreneurs. Explicit targeting is limited in the portfolio, but even projects targeting specific groups do not necessarily report results for the group that was targeted. Only 11 of 19 closed projects targeting gender in their design report results by gender.

Nine of 11 projects that IEG reviewed documented positive results for women. As the number of investment climate interventions with gender-relevant targeting (and even more the number of "gender-informed" projects) increases over time, it may be desirable for these projects to include gender-disaggregated indicators. This will allow a comparison of gender results achieved by interventions with explicit gender targeting (and gender-relevant actions) and those obtained by gender-neutral interventions, but with the potential to disproportionately benefit women. With the data currently available, such a comparison cannot be made.

Fragile and Conflict-Affected Situations

The small number of completed and evaluated investment climate projects in FCS suggests that effectiveness in FCS is significantly lower than in non-FCS. Evidence from country cases shows mixed results and indicates the importance of political feasibility, institutional capacity building, and implementation assistance as determinants of performance. For example, the difference in the design and implementation strategy between Sudan and South Sudan led to vastly different results. In Lao PDR, the Bank was cognizant of local capacity limitations and subsequently increased technical assistance during the progression of its budget support operations, leading to positive outcomes.

As highlighted in a recent IEG evaluation (IEG 2013), investment climate reforms are necessary but not sufficient conditions for PSD in FCS.

Industry-Specific Focus

The number of evaluated investment climate industry projects is small; therefore, it is hard to draw general findings. On average, IFC investment climate advisory projects in the agribusiness and tourism sectors are more likely to have positive development outcomes than the general investment climate portfolio (71 percent versus 55 percent). By contrast, World Bank investment climate investment projects in agribusiness and tourism on average are less successful than the general investment climate portfolio (71 percent versus 82 percent). The difference is not statistically significant for either IFC or the World Bank .

Assessing the Social Impacts of Regulatory Reforms

Governments typically implement regulatory reform to correct perceived market failures and improve market efficiency. Improving the social benefits of regulatory reform requires consideration of its impact on a range of important social stakeholders, practices, and institutions—not only businesses. The twin goals of poverty elimination and shared prosperity guiding the new World Bank Strategy demand that regulatory reform be understood in the context of broader social values. In practice, though, diagnostics, reform design, and implementation tend to focus primarily on business costs.

REGULATORY REFORM AND ITS EFFECTS: THEORETICAL FOUNDATIONS

Regulation is often treated in academic and policy discourses as a burden, cost, or constraint on business activity. This is principally because assessments of regulatory reform focus on the real or perceived impact on businesses rather than on the full range of stakeholders whom regulation affects. But regulation is not just a burden on businesses. It performs a necessary function in enabling markets to function and in protecting public health and safety. However, although regulatory reform often generates public goods, not all members of a population are guaranteed to benefit equally, and some may lose out.

APPROACHES TO ASSESSING THE SOCIAL VALUE OF REGULATORY REFORM

Social value means different things to different people. How societies define social value is likely to be influenced by a wide range of factors, including national policies, the level and distribution of wealth, availability of infrastructure, the role of civil society organizations, and demographic factors. Consequently, the appropriate analytical framework to measure this value comprises a theory of change connecting regulatory reform, the actions of businesses, and the wide variety of stakeholders with whom they interact (consumers, suppliers, employees, investors, and others), and a wide range of social value effects. Measuring the benefits and costs of regulatory reform is a difficult task. Various methodologies are available to measure social value, such as the social return on investment, the standard cost model, and regulatory impact assessment.

ANALYSIS OF CROSS-COUNTRY EVIDENCE

IEG reviewed all projects in the investment climate portfolio and identified 108 projects (87 for IFC and 21 for World Bank) with some assessment of social impacts. Some of the findings are as follows: (i) Formal impact assessments are conducted in only a minority of World Bank Group projects with investment climate interventions—about 15 percent of them; (ii) formal assessments do not always refer to all regulatory reforms implemented as part of an intervention; (iii) a large number of projects have no data, especially for the World Bank; (iv) only four in ten IFC evaluations, and three in ten World Bank evaluations, provided any data on the different kinds of social benefit for a variety of stakeholder groups; (v) in only 13 percent of IFC projects and 1 percent of World Bank projects were specific recipients of the social value of regulatory reform identified; and (vi) distributional issues were examined in only seven projects, corresponding to 2 percent of the IFC portfolio and none of the World Bank projects.

In general, projects do not define social value explicitly. There are some indications of a broader notion of social value making reference to environmental, health and safety, and other types of impact, and to nonbusiness stakeholders—but these are generally discussed briefly or do not appear to be fully integrated into the design, implementation, or evaluation of projects. Procedural indicators such as compliance cost savings do not tell us very much about social benefits. Business stakeholders are treated as paramount; nonbusiness stakeholders are barely visible. Moreover, compliance cost savings data are presented as though they are necessarily benefits for all businesses, yet such benefits are likely to be distributed unevenly, because some are better able to exploit regulatory change than others, and this might even generate adverse impacts for some businesses.

Factors Affecting Delivery and Performance

IEG reviewed World Bank Group investment climate projects to shed light on factors that help explain their success or failure. Implementation delays and the onset of a crisis are the most commonly encountered implementation problems in Bank Group investment climate projects. This is in part because political stability plays such an important part in the success of investment climate projects. Because most investment climate work relies on the enactment of laws, regulations, and coordination among different ministries and agencies, a committed and strong government is key to success.

In parallel, IEG's 25 country case studies show that political stability, political commitment, and reform champions are essential for the success of the regulatory reform process. This was the case in Kenya, Nepal, and Rwanda, for example. In Rwanda a high level of commitment enabled it to become one of the top reformers in regulations captured by the Doing Business indicators. In Kenya post-election violence in 2007–08 derailed the investment climate reform program. In addition, Bangladesh shows the importance of both political stability and commitment to sustain the reform process. Similarly, IFC did not have a constant client within the government of Nepal who could consistently champion the investment climate reforms.

Regression analysis shows that three factors under the Bank's control—complexity of design, inadequate risk assessment, and inadequate monitoring and evaluation—and two on the borrower side—borrower performance and crisis—are significant determinants of project effectiveness.

IEG's analysis attempted to identify the complex interactions among the various factors of performance. The results show that first, there are aspects under the control of the World Bank Group that can reduce or eliminate the negative effect of external factors. More specifically, inadequate borrower performance can be alleviated by having a simpler project design, whereas a crisis can be dealt with better if the project does not have a complex design, there is good supervision, and there is a good risk assessment. Second, two aspects of the project implementation—simplicity of design and good risk assessment—can reduce or eliminate most of the implementation problems. Finally, there is one factor for which no aspect of implementation can compensate: inadequate technical design.

FACTORS OF PERFORMANCE IN FRAGILE AND CONFLICT-AFFECTED SITUATIONS

Evidence from country case studies points to the fact that the World Bank Group effectiveness in FCS was contingent on a number of factors. In many FCS, overambitious projects—in terms of scope or timing—led to less than satisfactory results. Institutional capacity building and implementation assistance have been instrumental in determining the success of interventions. Government ownership is also a vital success factor in FCS. And the fragile political economy has, more than elsewhere, a fundamental bearing on the success of investment climate interventions.

FACTORS OF PERFORMANCE IN INDUSTRY-SPECIFIC PROJECTS

A review of project evaluations suggests that three factors are associated with success or failure: counterpart commitment; local capacity and human resource quality; and project complexity. For IFC, agribusiness and tourism investment climate projects are more likely to suffer from technical design issues and less likely to have implementation delays, although this is the leading problem identified for IFC investment climate industry projects. For the World Bank, projects are more likely to have too many components and are less likely to suffer from implementation delays. For Bank projects, monitoring and evaluation is the most common problem.

COLLABORATION ACROSS INSTITUTIONS

With the recent evolution of strategies for investment climate work, the World Bank Group has seen a substantial reorganization in the investment climate space since the mid-2000s. Major organizational change of the investment climate space occurred in FY14. Beginning in July 2014, all investment climate units will operate under the Trade and Competitiveness Global Practice. This global practice will be the most integrated practice in the new World Bank Group structure. In the investment climate portfolio, 33 projects with IEG ratings were characterized as having some form of coordination. Evidence indicates that the higher the degree of collaboration, the higher the probability of achieving the development objectives is. It must be recognized, however, that these findings rely on a small number of observations. Given this limitation, IEG reviewed projects with examples of collaboration to draw additional evidence. This led to the conclusion that successful collaboration rests on complementarity— of roles, of perspective, and of instruments.

IEG's staff survey results show that lighter collaboration is more frequent than deeper collaboration. Overall, half the time collaboration occurs, it refers to simple activities such as information sharing and peer reviewing. Only one-third of the collaboration is deep and involves design and implementation of projects.

The factors that play a role in fostering collaboration can be grouped in three categories: the role of the unit and its strategy; systems or formal organization; and informal organization. IEG's staff survey results point out to the primary role of informal factors in fostering collaboration. In contrast, systems and formal organization are seen as mostly discouraging collaboration, although they present a significant opportunity for changing this perception. Finally, factors related to roles and strategy can foster collaboration if properly handled.

IEG interviews and its survey of World Bank Group investment climate management and staff provide some insights on how to optimize value to clients with the new Global Practice. Most of the staff provided positive feedback, highlighting the complementarity and strengths of the World Bank and IFC business models. However, some concerns exist. The interviews indicate the concern that the merger cannot be a simple juxtaposition of current systems and programs under one roof. From an operational perspective, many staff hope that serious attempts will be made to remove impediments to collaboration found in the formal organization, for example, governance and accountability systems, funding, pricing, human resources policies, and operational systems.

Recommendations

Improving the investment climate has been and remains a key objective of countries in their pursuit of economic growth through PSD. In this evaluation IEG assesses the extent to which the World Bank Group has achieved its goal of helping client countries improve the investment climate in which firms operate. IEG looked at three main aspects of the World Bank Group activities: relevance, effectiveness, and social value of regulatory reforms.

RELEVANCE

At the corporate level and in a number of sectors, improving business climate is seen as key to stimulating private sector investment. At the country level, nearly all World Bank Group country partnership and assistance strategies identify enhancing the business environment as a main objective to foster PSD. However, although country strategies put a significant emphasis on improving the business environment, the client countries' own strategies put much less emphasis on it—only a few counties emphasized the role of investment climate in their vision.

IEG's mapping exercise provides evidence that, generally, World Bank Group interventions support relevant areas, that is, cover the full set of potential regulations of a country with a business-friendly regulatory environment. Using data from the Enterprise Survey, IEG was able to establish that the World Bank Group supports the reforms most needed by client countries and supports regulatory interventions in those countries that need them most.

When looking at the analytical relevance of the most common diagnostic tools used to determine regulatory reforms—Doing Business and Enterprise Surveys—IEG found that these tools do not cover all areas of the regulatory spectrum as identified in the comprehensive list of regulations mentioned earlier. Doing Business and Enterprise Surveys cover only areas—such as business registration, taxation, and trade—where most of the World Bank Group activities take place. Hence, although these diagnostic tools are often relied on to inform country strategies, they are less frequently used to design investment climate projects, especially in IFC.

Recommendation—Expand the coverage of current diagnostic tools and integrate them to produce comparable indicators so that these can capture the areas of the business environment not yet covered by existing tools.

SOCIAL VALUE

Improving the social benefits of regulatory reform requires consideration of its impact on a range of important social stakeholders, practices, and institutions—not only businesses. In practice, though, the discussion focuses only on business costs. Social value is not explicitly defined in World Bank Group projects. Procedural indicators such as compliance cost savings do not tell very much about social benefits. Reforms can have broader social and distributional impacts that go beyond the economic and beyond the effects on business. These effects need to be taken into account in the design and implementation of regulatory reforms.

Recommendation—Develop a differentiated approach to identify the social effects of regulatory reforms on all groups expected to be affected by them beyond the business community. The approach should identify which groups are expected to be affected by the regulatory reform(s) within and beyond the business community, in order to ensure that reforms "do no harm" to people and the environment. The assessment should be differentiated depending on the expected impact of the regulatory reform(s) and may include qualitative or quantitative methods. The approach should be employed both ex ante (during the design of the project) as well as ex post (to assess the achieved impact of the reform).

Such an approach should help better estimate the political economy risk associated with the reform, to identify potential groups that would sustain or oppose reforms and the extent of such support or opposition. The World Bank Group may also consider developing client capacity to conduct social value assessment in order to enable sustainability of investment climate reforms.

COORDINATION ACROSS THE WORLD BANK GROUP

The World Bank and IFC work in the same space and with the same clients through two distinct business models. The IFC business model is implemented through stand-alone advisory services. Projects are based on standardized, focused, short-term, and rapid interventions. They are mostly funded through internal budget and trust funds. The World Bank business model is implemented through lending and budget support and to a lesser extent through technical assistance. These projects are broader in scope and tend to be more long term than IFC projects.

Each model has unique features and stakeholders appreciate their differences. Stakeholders interviewed across countries often appreciated IFC's international technical expertise, quick response and delivery, and close support. However, according to stakeholders, IFC's ability to handle the political economy was not as strong, nor was its ability to move beyond standardized products. The World Bank's main strength is its institutional access to government institutions, its comprehensive services, and its ability to provide substantive funding. Yet there was a common sense that the World Bank is slow to respond and to implement projects.

Interviews with World Bank Group management and staff surveys indicated that there is collaboration among the institutions, to varying degrees. Survey results show that simple activities such as information sharing are more frequent than formal engagements. Different systems and organizational structure are perceived as the main bottlenecks to collaboration.

Recommendation—Ensure that the World Bank Group takes advantage of the complementarity and strengths of World Bank and IFC business models when designing the new Trade and Competitiveness Global Practice. Exploit synergies by ensuring that World Bank and IFC staff improve their understanding of each other's work and business models. Maintain the richness of the two delivery models while addressing factors that discourage collaboration.

References

IEG (Independent Evaluation Group). 2013. *Evaluation of the World Bank Group's Support for Investment Climate Reforms, Approach Paper*. Washington, DC: World Bank.

World Bank. 2011. *Doing Business 2012: Doing Business in a More Transparent World*. Washington DC: World Bank.

———. 2013. *A Stronger, Connected Solutions World Bank Group*. Washington, DC: World Bank.

World Bank Group Management Response

World Bank Group management would like to thank the Independent Evaluation Group (IEG) for undertaking a valuable and informative evaluation and welcomes the opportunity to provide its comments.

Overall Comments

Management acknowledges IEG's thorough, relevant, and comprehensive work to evaluate the World Bank Group's activities in the investment climate space and appreciates the systematic analysis contained in the report. Management recognizes the complexity of this task, given the institutional set-up, with multiple units involved in the World Bank Group work program on investment climate topics, the comprehensiveness of the issues, and the technical sophistication of different reform areas. The complexity of the issue presents significant challenges with regard to assessing the success of the different interventions undertaken during the period covered by IEG's report.

Management would like to underscore the timeliness of the report, given the important organizational changes taking place in the World Bank Group. The IEG report comes at an opportune time and has the potential to inform the future structures and strategies of the various players involved in investment climate activities, and the interactions and complementarities between these players, both within the new Trade and Competitiveness Global Practice as well as between this and other Global Practices and the five Cross-Cutting Solutions Areas. The report provides relevant analysis and observations on past investment climate work that can inform the operations of the Trade and Competitiveness Global Practice.

Management notes that the report is generally positive in its evaluation of the Bank Group's intervention on investment climate reforms. Management agrees with the report that World Bank Group interventions generally support reforms most needed by client countries and support regulatory interventions in those countries that need them most. The assessment demonstrates that the activities analyzed are relevant in a strategic and client-oriented context and shows evidence of positive results and the overall effectiveness of investment climate activities across the World Bank Group. Management appreciates the useful set of lessons and agrees with the recommendations, which it looks forward to implementing.

The World Bank Group Approach to Investment Climate Work

EVOLVING NATURE OF THE WORLD BANK GROUP'S INVESTMENT CLIMATE WORK

Management appreciates the discussion in the report of the evolution of the Bank Group's investment climate work over the years, including considerable innovation and restrategizing. As mentioned in the report, these innovations relate to (i) definition and scope of investment climate; (ii) strategies; (iii) monitoring and evaluation (M&E) frameworks (from output to outcomes/impact); (iv) institutional set-up/delivery models; and (v) consideration of political economy and reform sustainability. As the report mentions, an example is the evolution of the Foreign Investment Advisory Services (FIAS) strategy over the past three strategy cycles (FY05–07, FY08–11, and FY12–16). This shows major shifts in the strategy, focus areas, and approaches underlying investment climate work at least in the Investment Climate Department and Finance and Private Sector Development space, toward a stronger focus on results and impacts. It also shows shift toward more industry-specific investment climate reform activities, and importance of cross-cutting topics such as competition, transparency, inclusion, and green growth/climate change. The investment climate work will continue to evolve in the light of experience on the ground and in response to internal developments, such as the new Global Practice agendas.

COMPREHENSIVENESS AND SELECTIVITY

Management notes that the relevance of the World Bank Group's investment climate work is not defined solely by the comprehensiveness of the solutions offered. The Bank Group has a comparative advantage in offering advice and in aiding reforms and needs to consider carefully which types of reforms matter more for the desired outcomes. In many cases, the World Bank Group may be far more relevant by being able to effectively help countries enact reforms in a very narrow subset of areas than attempting to be comprehensive and ending up working on several areas in which it does not have specialized expertise or where there is little likelihood of reforms occurring. Management notes the report's acknowledgement of the need to consider the World Bank Group's comparative advantage in selecting priority areas of intervention in countries.

NEED FOR COMPLEMENTARY REFORMS

Management is pleased to note that, overall, World Bank Group interventions are relatively successful in reducing time, cost, and number of procedures in relation to setting up, operating, or exiting a business and that the rate at which reforms are undertaken does seem to accelerate with Bank Group support. However, practical experience across many areas shows that while regulatory reforms are indeed critical, they are not sufficient. Decisions to invest go beyond whether it is "easy to do business" and, particularly in difficult/unknown markets and markets for the poor, investment decisions are driven by the perceived market opportunity, the perception of firms about whether poor customers are willing to pay, and how technically difficult it is to reach them (including infrastructure constraints). This is the risk-reward trade-off. It is thus necessary to give more attention to reforms that address the broader operating context, as well as broader market conditions beyond the "enabling environment."

SETTING PRIORITIES: THE ROLE OF INDICATORS

Management believes that the combination of the Enterprise Surveys and the Doing Business indicators provides a powerful, complementary set of tools to help set priorities for World Bank Group work on the investment climate. The Enterprise Surveys and Doing Business are very different data sets. Although they do assess related areas, they measure different aspects of the same reality. These data sets should thus be used as complements, not as substitutes. The Enterprise Survey produces survey data where many different types of businesses are interviewed (a variety of business sectors, firm sizes, ownership types, subnational regions, and so forth), yielding a rich analysis that can be tailored to address particular sector/locational issues. This detailed, nuanced approach to business environment data is necessary for the World Bank Group to support investment climate interventions. The Doing Business indicators are based on expert inputs and provide granular information on specific regulatory processes that help identify reform actions. The Bank Group recognizes the limitations of both tools and does not rely solely on the two surveys' results. Management notes that, for some work areas, there are other indicators that are relevant and used in the World Bank Group's work and appreciates the report's recognition of this. Management also notes the move of the Global Indicators and Analysis Group, responsible for the Enterprise Surveys and Doing Business indicators, to the Development Economics Vice Presidency in October 2013 as part of the efforts to further revamp and expand the menu of investment climate indicators available to World Bank Group staff.

STRENGTHENED M&E AND IMPACT MEASUREMENT

Management agrees with the report's finding that the results framework underpinning the World Bank Group's work on investment climate has evolved over time, with a much strengthened emphasis on outcome and impact measurement, particularly in the International Finance Corporation (IFC). The focus is on literature reviews, target-setting methodologies, and impact evaluations of investment climate projects, as well analysis of value for money and sustainability of investment climate reform activities. Management will explore whether and how IFC's systematic approach to result and impact measurement can be replicated for the investment climate portfolio managed by the Bank and to the entire Trade and Competitiveness Practice.

POLITICAL ECONOMY AND PUBLIC-PRIVATE DIALOGUE

Management agrees with the report on the need to better understand and strengthen clients' commitment to reforms. Experience with investment climate work has highlighted the importance of proper engagement and it has shown that commitment at a strategy level (higher political level) is often not adequate and needs to be complemented by commitment at mid- and lower levels of government. The World Bank Group needs to work better to strengthen the links between the upstream strategy and downstream commitment at project level. Despite the repeated reference to the lack of emphasis or expertise in the area of political economy, there is no discussion of public-private dialogue in the report. Public-private dialogue plays a critical role as the primary tool by which the investment climate projects and programs seek to engage with a broad set of constituencies. The approach to public-private dialogue has evolved from being a separate "product" to a cross-cutting tool for addressing issues related to social value, including voice, transparency and accountability.

FRAGILE AND CONFLICT-AFFECTED SITUATIONS

Substantial efforts have been made over the years to increase the advisory services portfolio in fragile and conflict-affected situations (FCS). The early regulatory reforms in the FCS context focus on the simplification of typically overly burdensome or obsolete regulations. Many FCS countries have effectively used Doing Business indicators to frame their reform programs. According to the World Development Report 2011, an early emphasis on simplification of business regulations—rather than expansion or refinement—has proved effective in FCS. Management agrees that investment climate reforms alone are not sufficient for private sector development in FCS and emphasizes the importance of a complementary, and appropriately sequenced, package of interventions. The report identifies complexity of design and wavering political economy environment as factors explaining low performance, notably in FCS environments. Management also notes that the complexity of project design in FCS environments is often necessitated by the need to simultaneously intervene on several fronts and thus emphasizes the need to build in explicit and agile mechanisms to factor in redesign of the projects or exit in a timely manner if original project assumptions do not hold.

ADDRESSING GENDER IN INVESTMENT CLIMATE WORK

The report's finding is that projects targeting gender-related reforms do not consistently report disaggregated indicators. The report questions gender differentiation in several places and suggests that more attention be given to gender in projects. Many of the regulations under review do not formally treat women and men differently (with labor regulations being one of the exceptions), although sometimes there is discrimination in implementation and/or women find it more burdensome to comply with them. Management will consider whether the scope of investment climate interventions should also capture cases of gender discrimination, or if other parts of the World Bank Group are better positioned to address them. This will involve greater use of the Enterprise Survey data, which contain a wealth of information that can be disaggregated by ownership or top manager's gender and thus help World Bank task team leaders more effectively design and target their regulatory reform work.

DIAGNOSTIC TOOLS AND INDICATORS

Management is already undertaking multiple initiatives to develop new, and refine existing, diagnostic tools. For instance, in the area of trade, the World Bank Group is developing a series of tools (trade competitiveness diagnostic, the nontariff measures toolkit, the trade in services toolkit) to allow a solid assessment of the trade angle of the investment climate reform agenda. The Development Economics Vice Presidency Global Indicators and Analysis Group team is piloting new indicators in the areas of procurement and regulatory transparency, as well as developing suites of indicators for priority sectors such as agribusiness and sustainable energy. To increase the power of diagnostics, management will develop actionable indicators, along with undertaking empirical work, to identify binding constraints to growth. The operational priorities will be further fine-tuned through a dialogue with (and requests by) clients and stakeholders, in addition to being informed by indicators. In addition to the improvements in the business environment and quality of regulation, what matters is the actual implementation of regulation.

SOCIAL VALUE

In the currently formulated and implemented investment climate reform interventions, social effects are taken into consideration in a variety of ways. Investment climate projects mostly aim at increased levels of investments and higher levels of economic exchange. The empirical evidence suggests that these goals—if achieved—should generate social benefits, through increased employment, entrepreneurial opportunities, and higher levels of economic inclusion. Impact evaluations, including a lens on the social dimension of investment climate reform, are being carried out under the investment climate business line's Impact Program, including an evaluation looking rigorously at effects on informality in Benin/Malawi.

Management agrees that there is, nonetheless, scope to do more in-depth social value assessments on a selective basis and understands IEG's recommendation about a differentiated approach in that spirit. Social value exercises require specific expertise and significant resources and will need to be done selectively. Measuring "social" impact is typically associated with household-level data and generally with the economic analysis of welfare, while investment climate work is traditionally associated with firm-level data. There is a need for a nuanced approach that distinguishes between reforms that attempt to do away with laws and regulations that convey very little in way of social benefits and reforms inducing trade-offs between business interests and social interests. Therefore, management plans to develop a set of criteria to help prioritize interventions for which social value assessments would be done and in what form, and to implement a selective approach to assessing the social effects of regulatory reforms.

COMPLEMENTARITY AND STRENGTHS OF WORLD BANK AND IFC BUSINESS MODELS

The Trade and Competitiveness Global Practice will help stimulate collaboration across different business models and approaches pursued within the Group. The Trade and Competitiveness Global Practice (together with the Finance and Markets Practice, which is also being set up as a fully integrated joint Bank/IFC Global Practice), will lead work in this area, especially through outreach, communication, and partnership with other networks/ Global Practices on approaches, diagnostic tools, and lessons. As the report notes, different parts of the World Bank Group have demonstrated their comparative advantages, suggesting that a synergistic approach may help to leverage strengths and overcome past weaknesses. The complementarity of interventions that are specific to parts of the Group is often grounded in the complementarity of their skills mix, and in the differences between short- and long-term reforms.

MULTILATERAL INVESTMENT GUARANTEE AGENCY SUPPORT

Since the Multilateral Investment Guarantee Agency (MIGA) subcontracted its technical assistance function with respect to foreign direct investment promotion to FIAS in 2005, the scope of the IEG evaluation excludes explicit references regarding MIGA support for investment climate reforms. However, FIAS remains a donor-funded mechanism supporting investment climate operations across the three institutions. Within the ambit of investment climate interventions discussed in the report for improving the business environment for entry, operations, and exit, Investment Policy and Promotion interventions (part of Operations) supported through FIAS is most relevant for MIGA, both in terms of facilitating investments and reducing political risks.

Management Action Record

Expand Coverage of Diagnostic Tools and Their Integration

IEG FINDINGS AND CONCLUSIONS

Over the years a number of diagnostic tools have been used to design investment climate interventions. Recently new tools have been developed for specific areas of the regulatory environment. Although these tools cover in detail individual areas of the regulatory environment, there is no comprehensive tool that allows an assessment of all regulatory aspects in client countries. Such a tool would help determine which area is the most problematic in client countries.

IEG presented evidence that the Doing Business indicators and Enterprise Survey data—the most commonly used diagnostic tools—are incomplete; that is, they do not cover all areas of regulation as identified in the best practice list (Table 1.3). Doing Business and Enterprise Surveys cover only some aspects—such as business registration, taxation, and trade—where most of the World Bank Group activities take place.

IEG RECOMMENDATION

Expand the coverage of current diagnostic tools and integrate them to produce comparable indicators so that these can capture the areas of the business environment not yet covered by existing tools.

ACCEPTANCE BY MANAGEMENT

Agree

MANAGEMENT RESPONSE

Management agrees that diagnostic tools and indicators should evolve over time in the light of operational experience, evolving priorities, and advances in the academic literature. Management is undertaking multiple initiatives to develop new, and refine existing, diagnostic tools.

Management plans to review how indicators and other benchmarking tools are being utilized by the World Bank Group to inform investment climate activities, with a view to expand the utilization of indicators as an engagement tool. Management also notes the move of the Global Indicators and Analysis Group, responsible for the Enterprise Surveys and Doing Business indicators, to the Development Economics Vice Presidency in October 2013 as part of the efforts to further revamp and expand the menu of investment climate indicators available to World Bank Group staff.

Develop a Differentiated Approach to the Social Effects of Reforms

IEG FINDINGS AND CONCLUSIONS

Business regulations govern markets to enhance or protect certain social values, such as public health, safety, and the environment. IEG's review shows that social value is not explicitly defined or accounted for in regulatory reforms supported by the World Bank Group in client countries. Without that it is difficult to establish whether particular reforms have generated any particular benefits (or losses), or to identify distributional effects.

The Bank Group impact indicators include measures of aggregate compliance cost savings for businesses or increases in private sector investment. Separate measures are needed to capture a wider range of benefits and costs (social, economic, and environmental) if existing regulations are changed. Some groups may benefit from regulatory reform, but other (potentially vulnerable) groups may lose out, with regard to incomes; employment; access to goods, services, and infrastructure; or other indicators. A social value framework suggests that projects should identify relevant stakeholders; an exclusive focus on businesses is too narrow. Nonbusiness stakeholders need to be incorporated within any evaluation of regulatory reform.

Furthermore, a better assessment of political commitment is key in determining the success of investment climate projects. In many cases, IEG found that unsuccessful efforts in regulatory reforms focused on improving the technical quality of legislation but ignored the importance of the political process. Although the World Bank and IFC cannot and should not be engaged in these processes, successful regulatory reform requires understanding this part of the policy-making process and informing relevant stakeholders. This is especially important in FCS, where the political process is even more unstable.

IEG RECOMMENDATIONS

Develop a differentiated approach to identify the social effects of regulatory reforms on all groups expected to be affected by them beyond the business community. The approach should identify which groups are expected to be affected by the regulatory reform(s) within and beyond the business community, to ensure that reforms "do no harm" to people and the environment. The assessment should be differentiated depending on the expected impact of the regulatory reform(s) and may include qualitative or quantitative methods. The approach should be employed both ex ante (during the design of the project) as well as ex post (to assess the achieved impact of the reform).

Such an approach should help better estimate the political economy risk associated with the reform, to identify potential groups that would sustain or oppose reforms, and the extent of such support or opposition. The World Bank Group may also consider developing client capacity to conduct social value assessment to enable sustainability of investment climate reforms.

ACCEPTANCE BY MANAGEMENT
Agree

MANAGEMENT RESPONSE
Management agrees on the importance of considering both the economic and social impact of regulatory reforms. It concurs with the recommendation for a differentiated approach that takes into account the expected scale of impact.

In investment climate reform interventions, management takes into consideration social effects in a variety of ways. Scaling up a social welfare/value assessment requires specific expertise and significant resources. A nuanced approach is needed and management plans to develop a selective approach that distinguishes between reforms that attempt to do away with laws and regulations that convey very little in way of social benefits, and reforms inducing trade-offs between business interests and social interests. Management plans to develop a set of criteria to help prioritize interventions for which social value assessments would be done and in what form.

Take Advantage of Complementarity of World Bank and IFC Business Models in the Trade and Competitiveness Global Practice

IEG FINDINGS AND CONCLUSIONS

The World Bank and IFC work in the same space and with the same clients through two distinct business models. The IFC business model is implemented through stand-alone advisory services. Projects are standardized, focused, and short-term and include rapid interventions. They are mostly funded through internal budget and trust funds. The World Bank business model is implemented through lending and budget support and to a lesser extent through technical assistance. Projects are comprehensive and tend to be more long term. The client or the Bank executes the project. Each model has unique features, and stakeholders appreciate their differences. Stakeholders interviewed across countries often appreciated IFC's international technical expertise, quick response and delivery, and close support. However, IFC's ability to handle the political economy was not as strong, nor was its ability to move beyond standardized products. The World Bank's main strength is its institutional access to government institutions, its comprehensive services, and its ability to provide substantive funding. Yet there was a common sense that the World Bank is slow to respond and to implement projects.

IEG's interviews with World Bank Group management and staff surveys indicated that there is collaboration among the institutions to varying degrees. Survey results show that simple activities such as information sharing are more frequent than formal engagements. Evidence shows that different operating environments of IFC and the World Bank make collaboration difficult. Systems and organizational structures—such as different pricing policy, accountability matrix, results framework, and human resources policies and staff incentives—are perceived as the main bottlenecks to collaboration. Also, the interviews with investment climate management and staff indicate that staff have a positive perception of complementarity and strengths of the institutions with the new Trade and Competitiveness Global Practice; however, some concerns exist regarding the dominance of one institution model over the other.

IEG RECOMMENDATIONS

Ensure that the World Bank Group takes advantage of the complementarity and strengths of World Bank and IFC business models when designing the new Trade and Competitiveness Global Practice. Exploit synergies by ensuring that World Bank and IFC staff improve their understanding of each other's work and business models. Maintain the richness of the two delivery models while addressing factors that discourage collaboration.

ACCEPTANCE BY MANAGEMENT

Agree

MANAGEMENT RESPONSE

The Trade and Competitiveness Global Practice (together with the Finance and Markets Practice, which is also being set up as a fully integrated joint Bank/IFC Global Practice) will lead the World Bank Group engagement in this area and accordingly strengthen its outreach, communication, and partnership with other networks/Global Programs on approaches, diagnostic tools, and lessons.

Chairperson's Summary:
Committee on Development Effectiveness

The Committee on Development Effectiveness met to consider the evaluation entitled *Investment Climate Reforms: An Independent Evaluation of World Bank Group Support to Reforms of Business Regulations* and the draft Management Response.

Summary

The Committee welcomed the evaluation's findings and recommendations and agreed they highlight the main challenges facing the World Bank Group in investment climate activities. They were pleased to see that overall the World Bank Group has targeted the right countries, supported the right reforms, and been effective in improving the regulatory environment of client countries, particularly in terms of reducing procedures, time, and costs for business. Members found the evaluation timely, given the internal changes in the World Bank Group and the new Global Practices and Cross-Cutting Solutions Areas. As investment climate moves into the joint Trade and Competitiveness Global Practice, they saw this as an opportunity to take advantage of the complementarities and strengths of the Bank and International Finance Corporation delivery models to provide collaborative solutions to clients. Members concurred that the current diagnostic tools should be enhanced and integrated to produce comparable indicators to capture areas of the business environment not yet covered; they encouraged management to enhance coordination and collaboration with other multilateral development banks, donors, and institutions in this respect.

Members agreed with the need to develop a differentiated approach to identify the environmental and social effects of regulatory reforms. Members welcomed management's intent to try to standardize environmental and social considerations in order to measure the impact of investment climate reforms on the bottom 40 percent, women, and fragile and conflict-affected countries. They underscored the importance of conducting ex ante social impact assessments and building client capacity on this front. Members highlighted that gender-focused investment climate projects still correspond to a small proportion of all investment climate reform-targeted projects. They urged management to strengthen the gender focus in the World Bank Group's investment climate activities.

Juan José Bravo
CHAIRPERSON

1 Introduction and Portfolio Review

HIGHLIGHTS

- Extensive literature shows that a good business environment benefits firm productivity and growth.

- Over the period FY07–13, the World Bank Group supported 819 projects with investment climate interventions, of which 476 were for the World Bank and 343 for the International Finance Corporation (IFC), for a total estimated value of $3.7 billion. Investment climate interventions aim to simplify and streamline regulatory procedures, remove sector specific administrative constraints, revise the legal framework and institutions, establish effective dialogue systems between private and public sectors, and harmonize procedures and systems.

- Although both institutions operate in the same space, the scope of their investment climate interventions is generally different, with some overlap. The World Bank focuses more on higher level reforms, such as revising and harmonizing laws and codes, reforming institutions, developing strategies, and coordinating government agencies and ministries. IFC, in contrast, mostly focuses on streamlining and simplifying procedures and processes, providing technical assistance, and automating systems.

Motivation

The rationale for World Bank Group engagement in investment climate activities rests in the understanding that support to investment climate reforms is an integral part of World Bank Group efforts to eliminate extreme poverty and boost shared prosperity. Private firms are at the forefront of the development process, as they contribute to improving standards of living by providing more than 90 percent of the jobs, supplying goods and services, and representing the main source of tax revenues. In turn, the contribution that firms make to society is determined by the quality of the investment climate (World Bank 2004b).

Furthermore, social equity and inclusion is critically influenced by the investment climate. The notion of a "level playing field," where economic players have equal opportunities to succeed, is a fundamental focus of investment climate interventions. Barriers to dynamic and well-functioning markets may benefit privileged economic participants at the expense of competitors, potential entrants, and consumers.

This evaluation is part of a programmatic series of assessments by the Independent Evaluation Group (IEG) of critical aspects of the World Bank Group's support for financial and private sector development. It aims to assess the extent to which the World Bank Group has achieved the goal of helping its client countries improve the investment climate in which firms operate. The evaluation coincides with the establishment of the global practice on trade and competitiveness, which will be the focal point of World Bank Group work on investment climate reforms. The findings and conclusions of this evaluation are thus intended to offer insights into this aspect of the Bank Group change process.

Theoretical Foundations

Private sector development (PSD) drives economic growth.[1] Driven by the quest for profits, private firms invest in new ideas and strengthen the foundation of economic growth and prosperity (World Bank 2004b).

There are two main avenues through which the private sector drives growth: private investment and productivity improvements. In their study of the determinants of growth, Levine and Renelt (1992) show that investment is the only robust determinant of economic growth among the 50 measures of trade policy, fiscal policy, and other economic variables that they consider.[2] They also find, along with others (Sala-i-Martin 1997; Phetsavong and IchiHashi 2012; Deverajan, Easterly, and Pack 2003), that private—but not public—investment is robustly correlated with growth.[3]

Sustained and broad-based growth in private investment will only occur when the business environment is favorable. If private firms do not believe that their investment is secure, that regulation is too burdensome or unpredictable, or that infrastructure is poor, they will not invest in new machinery and equipment (World Bank 2004b, figure 1.10). Sala-i-Martin and Artadi (2002) show that in the Arab world high investment rates did not translate into larger growth rates because of a hostile environment.

Although private investment is important for growth, it is not the only driver of long-run economic growth. Summarizing the theoretical literature on economic growth, Athreya argues (2013, p. 251) that without improvements in productivity, diminishing marginal returns to capital will eventually result in stagnating living standards. The business environment affects firm productivity. Many firm-level studies, often using data from the World Bank's Enterprise Surveys, show that total factor productivity is higher in countries and regions within countries where the business environment is more hospitable.[4]

Private sector investment is typically constrained by market failures that are especially severe in developing countries. Governments use regulations to correct perceived market failures and improve market efficiency (Veljanovski 2010). In doing so, policy makers need to take broad social interests into account, including employee and consumer interests and concerns for the environment. Regulatory reforms therefore require consideration of the interests of a range of stakeholders—not only businesses.

World Bank Group strategies, especially those of the Facility for Investment Climate Advisory Services (FIAS), also emphasize cross-cutting themes such as gender, fragile and conflict-affected states (FCS), and industry. These strategies recognize that certain obstacles make it harder for women than for men to start and grow enterprises. FCS are seen as a priority because of their urgent need to attract local and foreign direct investment (FDI). Tourism and agribusiness are prioritized because of their potential for employment creation.

GENDER

Whether investment climate interventions should explicitly target specific subgroups of the population rather than promoting reforms to improve the general business environment of a country is a question with no immediate and obvious answer. On the one hand, reforms by their own nature are supposed to be general and any specific provision could be perceived as a politically unpalatable affirmative action. On the other hand, it is normally the case that the playing field is not leveled for everybody, and certain entrepreneurs or firms, current or potential, experience obstacles that are specific to their group and, if not addressed, not only raise issues of fairness and equity, but can also hinder the growth potential of the whole economy. Furthermore, traditionally disadvantaged groups may be less able to take advantage of a level playing field.

The disadvantageous position of women in entrepreneurship has been widely documented. Fewer women than men own and manage businesses worldwide (Kelley and others 2012). Also, in all regions of the world, including in developed economies, female-owned enterprises are substantially and significantly smaller than those owned by men (Bardasi, Sabarwal, and Terrell 2011; Minniti 2010). This is partly because women are more likely than men to operate in industries where firms are smaller and less efficient, but also because women face disproportionate obstacles in accessing finance, accessing markets, obtaining licenses and permits (because of limited mobility, time constraints, and sometimes discrimination and higher exposure to bribes and sexual harassment), accessing courts and dispute-resolution systems, accessing networks, and accessing assets and property.

The identification of the obstacles faced by specific groups—such as youth and women—or types of firms—such as exporters, informal firms, or firms located in specific industries or regions—is essential at the diagnostic stage. The type of interventions that can reduce those obstacles, however, may not explicitly target a subgroup and because of their own nature, may be disproportionately beneficial to women, youth, or a specific industry.

For example, as female entrepreneurs are disproportionately penalized by lengthy and cumbersome registration procedures (Simavi, Manuel, and Blackden 2010), reforms meant to simplify business registration are disproportionately beneficial to women, even when women are not explicitly targeted by the reform. Similarly, reforms introducing one-stop shops, setting up alternative dispute-resolution systems, or reducing administrative barriers can be especially advantageous to current and potential women entrepreneurs. Access to finance and start-up financing, simplification of the administrative and regulatory framework, and business assistance and support have been identified as key crucial factors to address in policies and programs to support youth entrepreneurship (Schoof 2006).

FRAGILE AND CONFLICT-AFFECTED STATES[5]

PSD in FCS only started to gain attention from policy makers, donors, and nongovernmental organizations in the last decade (del Castillo 2008; Cramer 2009; Paris 2004). With some 1.5 billion people living in fragile or conflict-affected parts of the world, donors began to envision a complementary role for the private sector to meet the challenges of fragility in the 21st century.[6] The private sector contributes not only to jobs, wealth, and a country's tax base, but also to delivering public services and rebuilding social trust that has been fractured by war. These activities promote economic growth and improved livelihoods, which in turn help cement peace dividends and lasting recovery (Bagwitz and others 2008, p. 4; MacSweeney 2008, p. 10; Mills and Fan 2006, p. 27; and Peschka 2010, p. 1).

The relatively recent attention to PSD in fragile situations means that only a small body of literature exists on the topic. Within this literature, which is dominated by practitioner reports, there is general agreement that building competitive, inclusive markets and businesses is crucial for postconflict recovery, just as fragile situations present special challenges and opportunities for PSD. Most studies are quick to point out that the private sector never completely disappears in war, even if it becomes disrupted and distorted by conflict, functioning typically on an informal level. This happens in the context of weak political and economic institutions, low governing capacity and legitimacy, limited policy and administrative functions, displaced populations, damaged infrastructure, ongoing guerrilla or irregular warfare, and high corruption and rent-seeking behavior—common features of fragile environments—which make PSD work in FCS especially challenging and different than in other developing countries (Bagwitz and others 2008). Still, most studies agree that PSD is worthwhile for countries coming out of conflict. As fragile states rebuild their institutions, PSD-friendly policies should be a part of early interventions, included in the first round of reforms to ensure future growth and reform (Kusago 2005; Mills and Fan 2006, pp. 27–28; and Piffaretti 2010, p. 19).

In spite of the agreement on the challenges and opportunities of PSD in FCS, there is significant disagreement over how exactly it should be carried out. There is no clear consensus over the most effective starting point in FCS. Much of the debate is centered on whether investment climate or early interventionist approaches should be prioritized to encourage PSD in conflict-affected areas. This debate is essentially about sequencing, whether "doing reforms" to improve the investment climate or "doing deals" with targeted enterprises and sectors should come first in these environments.

Proponents of the first approach—prioritizing investment climate reform—can be divided into three groups. A first group supports regulatory reforms early in the reform process. This group stresses that regulatory reforms in FCS[7] should focus on simplification of typically overly burdensome or obsolete regulations, as they are best suited to limit problematic rent seeking when, in particular, they aim to foster FDI and a repatriation of finance (Piffaretti 2010; MacSweeney 2008, pp. 14, 19–20, 29; and Euser 2011, pp. 42–43). Piffaretti (2010) puts a clearer emphasis on regulatory reform before institution building.

A second group that supports this approach argues that institutional reforms should precede regulatory reforms. Collier and Hoeffler emphasize that institutional governance and social policies should come ahead of sectoral and macrolevel policies (Collier and Hoeffler 2000; 2002, p. 13). Some World Bank Group work sides with this point, advocating for priority attention to infrastructure development and legal and regulatory reform in PSD programming in FCS (IFC 2004).[8] Others point out that certain states or government actors are not in a position to promote an early reform agenda when they have been culpable in conflict, because of weak trust in the officials.[9] Donors and governments cannot just set up a regulatory environment and assume that foreign and local enterprise will sprout. Reform of the justice and security sector must also be a priority above and beyond business regulations to enforce the regulations and contract rights in the first place.

Finally, a third group stresses that early simplification of regulations restores investor confidence and attracts businesses and entrepreneurs. However, other reforms are equally important, if not more significant to investors, such as rule of law, infrastructure development (electricity and roads), finance, and confronting corruption (World Bank 2010; Mills and Fan 2006). The only issue is that both the World Development Report and Mills and Fan remain unclear on the details of sequencing these institution-building steps in terms of investment climate regulatory reforms (see World Bank 2010, pp. 157, 160–61).

A second approach—prioritizing early direct interventions, a so-called "interventionist" approach[10]—has become popular but has received limited attention from the World Bank Group. Although proponents of interventionism are clearly convinced of the case for early proactive PSD activities in fragile states, there is internal disagreement over which activities to prioritize, and the pros and cons of each.

A leading Donor Committee for Enterprise Development report cites a difference of opinion among practitioners over whether interventions should target particular industries or entire systems and value chains (MacSweeney 2008, pp. 51, 73). Each donor or nongovernmental organization tends to emphasize its favored approaches. The German Organization for Technical Cooperation guidebook on PSD in (post-) conflict situations heavily promotes public-private partnerships as a way to assist fragile states in public service delivery (Bagwitz and others 2008, pp. 7, 33, 94–97), but others point out that such partnerships can become hijacked by powerful competing interest groups.[11] A study by the Center for Strategic and International Studies on PSD in fragile, conflict-affected, and violent countries argues that promoting domestic small and medium-size enterprise (SME) development above and beyond FDI is more sustainable over the long run in resource-rich fragile states (Hameed 2013, pp. 7–10; Kusago 2005).

Most studies on PSD in FCS inside and outside of the World Bank Group emphasize a third, integrated approach unfettered by concerns for sequencing. These studies argue, directly and indirectly, that regulatory and interventionist approaches should not be viewed as mutually exclusive, but as complementary in encouraging growth in fragile environments.

The World Development Report 2011 (World Bank 2010) leans in this direction by highlighting both investment climate reforms and direct interventions as important for fragile states. In particular, the report gives attention to the positive role that direct interventions can make in stimulating the private sector through new market and value chain programming in case study examples of Kosovo dairy and Rwanda coffee ventures (2010, pp. 157–59). It recognizes that creating the right business climate is often not enough to attract investment in violent situations. This is just as too much focus on reforming political and security institutions runs the risk of ignoring key economic dynamics behind conflict (Collier and Hoeffler 2002).

An IFC draft report recognizes that both approaches are ultimately needed in order not to miss opportune moments to support economic growth in FCS (Masinde and Harwit 2014, p. 4; Peschka 2010; del Castillo 2001; Kusago 2005).[12] Development practitioners most frequently use a mix of context-specific approaches (UNIDO-GTZ 2008, pp. 53–4; MacSweeney 2008; Peschka 2010, p. 41). The Donor Committee for Enterprise Development—which has produced the most comprehensive practitioner report on PSD in FCS (MacSweeney 2008)—sees development moving toward this integrated approach.

The guidebook from the German Organization for Technical Cooperation (Bagwitz and others 2008) does the best job of steering practitioners toward a mix of investment climate and direct interventions, depending on particular conflict drivers and development goals (see also Curtis and others 2010).[13] The conclusion is that context should dictate PSD programming and the appropriate balance and sequencing of investment climate and direct interventions (see Curtis and others 2010, pp. 46–48).

In sum, the Bank Group tends to lean toward investment climate or integrated programming in FCS, but there appears to be burgeoning attention in the Bank Group to targeted early interventions in and of themselves; this is clear in a new report on value chain promotion in fragile areas of Africa (Dudwick and others 2013). Outside the World Bank Group, most practitioner and scholarly literature supports an integrative approach.

Proponents of all approaches do agree that there is no one solution or set of best practices on PSD in FCS, but rather context and conflict-specific "best fit" approaches that must be pursued to affect lasting growth and recovery. The interventionist approach is the most fractured and divergent, with each donor emphasizing different interventions and with practically no concern for sequencing direct interventions.

INDUSTRY

Although some aspects of the investment climate apply to all firms participating in the economy, others are far more specific and can create a "micro" investment climate for firms of particular characteristics in a particular region or sector. Industrial sectors may have laws and regulations specific to an industry or field of economic activities, such as licensing and registration requirements or tax treatment. For example, in 2009, the Investment Climate Advisory Services of the World Bank Group issued a mining sector licensing study "to provide guidance on best practices in mining licensing" by identifying "certain common features of successful mining licensing regimes worldwide" (World Bank 2009, p. vii).

At the end of 2011, the Bank's Vice-Presidency of Financial and Private Sector Development (FPD) created the Investment Climate for Industry team, focusing on supporting investment climate reform and facilitating investment in key sectors of the economy, principally agribusiness and tourism. It aimed to "support industry-specific interventions that help streamline the effectiveness of industry regulations, generate sustainable investment, and create jobs in sectors critical to economic diversification and poverty reduction"[14] (World Bank 2011, pp. 1–2).

Initially focusing on agribusiness and tourism, this practice sought to deepen engagement in strategic industries and improve the business environment and growth prospects for light manufacturing. Interviews with members of the practice suggest that it took some time to find a focus and that its ultimate scope extends beyond the legal and regulatory focus of the broader investment climate practice. Instead, it also includes activities relating to strengthening value chains, investment promotion (especially foreign direct investment promotion), strengthening sectoral institutions and standards, promoting specialized financing mechanisms (such as warehouse receipts), and a variety of other activities. In its own words, the practice applies "the full range of economywide supported products in the delivery of sector-specific advisory services."

The remainder of this chapter discusses the definition of investment climate IEG adopted in this study, the World Bank Group engagement in investment climate and business models, the evaluation design and methodology, the good practice standard for business regulations, and a description the Bank Group investment climate portfolio. Chapter 2 reviews the relevance of the World Bank Group from three different perspectives: strategy, interventions, and diagnostic tools. Chapter 3 assesses the effectiveness of the Bank Group investment climate portfolio at two levels: the project level—in terms of the achievement of the development objectives—and the intervention level—in terms of the achievement of intermediate outcomes. The chapter also provides insights on the effectiveness of investment climate interventions focusing on gender, FCS, and industry. Chapter 4 reviews the methods used by the Bank Group to assess the social benefits of regulatory reform. Chapter 5 provides insights into factors affecting the performance of investment climate interventions, collaboration across the Bank Group institutions, and country perspectives. The last chapter provides conclusions and offers recommendations.

Investment Climate Definition

Different definitions of investment climate have been proposed in the literature. Nicholas Stern, who as the World Bank Group Senior Vice President and Chief Economist in the early 2000s elevated investment climate to an important area of focus for the World Bank Group, defined it as "the policy, institutional, and behavioral environment, both present and expected, that affects the returns and risks associated with investment"(Xu 2011, p. 1). The World Bank's *Productivity and Investment Climate Survey Implementation Manual* (World Bank 2003) was designed to give World Bank task managers guidance on preparing investment climate surveys and completing Investment Climate Assessments. It adopted a similarly broad definition by suggesting that studies of the investment climate should discuss "factors constraining the effective functioning of product markets, financial and nonfinancial factor markets, and infrastructure services, including, in particular, weaknesses in an economy's legal, regulatory and institutional framework" (World Bank 2003). In 2005 the World Bank's flagship World Development Report focused on the investment climate[15] and defined it in a similar way as "the set of location-specific factors shaping the opportunities and incentives for firms to invest productively, create jobs, and expand" (World Bank 2004b).

Although at a diagnostic level assessments of the investment climate have been fairly inclusive, in practice "investment climate" is associated with a distinct and narrow set of regulatory requirements for businesses to operate, trade and invest across borders, and function in key sectors. In line with this practice, IEG will refer to "investment climate" as the support for policy, legal, and institutional reforms intended to improve the functioning of markets and reduce transaction costs and risks associated with starting, operating and closing a business in the World Bank Group's client countries. Within this context World Bank Group efforts aim to promote reforms to improve the conditions for firms to enter, operate, and exit both in domestic and international markets as well as in key sectors. Consequently, all projects that aim to reform the regulatory environments for businesses, irrespective of the sector and source of financing, will be part of the scope of this evaluation.

World Bank Group Engagement in Investment Climate

Investment climate activities have been part of the World Bank's PSD strategy since the late 1980s, under various names, including "business environment" or "enabling environment." In fact, improving the business environment was one of four strategic pillars of the 1989 PSD Action Plan. The 1980s also witnessed increased attention to the promotion of foreign investments with IFC's establishment of FIAS in 1985 and, soon after that, the creation of the

Multilateral Investment Guarantee Agency (MIGA). This strategy also called for an expansion of the FIAS program.

In the 1990s, the Bank Group realized that macroeconomic reforms alone would not guarantee long-term growth. Hence, a second generation of reforms, focused on microdeterminants of growth, took center stage in the Bank's strategies. Priorities shifted toward making reforms that improved the "business environment" in which the private sector operated. Three-quarters of the World Bank's development policy operations at the time aimed to help countries create a supportive business environment. The key goal was to foster competition. The focus of the FIAS program expanded from its original mandate of FDI advisory to provide support for reforms needed to improve the client country's investment climate for domestic and foreign investment.

It was not until the early 2000s that the term "investment climate" replaced what had been referred to as "business environment" or "enabling environment." This change in terminology was accompanied by significant organizational restructuring across the Bank Group within the PSD domain. FIAS was merged into the newly created joint IFC/World Bank Investment Climate Department (CIC).[16] CIC became an anchor unit connecting investment climate activities of the Bank, IFC, and FIAS. Though technical assistance to promote FDI is part of MIGA's mandate, in 2005 the decision was taken to subcontract this activity to FIAS[17] (World Bank 2006) with full integration becoming effective in 2007.

During the review period, the World Bank Group PSD strategy—which includes investment climate activities—did not change, and the FIAS strategy evolved with three strategy cycles (FY05–07, FY08–11, and FY12–16). Earlier FIAS strategies focused on diagnostic tools, and more recent strategy put a stronger emphasis on clearly defined activities; on results and impacts; on industry-specific interventions; and on cross-cutting topics such as competition, inclusion, and green growth/climate change.

At the operational level, in July 2011, the FPD Network was realigned into six global practices, cutting across regions and FPD's key thematic areas. The FPD Investment Climate Global Practice, one of the six practices, became the only joint practice, covering IFC and Bank investment climate activities and staff. CIC acts as a central anchor, providing knowledge, expertise, and analytical support for investment climate advisory work that is implemented by IFC's Investment Climate Business Line and FPD's Investment Climate Global Practice. FIAS remains a donor-funded mechanism, supporting investment climate operations across the three institutions. It changed its name from FIAS to Facility for Investment Climate Advisory Services. The FPD sector board is in charge of the overall planning and quality control of the investment climate program.

In addition to CIC and the FPD Investment Climate Global Practice, two other groups within the World Bank Group are involved in investment climate reform work. The IFC Investment Climate Business Line is IFC's operational arm, focusing on providing investment climate advisory work from the field. In the Bank, other sector units, such as the Poverty Reduction and Economic Management Network (PREM), the Human Development Network, and the Sustainable Development Network (SDN), also operate in the investment climate space. In fact, as shown in the portfolio review for this evaluation, the majority of investment climate projects within the World Bank investment climate portfolio are run outside the FPD sector.

To support investment climate reform work, the Bank Group uses a number of indicators and benchmarking tools to help shed light on the characteristics and quality of the investment climate in a country, identify areas for reform, and monitor progress. In recent years new tools have been developed for specific areas of the regulatory environment. These tools cover in detail individual areas of the regulatory environment. The diagnostic tools include surveys (for example, Enterprise Surveys and Tax Compliance Cost Surveys), indicators and indices (for example, Doing Business; Women, Business, and the Law; Investing Across Borders; and Logistics Performance Index), and assessments (for example, Investment Climate Assessments, marginal effective tax rate, and standard cost model). The Development Economics Vice Presidency, PREM, and Global Indicators and Analysis are some of the Bank Group units involved in this type of work.

The Investment Climate Department—in particular, IFC's Investment Climate Business Line—is designing a new framework to track the development impact of investment climate interventions; IEG could not assess this within the timeframe covered in this evaluation. The approach followed includes literature reviews, target-setting methodologies, analysis of value for money (such as standard cost model), and sustainability of reforms. In addition, the department has initiated an impact evaluation program both at a global level (Joint Bank Group-Donor Program on Impact, Sustainability and Value for Money of Investment Climate Reform) and a regional level (for example, Investment Climate Africa Impact Initiative). Some impact evaluations cover limited social dimensions such as informality (in Benin/Malawi) and patient safety (in Kenya). Finally, over the past few years FIAS has undertaken a number of external evaluations (evaluation of the FIAS FY08–11 strategy cycle, 2011; the external evaluation of the Business Regulation Product under IFC's Investment Climate Business Line, 2012; and the external evaluation of four IFC Africa Region investment climate projects, 2013.

There was a major organizational change of the investment climate space in FY14. In the World Bank Group's ongoing reorganization, all staff mapped to investment climate work

(CIC, FPD/investment climate regional staff, and IFC/investment climate regional staff) are expected to join the Trade and Competitiveness (T&C) Global Practice, the most intensively integrated practice in the new World Bank Group structure.

In supporting investment climate reforms, the Bank Group has adopted two distinct business models. The IFC business model is implemented only through stand-alone advisory services. These are structured under a set of defined products within the IFC Investment Climate Business Line and tend to form focused, concrete, short-term, and rapid interventions. They are mostly funded through internal budget and trust funds, with some client contribution, and are executed by IFC or CIC.

There is also the World Bank business model, which is implemented through not only advisory services, but also through investment and policy-based lending. When not funded through the loans, advisory services are generally funded through trust funds or reimbursable advisory services. The client or the Bank executes the project (Table 1.1).

Regardless of the differences between the business models, the two institutions work in the same space and with the same clients. In general, the services provided by the institutions complement each other. The World Bank is generally involved in upstream policy dialogue on PSD and overall economic reforms and supports interventions that tend to have a wider and

TABLE 1.1 Characteristics of the World Bank and IFC Business Models

Business Model	Main Managing Departments	World Bank Group Activities	Funding	Executing Agency	Model Characteristics
IFC	CIC and IFC Investment Climate Business Line	IFC and CIC stand-alone advisory services	Trust funds, internal budget, client contribution	IFC Investment Climate Business Line, CIC	Product-based, focused, rapid, short term
World Bank	World Bank sector units	World Bank stand-alone advisory	Trust funds, RAS, loans	Client government, World Bank	Wider and deeper scope, long term
		World Bank policy and investment loans	Investment loans and/ or budget support	Client government	Wider and deeper scope, multiyear

SOURCE: IEG.
NOTE: CIC = investment climate practice; RAS = reimbursable advisory services.

deeper scope and to be of longer term; IFC supports interventions that tend to be standardized and narrowly focused. Each business model has its own strengths and weaknesses.

Evaluation Design and Methodology

The conceptual framework for this evaluation is represented in Figure 1.1, which shows the logical connections of investment climate priorities and interventions with outputs, outcomes, and ultimate goals. This framework is a combination of theoretical literature and World Bank Group strategic priorities and objectives. It starts with the strategic priorities. The priories are outlined in the World Bank, IFC, and FIAS investment climate strategies. They enhance the regulatory environment to foster business creation and growth, international trade and investment, investment in key sectors, and investment in focus countries (for example, FCS).

The strategies mainly focus on enterprises and don't include the broad social interest of different stakeholders beyond businesses, such as consumers, employees, investors. The logical model identifies specific areas of intervention—entry, operation, and exit—and, within them, specific topics such as registration, commercial law, and bankruptcy, which represent a good practice standard in business regulations. These topics are embodied in diagnostic, advisory, and investment work.

IEG then examines these interventions in light of specific indicators of output and outcomes that are directly attributable to them. Finally, IEG relates these outcomes to a number of economic development goals—including productivity, investment, employment growth, and greater economic inclusion. However, because of the complexity and multiplicity of determinants, some well outside the scope of this study, IEG does not quantify this level of impact in this evaluation.

The overarching question that IEG seeks to answer in the evaluation is: "Has the World Bank Group been successful in helping client countries to improve their business regulatory environment while taking into account the impact on different stakeholders in society?" This question addresses the extent to which Bank Group–supported regulatory reforms have achieved the policy objective of improving the regulatory environment in which business operates, taking into account that regulatory reforms should improve outcomes for society as a whole, not only for businesses. As a matter of fact, regulatory reforms impact a wide set of stakeholders in society, not just businesses. Furthermore, not all stakeholders are impacted evenly. Consequently, both at the design stage of reforms (ex ante) and when estimating its impact (ex post), it is important to estimate the increase or reduction in cost and benefits of these reforms.

FIGURE 1.1 Conceptual Framework of the Evaluation

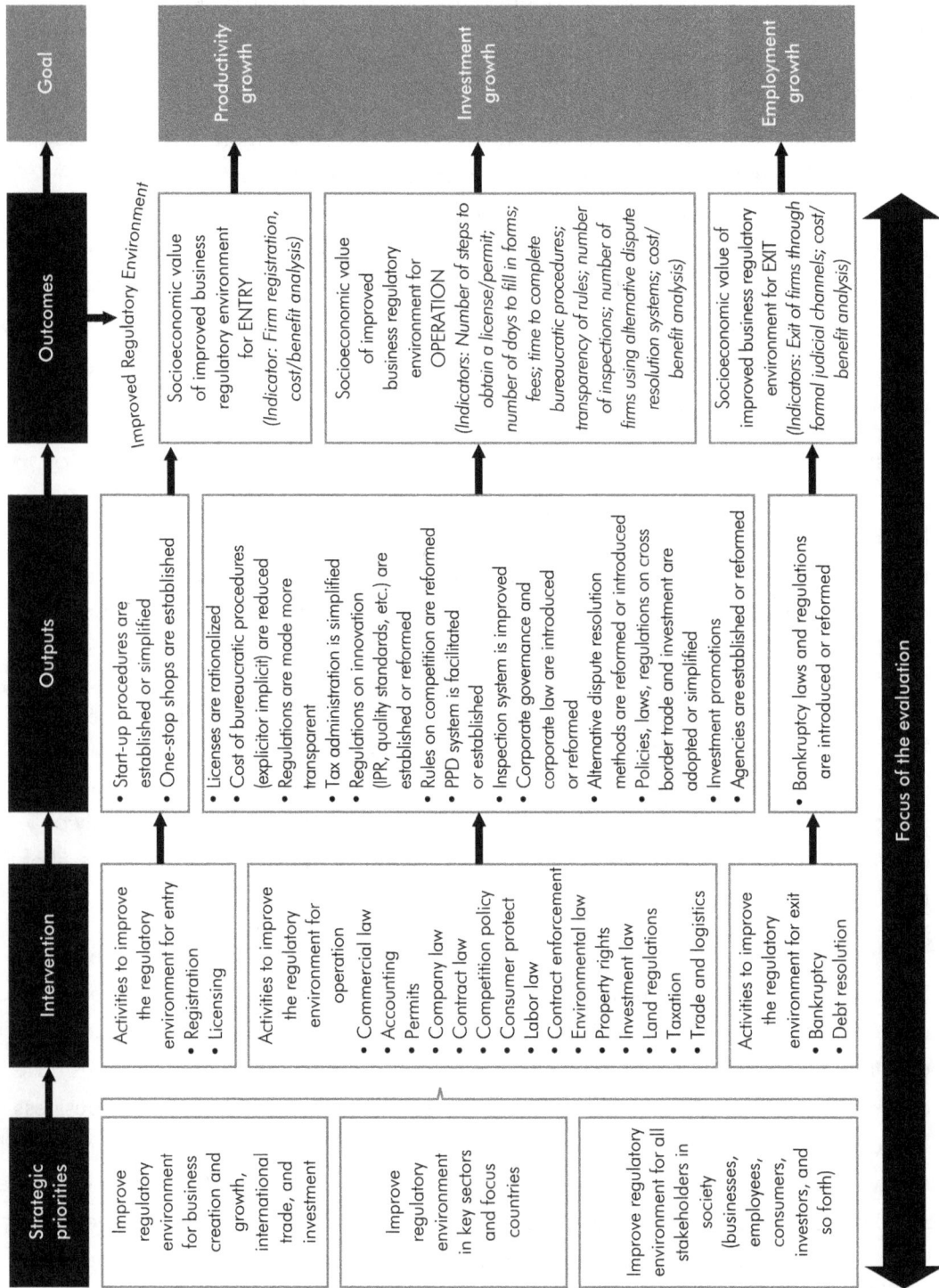

Strategic priorities	Intervention	Outputs	Outcomes	Goal

Strategic priorities

Improve regulatory environment for business creation and growth, international trade, and investment

Improve regulatory environment in key sectors and focus countries

Improve regulatory environment for all stakeholders in society (businesses, employees, consumers, investors, and so forth)

Intervention

Activities to improve the regulatory environment for entry
- Registration
- Licensing

Activities to improve the regulatory environment for operation
- Commercial law
- Accounting
- Permits
- Company law
- Contract law
- Competition policy
- Consumer protect
- Labor law
- Contract enforcement
- Environmental law
- Property rights
- Investment law
- Land regulations
- Taxation
- Trade and logistics

Activities to improve the regulatory environment for exit
- Bankruptcy
- Debt resolution

Outputs

- Start-up procedures are established or simplified
- One-stop shops are established

- Licenses are rationalized
- Cost of bureaucratic procedures (explicit or implicit) are reduced
- Regulations are made more transparent
- Tax administration is simplified
- Regulations on innovation (IPR, quality standards, etc.) are established or reformed
- Rules on competition are reformed
- PPD system is facilitated or established
- Inspection system is improved
- Corporate governance and corporate law are introduced or reformed
- Alternative dispute resolution methods are reformed or introduced
- Policies, laws, regulations on cross border trade and investment are adopted or simplified
- Investment promotions
- Agencies are established or reformed

- Bankruptcy laws and regulations are introduced or reformed

Outcomes

Improved Regulatory Environment

Socioeconomic value of improved business regulatory environment for ENTRY

(*Indicator: Firm registration, cost/benefit analysis*)

Socioeconomic value of improved business regulatory environment for OPERATION

(*Indicators: Number of steps to obtain a license/permit; number of days to fill in forms; fees; time to complete bureaucratic procedures; transparency of rules; number of inspections; number of firms using alternative dispute resolution systems; cost/benefit analysis*)

Socioeconomic value of improved business regulatory environment for EXIT

(*Indicators: Exit of firms through formal judicial channels; cost/benefit analysis*)

Goal

Productivity growth

Investment growth

Employment growth

Focus of the evaluation

SOURCE: IEG.

NOTE: IPR = intellectual property rights; PPD = public-private dialogue.

The overarching question will be answered by looking at three different dimensions:

- **Relevance:** Has the World Bank Group support for regulatory reforms been relevant to client countries?

- **Effectiveness:** Has the World Bank Group support for regulatory reforms achieved its intended objectives?

- **Social Value:** Has the World Bank Group taken into account the social impact in its regulatory reform work?

The review covers the FY07–13 period. It includes analysis at two levels: (i) interventions (such as regulations for entry, bankruptcy law, and so forth) and (ii) client countries, as reforms produce results at the country level and are not implemented in isolation; rather, they are the consequence of a sustained and prolonged engagement with the client country.

The different sources and methods used for this evaluation include (i) internal and external literature reviews on regulatory reforms, both broad and with a gender, industry, and FCS focus; (ii) a portfolio review of World Bank Group projects and interventions in the area of business regulatory environment; (iii) a review of policy and strategy documents at country and corporate levels; (iv) 25 country case studies; (v) 5 field-based country cases; (vi) interviews with World Bank Group staff and management; (vii) opinions and insights from World Bank Group donors; and (vii) a World Bank Group staff survey to seek insights into the factors that foster or hinder collaboration.

The evaluation builds on IEG reviews and evaluations of World Bank Group interventions including Country Assistance Strategy Completion Report Reviews (CASCR Reviews), Project Performance Assessment Reviews, Implementation Completion and Results Reports (ICRs), Expanded Project Supervision Reports, Project Completion Reports (PCRs), and Country Program Evaluations. In addition, IEG uses World Bank Group databases including Enterprise Surveys, Doing Business Indicators, investment climate indicator databases, and World Bank Group entrepreneurship databases, as well as external databases such as the Organisation for Economic Co-operation and Development regulatory reform database and the World Economic Forum (WEF) competitiveness database.

Investment Climate Good Practice Standard

Given the absence of a comprehensive list of regulatory reforms, IEG developed a good practice standard of regulatory areas as follows: first, IEG identified the five countries with the best regulatory environment, according to the WEF and Doing Business (World Bank 2013).

This generated a list of eight economies: Denmark; Finland; Hong Kong SAR, China; New Zealand; Qatar; Rwanda; Singapore; and the United States.

Second, for each of these economies, IEG reviewed the law library compiled by the Doing Business program (http://www.doingbusiness.org/law-library) and classified the key regulatory areas.[18] Finally, this list is taken as a good practice standard of the set of regulatory areas a typical country with the best regulatory environment would have (Table 1.2).

IEG reviewed evidence of the extent to which diagnostic tools cover the good practice areas identified above. As noted earlier, the PSD strategy update (2002) put particular emphasis on the role of diagnostic tools in the design of regulatory reforms. In line with this priority, IEG reviewed the two most commonly used diagnostic tools for regulatory reforms, the Doing Business and the Enterprise Surveys data, and conducted a mapping exercise of the areas covered in these tools with the list of good practice areas identified earlier (Table 1.3).[19]

The table shows in blue the regulatory areas that are covered by these instruments and in grey the areas not covered by either of them. This evidence shows that only about half of the regulatory areas are covered by these diagnostic tools. Some neglected areas are contract law, competition policy, consumer protection, intellectual property rights, employment law, and Alternative Dispute Resolution (ADR). This implies that these two diagnostic tools are only partially helpful in identifying regulatory areas of intervention.

World Bank Group Investment Climate Portfolio

PROJECTS

To identify the relevant portfolio of investment climate projects, IEG followed two separate approaches for IFC and the World Bank. For IFC, the identification of the investment climate portfolio was straightforward because of the existence of the Investment Climate Business Line database. The IEG team obtained the universe of IFC Advisory Services projects and filtered the projects within the investment climate business line approved on or after FY07 through FY13.

For the World Bank, in contrast, given the absence of a classification for investment climate projects, IEG followed two approaches for lending projects closed from FY07 and approved not earlier than FY03 through FY13: (i) Operations Policy and Country Services theme code method, that is, projects that charged 20 percent or more in volume of commitment to one or more of 10 of these "theme codes" relevant to investment climate; and (ii) a keyword search method, that is, for projects whose objective description matched one of approximately 100 investment climate key words.[20] Finally, all projects identified were reviewed individually.

TABLE 1.2 Comprehensive Menu of Regulatory Areas

Stage	Regulatory Topics
Entry	Commercial laws
	Business registration
	Business licensing
Operations	**Commercial laws**
	Accounting and auditing
	Registration
	Business licensing/permits
	Company laws (business regulations, inspections)
	Contract laws
	Competition policy
	Consumer protection
	Courts and proceedings (that is, contract enforcement)
	Environmental laws
	Property rights
	Property law
	Intellectual property and other goods protection (privacy laws, copyrights/ patents/ trademarks/ unfair business practices act)
	Investment policy/promotion
	Labor laws
	Employment law
	Labor protection
	Apprenticeships and training
	Labor safety and health
	Land regulations
	Taxation
	Trade and logistics
Exit	**Bankruptcy**
	Debt resolution and insolvency/Alternative Dispute Resolution
Other	**Industry/Sector specific**

SOURCE: IEG.

TABLE 1.3 Mapping of Doing Business and Enterprise Surveys to the Menu of Regulatory Reforms

Stage	Regulatory Topics	Enterprise Surveys/ICAs	Doing Business
Entry	**Commercial laws**		
	Business registration	Yes	Yes
	Business licensing	Yes	Yes
Operations	**Commercial laws**		
	Accounting and Auditing	No	No
	Registration	Yes	Yes
	Business licensing/permits	Yes	Yes
	Company Laws (business regulations, inspections)	Yes	Yes
	Contract laws	No	No
	Competition policy	No	No
	Consumer protection	No	No
	Courts and Proceedings (that is, contract enforcement)	Yes	Yes
	Environmental laws	No	No
	Property rights		
	Property law	Yes	Yes
	Intellectual property and other goods	No	No
	Protection(privacy laws, copyrights/patents/trademarks, unfair business practices act)		
	Investment policy/promotion	No	No
	Labor laws		
	Employment law	No	No
	Labor protection	No	Yes[a]
	Apprenticeships and training	Yes	Yes
	Labor safety and health	No	No
	Land regulations	Yes	Yes
	Taxation	Yes	Yes

Stage	Regulatory Topics	Enterprise Surveys/ICAs	Doing Business
Exit	Trade and logistics	Yes	Yes
	Bankruptcy	No	Yes
	Debt resolution and insolvency	No	Yes
	Alternative dispute resolution	No	No

SOURCE: IEG.
NOTE: Accounting and auditing standards are handled by the International Monetary Fund or the World Bank through the Reports on the Observance of Standards and Codes (http://go.worldbank.org/DJG7D61RB0). This evaluation did not cover financial markets regulations. ICA = Investment Climate Assessment.
a. Doing Business stopped indexing its indicators on employment regulations but continues to report them.

Over the period FY07–13,[21] the World Bank Group supported 819 projects with investment climate interventions in 119 countries, of which 476 were for the World Bank and 343 for IFC, for a total estimated value of $3.7 billion, of which $346 million was for IFC and $3.325 billion for the World Bank[22] (Figures 1.2 and 1.3).

In terms of number of projects, PREM, SDN, and FPD are the main networks that support investment climate projects. In terms of value, PREM supported projects with investment climate components for a value of $1.719 billion, SDN $866 million, and FPD $713 million. Investment climate projects represent approximately 20 percent of all IFC Advisory Services, with a total volume of $346 million (29 percent of total volume of Advisory Services) (Table 1.4). In absolute terms, PREM has the highest number of projects with investment climate interventions—often in the context of development policy lending. However, within networks, FPD has the highest proportion of network operations with investment climate interventions. In fact, 28 percent of FPD network lending is represented by investment climate interventions, compared to 8 percent of PREM and 14 percent of SDN. Further, FPD has on average 2.9 investment climate interventions per project, compared to 2.2 of PREM and 1.5 of SDN. Finally, IEG estimated that FPD staff support the implementation of investment climate interventions in the majority of PREM projects.

Across the two networks with the highest relative[23] share of investment climate projects— PREM and FPD—IEG observed that in PREM approximately one in three projects has an investment climate component; in FPD this is one in four. Similarly, one in three and one in four of development policy projects led by PREM and FPD, respectively, includes investment climate components. Half of the FPD investment climate projects are in Sub-Saharan Africa, and every year FPD has five active investment climate projects. In PREM, every year

FIGURE 1.2 World Bank Group Investment Climate Intervention, by Volume ($)

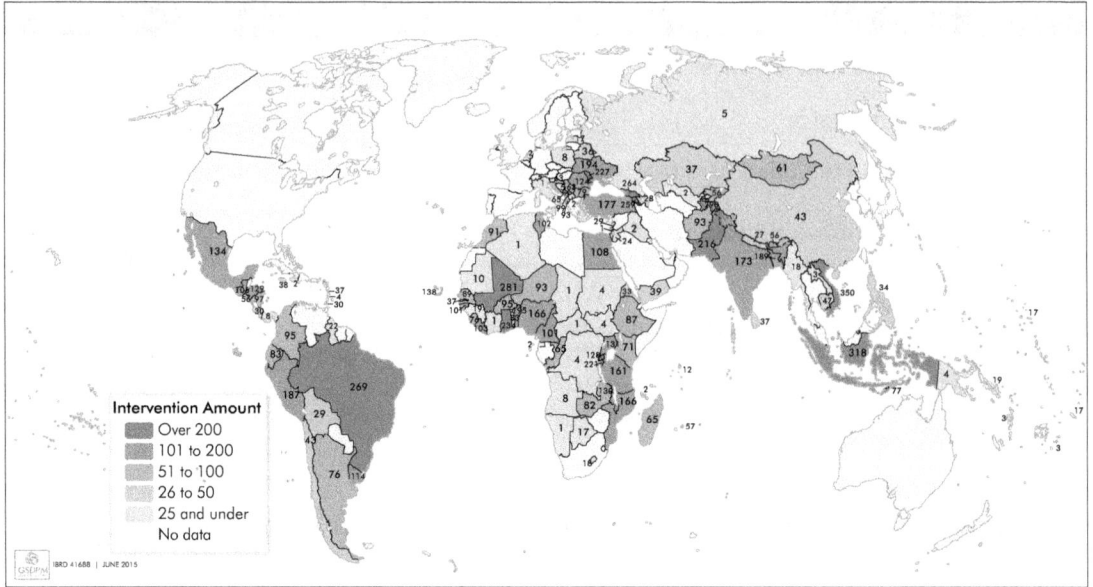

Intervention Amount
- Over 200
- 101 to 200
- 51 to 100
- 26 to 50
- 25 and under
- No data

IBRD 41688 | JUNE 2015

SOURCE: IEG.

FIGURE 1.3 World Bank Group Project Portfolio Composition

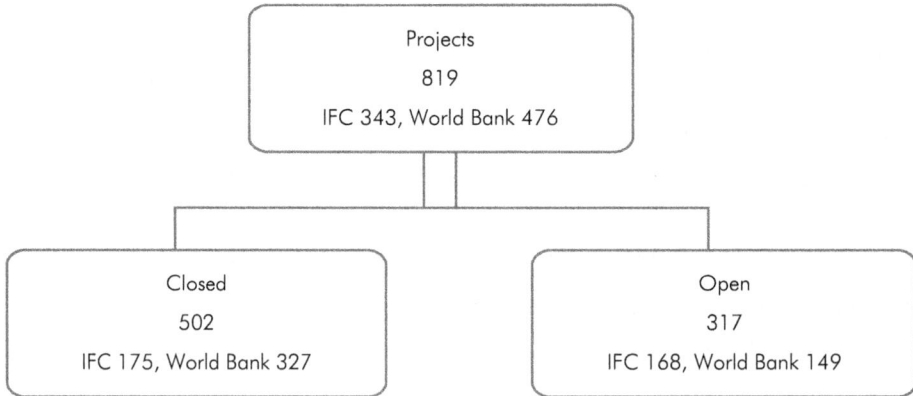

Projects
819
IFC 343, World Bank 476

Closed
502
IFC 175, World Bank 327

Open
317
IFC 168, World Bank 149

SOURCE: IEG portfolio review.

TABLE 1.4 Basic Characteristics of Portfolio, by Project

World Bank			IFC		
Network	Number	% of Network Portfolio	Business line	Number	% of AS Portfolio
FPD	61	26	Investment Climate	343[a]	22
HDN	13	2	Access to Finance	507	32
PREM	219	36	PPP	197	12
SDN	183	10	SBA	549	34

SOURCE: IEG portfolio review.
NOTE: AS = Advisory Services; PPP = public-private partnership; SBA = Sustainable Business Advisory. **Networks:** FPD = Finance and Private Sector Development; HDN = Human Development; PREM = Poverty Reduction and Economic Management; SDN = Sustainable Development.
a. 13 projects are mapped to Access to Finance, PPP, and SBA but include investment climate products.

approximately 20 projects have an investment climate component, although in terms of share it is approximately the same as for FPD.

Finally, it is important to note that although IFC investment climate projects are only advisory, the World Bank includes investment climate components in both investment and development policy operations, in approximately equal proportions. However, in terms of share, one in three development policy operations includes investment climate components, but only one in ten lending operations includes investment climate components. Not surprisingly, most (80 percent) of the adjustments with investment climate components are led by PREM, and most of the lending projects with investment climate (65 percent) are implemented by SDN, followed by FPD (17 percent).

INTERVENTIONS

Interventions are specific investment climate issues or dimensions that projects intend to address (such as land registration or construction permits). The World Bank Group activities in investment climate can be grouped in three main categories: those aimed at improving the business environment for entry, operation, and exit. Within each of these groups, the Bank Group implements a number of different interventions (Table 1.5).[24] These interventions aim to simplify and streamline regulatory procedures, remove sector-specific administrative constraints, revise the legal framework and institutions, establish effective dialogue systems between private and public sectors, and harmonize procedures and systems (Table 1.6).

TABLE 1.5 Distribution of Investment Climate Interventions

							Value ($ millions)[b]			
			IFC	World Bank	Total	Length (months)	IFC	World Bank	Active	Closed
Entry	Licensing		50	23	73	36	0.7 (46)	0.3 (1)	39	34
	Registration		40	36	76	23	0.5 (35)	3.4 (1)	25	51
		Total	90	59	149				17	42
Operations	Competition policy		3	23	26	29	0.2 (2)	12 (6)	9	17
	Contract enforcement		11	25	36	33[a]	0.7 (7)	0.3 (2)	10	26
	Doing Business indicators		36	0	36	45	0.7 (34)		19	17
	Investment policy and promo		52	107	159	29	0.6 (50)	9.7 (33)	59	100
	Labor		1	30	31	24[a]	0.3 (1)	0.2 (1)	2	29
	Property rights		14	99	113	24	0.2 (12)	13.1 (40)	37	76
	Public-private dialogue		30	25	55	42	0.7 (27)	6.6 (7)	23	32
	Regulations[c]		89	95	184	27	1.8 (84)	8.4 (20)	65	119
	Special enforcement zone		17	0	17	29[a]	1.1 (17)		9	8

			IFC	World Bank	Total	Length (months)	Value ($ millions)[b] IFC	Value ($ millions)[b] World Bank	Active	Closed
	Tax		39	65	104	32	1.2 (36)	12.1 (12)	44	60
	Trade logistics		36	136	172	31	0.9 (26)	7.8 (28)	50	122
	Other				4					
		Total	332	605	937				374	649
Exit	Alternate Dispute Resolution		21	10	31	32	0.8 (18)	2.2 (2)	11	20
	Bankruptcy		1	6	7	20[a]			0	7
	Debt resolution/ insolvency		11	24	35	27[a]	1.2 (10)	0.1 (2)	14	21
		Total	33	40	73				25	48
Sector reform			84	256	336				133	207
Total					1,499	23			549	947

SOURCE: IEG portfolio review.
NOTE: Length is based on single component project and major (for World Bank).
a. Based on multicomponent project.
b. Value refers to each intervention. Number of observations refers to the number of interventions for which there is direct report of amount.
c. Regulations is a broad category as it appears in project documents and includes licensing, permits, and administrative barriers.

TABLE 1.6 Description of Investment Climate Interventions

Intervention	Description
Licensing	This intervention aims to review, simplify, and streamline procedures needed to obtain a business license. This includes administrative reform programs, establishment of electronic registries of all valid licenses, design of screening mechanisms for new licenses to ensure necessity and quality, implementation of one-stop shops for licensing needs, and drafting and submission of new laws and amendments. Licenses addressed include those for business operations, construction, and environmental permits.
Registration	Registration includes procedures that are officially required, or commonly done in practice, for an entrepreneur to start up and formally operate an industrial or commercial business, as well as the time and cost to complete these procedures and the paid-in minimum capital requirement.
Competition Policy	The interventions aim to remove sector-specific constraints that affect market competition, enact the law on competition, and work with the competition council and other line ministries on reducing the concentration in key sectors. Interventions in this area support regulatory and competition assessments of businesses in the services sector and the creation of relevant toolkits and manuals.
Contract Enforcement	This intervention seeks to revise and harmonize commercial laws and codes, civil procedure laws, and laws regarding the functioning of the judiciary and court systems. Transfer judicial services from central courts and judges to municipal courts and clerks, establishment of new courts, automation of judicial procedures, and capacity building and training for lawyers, judges, and clerks are activities that help to improve enforcement mechanisms for businesses.
Doing Business Indicators	This intervention aims to prepare subnational and national indicators related to nine of the Doing Business areas. This includes training with local partners on the Doing Business methodology, report preparation and disseminaition, and technical assistance to implement reform proposals and recommendations.
Investment Policy and Promotion	Under this intervention, laws and strategies to promote increased investment, both from foreign and domestic investors, and in key sectors and locations, are adopted. Investment promotion trainings and workshops are conducted, investor aftercare programs developed and implemented, and investment oversight committees and agencies formed.

Intervention	Description
Labor	This intervention aims to revise the legal framework governing the labor market to improve labor market flexibility, improve employment relations and compensation schemes, reform pension systems, and make the hiring of foreign labor more flexible. This is done through new or amended labor laws, addressing wage-setting mechanisms and hiring quotas, and revising residency permits for foreign skilled workers.
Property Rights	This intervention addresses access to land, registering property, and protecting intellectual property rights. Review of legislation, digitization of property records and development of cadaster systems, and one-stop shops for property registration are among the activities used to promote property rights. Cadastres or surveys, together with land registries, are tools used around the world to map, prove, and secure property and use rights.
Public-Private Dialogue	Public-Private Dialogue interventions support programs that improve the quality and sustainability of policy reforms by providing flexible and robust mechanisms that address shortfalls in representation, communication, and coordination between relevant stakeholders.
Special Economic Zones	Interventions aim to develop SEZ regulatory regimes, draft laws for the industrial zone, enable environmental monitoring, and set up management of PPP arrangements inside the zone. This is done through market demand analysis and feasibility studies, best practices frameworks, and identification of land, investors, and developers for the zone.
Business Taxation	This intervention aims at streamlining burdensome tax payment and administration procedures for businesses by implementing small business tax regimes, electronic filing, and taxpayer education and services. Other activities and tax laws work to harmonize the tax system and reduce certain taxes, while at the same time eliminating exemptions.
Trade Logistics	Trade logistics comprises three core areas of reforms: (a) simplifying and harmonizing trade procedures and documentation, integrating risk management systems into border inspections and clearance, and implementing electronic processing, automation, and single window systems; (b) industry-specific reforms focus on agribusiness supply chains and on improving national logistics and distribution services; (c) regional integration reforms seek to improve trade logistics systems and services and border clearance at the regional level and foster mutual recognition of international standards, accreditation, and certification.

continued on page 26

Intervention	Description
Alternative Dispute Resolution	These interventions aim at establishing a system of court-annexed mediation, providing capacity building to mediators and judges, and establishing a regional forum for consensus building and ADR, preparing manuals on ADR, and enacting Laws on enforcement, bailiffs, and the execution of cash assets to accelerate enforcement of commercial disputes resolution.
Bankruptcy	These interventions aim at identifying weaknesses in existing bankruptcy law and the main procedural and administrative bottlenecks in the bankruptcy process in order to implement good practices to improve both the efficiency and the outcome of insolvency proceedings. Activities include improvements in existing regulations on company reorganization, through amendments to national bankruptcy acts and laws.
Debt Resolution/ Insolvency	This intervention aims to improve insolvency laws, based on global best practices, with regard to provisions relating to assets of the debtor, avoidance of transactions proceedings, reorganization, creditor rights, and secured lending. It improves institutional capacity for speedy resolution of disputes and technical assistance to improve court capacity.

SOURCE: IEG portfolio review.

It is important to note, however, that although both institutions operate in the same space, the scope of their investment climate interventions is generally different, with some overlap. The Bank focuses more on higher-level reforms, such as revising and harmonizing laws and codes, reforming institutions, developing strategies, and coordinating government agencies and ministries. In contrast, IFC mostly focuses on streamlining and simplifying procedures and processes, providing technical assistance, and automating systems.

Excluding sector reforms, which account for some 20 percent of all interventions, both institutions focus the great majority of interventions (80 percent) on firm operation, with 15 percent on entry and the remaining 5 percent on exit. Across interventions, regulations, trade, and investment promotion account for almost half of all interventions. There is an interesting "division of labor" among the two institutions. The World Bank conducts almost exclusively (over 80 percent of all) interventions in trade and property rights, as well as the majority of interventions on investment promotion. In IFC projects, in contrast, the majority (60 percent) focus on licensing and registration. Both institutions operate equally in regulation and public-private dialogue. Interestingly, IFC is the only institution that classifies some interventions as Doing Business indicators.

In terms of value, investment climate interventions in the World Bank are very small; the value is even smaller for IFC: less than $6 million for the Bank and less than $1 million for IFC. Typically the amounts related to investment climate interventions under Bank (lending) projects are significantly higher than those related to IFC advisory services, given the different nature and delivery models of the respective activities.

The distribution of interventions over time shows a remarkably similar trend for the two institutions. Over the FY07–13 period, the World Bank and IFC both supported a similar number of investment climate interventions (85 and 78 interventions per year, respectively), for a total of 597 for the World Bank and 547 for IFC (Figure 1.4). In terms of value, however, the two institutions provide a significantly different amount of support. The estimated value of World Bank investment climate interventions is equivalent to an estimated value of $475 million per year for the World Bank and $50 million for IFC (Figure 1.5).

The distribution of investment climate interventions across regions (Figure 1.6) and income levels shows that both the World Bank and IFC intervene most in Sub-Saharan Africa (37 percent of all interventions for both institutions) and Europe and Central Asia (24 percent for World Bank and 17 percent for IFC), followed by in Latin America and the Caribbean for the World Bank (17 percent) and East Asia and Pacific for IFC (15 percent). The Middle East and North Africa and South Asia Regions have the fewest interventions (4 percent

FIGURE 1.4 Number of Investment Climate Interventions Over Time, by Approval Year

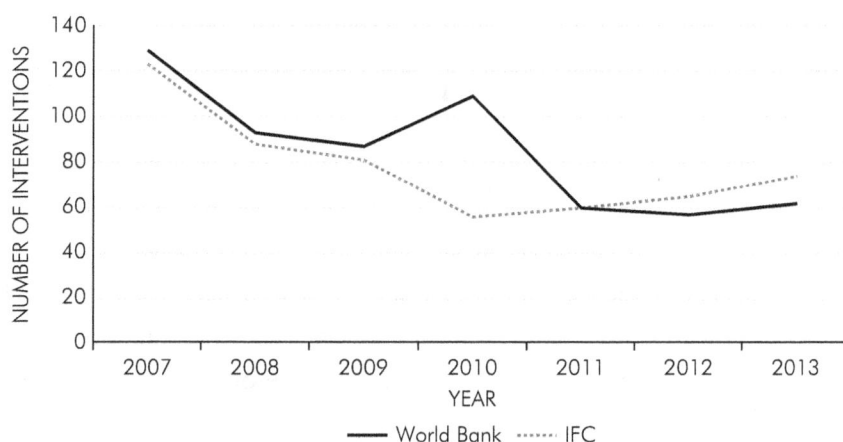

SOURCE: IEG portfolio review.

FIGURE 1.5 Value of Investment Climate Interventions Over Time, by Approval Year

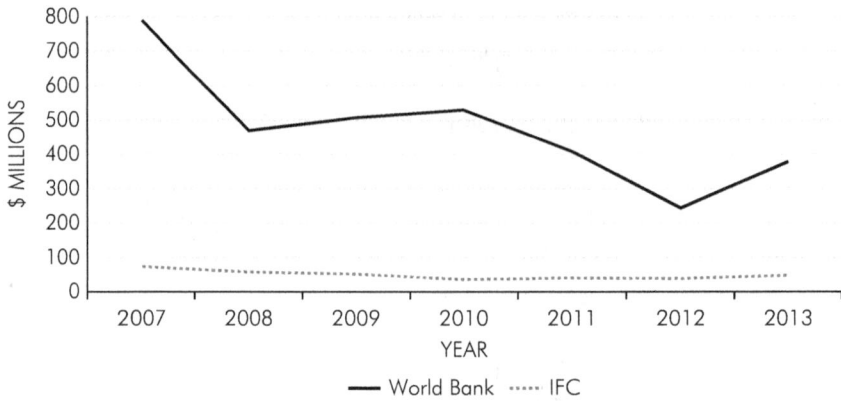

SOURCE: IEG portfolio review.

FIGURE 1.6 Distribution of Investment Climate Interventions, by Region and Status

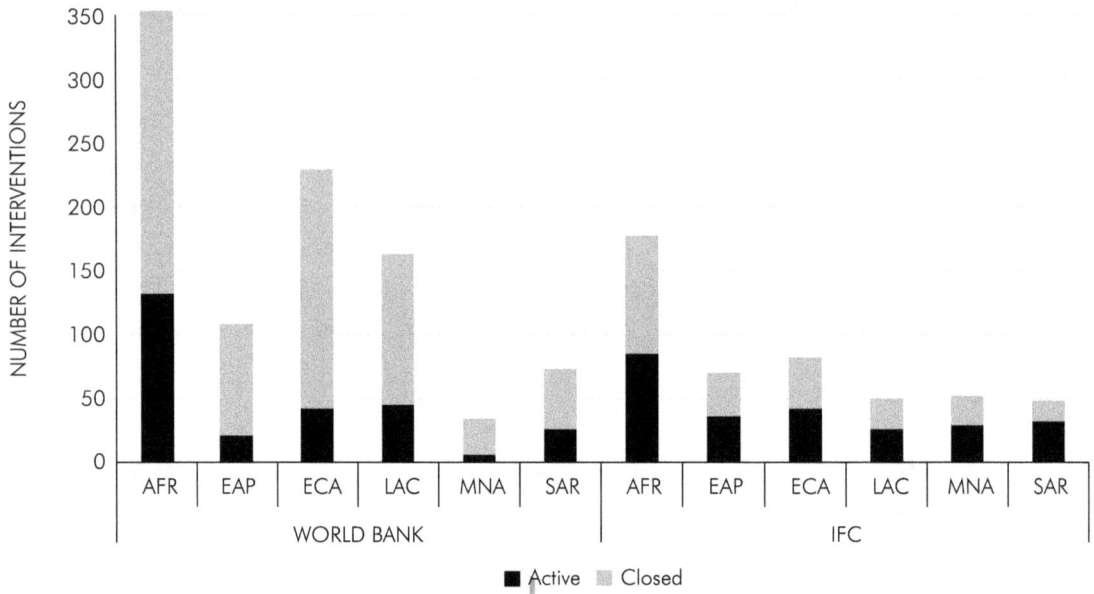

SOURCE: IEG portfolio review.
NOTE: AFR = Africa Region; EAP = East Asia and Pacific Region; ECA = Europe and Central Asia Region; LAC = Latin America and the Caribbean Region; MNA = Middle East and North Africa Region; SAR = South Asia Region.

for World Bank and 10 percent for IFC, respectively). It is interesting to note that although both institutions have the highest number of active projects in Africa and Europe and Central Asia, they complement each other in the distribution of new projects (active) in Latin America and the Caribbean and the Middle East and North Africa, with the World Bank focusing more in the former and IFC more in the latter. Similarly, both institutions pay particular attention to lower- and lower-middle-income countries, where 8 of 10 interventions are implemented.

All interventions[25] have active projects, with regulation, investment policy, trade, and tax being the most common and competition and labor the least. Bankruptcy is the only intervention for which there are no active projects as of the end of FY13. On average, investment climate interventions are implemented in less than 3 years (32 months). However, when in the World Bank these are part of lending operations, the average length is substantially higher. World Bank development policy operations with investment climate components are completed on average in less than two years; projects that include mostly investment climate components are implemented on average over six years.

With very few exceptions, namely bankruptcy and ADR, the distribution of interventions across regions shows that Africa is the region where the majority of interventions take place, followed by Europe and Central Asia and Latin America and the Caribbean (Table 1.7). In terms of income the distribution of interventions shows that almost half of interventions are in low-income countries, whereas entry and exit almost equally distributed between the three income groups.

In a few countries, for example, Cambodia, interventions focus on specific areas such as trade promotion. The World Bank Group did several things to promote trade: developed a guide to the World Trade Organization to inform businesses about the implications of entry into that organization; provided support for the development of an alternative dispute resolution system for commercial disputes; helped establish a legal and institutional framework for special economic zones (SEZs); and supported reductions in trade and investment-related processes and procedures through a single window system.

Often the World Bank Group, particularly IFC, also supports business regulations through programmatic approaches that cover many different aspects of investment climate. In Vietnam, the World Bank supported investment climate reform through five Poverty Reduction Support Credits. These projects supported trade and economic integration, tax regulations, land regulations, and labor skills. IFC projects supported licensing, land, and tax reforms.

In Bangladesh, IFC had a major programmatic approach through the Bangladesh Investment Climate Fund. One advantage of this approach is that it allowed the Bangladesh Investment Climate Fund (BICF) to re-engage with the line ministries at all levels to push a program forward after a change in government. The BICF covered a set of regulatory reforms and economic zones. The program supported drafting and approval of an economic zoned act and assisted the Bangladesh Export Processing Zones Authority in developing an

TABLE 1.7 Distribution of Investment Climate Interventions across Regions

	Share of Intervention by Regions (%)					
	AFR	EAP	ECA	LAC	MNA	SAR
Entry						
Licensing	34	13	23	18	6	7
Registration	39	11	16	19	8	7
Total	**37**	**12**	**19**	**19**	**7**	**7**
Operation						
Competition policy	44	8	20	20	8	
Contract enforcement	67	6	19	8		
Doing business indicators	32	19	13	13	19	3
Investment policy	35	20	11	17	5	11
Labor	42	0	26	13	3	16
Property rights	33	13	32	18	2	2
Public private dialogue	58	9	4	8	8	13
Regulation	29	10	28	15	9	9
Special economic zone	40	20		7		33
Tax	26	18	27	17	7	5
Trade logistics	36	17	18	18	3	8
Total	**36**	**14**	**21**	**16**	**6**	**8**
Exit						
Alternate dispute resolution	23	17	27	7	23	3

	Share of Intervention by Regions (%)					
	AFR	EAP	ECA	LAC	MNA	SAR
Bankruptcy	29		71			
Debt resolution	39	3	36	12	6	3
Total	**31**	**9**	**36**	**9**	**13**	**3**

SOURCE: IEG portfolio review.
NOTE: Regional projects are excluded because they mostly include knowledge management activities, data collection, and analytical products. **Regions**: AFR = Africa; EAP = East Asia and Pacific; ECA = Europe and Central Asia; LAC = Latin America and the Caribbean; MNA = Middle East and North Africa; SAR = South Asia.

environmental and social management system and in streamlining and automating its administrative processes.

In Kenya, IFC intended to develop a programmatic approach, as demonstrated by the establishment of a regulatory reform unit. In Nepal, a mini-diagnostic noted that the reform agenda should not be viewed as a series of consecutive discrete actions; sequencing and synergies between reforms had to be factored in to help the government design a PSD reform program most appropriate for the country. The investment climate reform program was designed as a programmatic series of Advisory Services operations. Following the completion of the Improving Climate Resilience Project, the second phase of the program was designed with connections across projects and between IFC and the Bank.[26]

INVESTMENT CLIMATE PORTFOLIO: GENDER

In the investment climate portfolio, explicit targeting—based either on the entrepreneur on the firm characteristics—is not common. IEG considered six "targeting dimensions," three regarding the entrepreneur's characteristics (gender, age, geographical location) and three regarding the firm's characteristics (formality status, exporting status, industry). Projects were coded based on whether they included an explicit targeting criterion for the beneficiaries of the intervention and whether they reported results for the specific group that was targeted. Only 8 percent of all projects specifically aimed to target women, and a similar percentage targeted firms based on their industry and formality status.

Targeting based on age, geographical area, or export status is even rarer (Table 1.8). Moreover, only a minority of projects with a specific target actually report on results for the

TABLE 1.8 Targeting in Investment Climate Portfolio

Targeted Group	All Projects % with Specific Targeting	Closed Projects % with Specific Targeting	% with Specific Targeting Reporting Results
Gender	8.1	5.7	37.9
Age	1.6	2.4	25.0
Geographic	1.2	0.8	25.0
Formality status	8.0	7.1	22.2
Export status	3.0	3.4	41.2
Industry	7.9	8.3	33.3

SOURCE: IEG portfolio review.

targeted group; for example, only 22.2 percent of those projects specifically targeting firms based on their formality status do. As for gender, fewer than 4 of 10 closed projects that had a gender target report any gender-disaggregated result or gender-relevant results.

Targeting by gender increased in FY12 and especially FY13, with respect to the previous years (Figure 1.7). Significant changes over time did not occur for other targeting criteria. The increase in gender targeting in the last two fiscal years likely reflects the renewed focus on gender mainstreaming by the World Bank Group. Since FY13, a "gender flag" was introduced to identify "gender-informed" operations. The gender flag—self-assigned by the project team—rates an operation as "gender informed" if the project documents integrate gender in either one of three dimensions: analysis, actions, or monitoring and evaluation (M&E).

The definition of gender targeting adopted by IEG for this evaluation is narrower than the definition of gender-informed according to the gender flag, although both are based on the same appraisal documents and on the identification of an explicit focus on gender (for this evaluation, "gender-targeting" is defined as an explicit aim to target women with specific activities).[27] An analysis of the overlap between the gender flag and the investment climate gender targeting in design for FY13, after limiting the sample to World Bank operations, reveals very little overlap. According to the gender flag, 66 percent of World Bank investment climate operations are gender informed; based on the targeting criteria, however, only 23 percent are.

FIGURE 1.7 Projects Targeting Beneficiaries by Gender in Their Design, by Approval Year

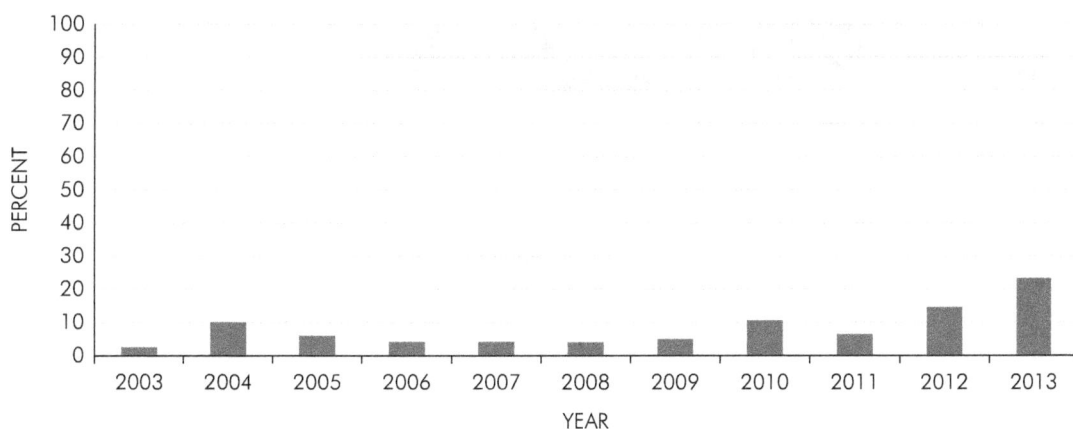

SOURCE: IEG portfolio review.

The prevalence of specific targeting in project design also varies by networks and regions. Of projects in all regions, those in the Middle East and North Africa are more likely to include in their design a target by gender as well as by firm formality status There are also differences across networks in the propensity to target specific groups, with IFC more likely to target specific firms (by formality status and industry; Table 1.9) and the Human Development Network to target youth (Table 1.10). Most of these correlations are confirmed in the multivariate analysis[28]—gender targeting was higher in FY13 than in previous years and lower in the Latin America and the Caribbean Region. Targeting of firms based on their formal/informal status is less common in PREM and SDN than in other networks, and most common in the Middle East and North Africa Region. Targeting of specific industries is also less common in PREM and SDN.

A close analysis of projects targeting gender reveals that many are small in size and mostly focused on capacity-building activities or on filling an information gap relative to gender-based barriers in the business enabling environment. Most of those projects target women as participants of training or consultative working groups rather than as entrepreneurs (or potential entrepreneurs) who may directly benefit from investment climate reforms. The gender dimension was also more easily found in activities aimed to produce diagnostic and baseline assessments.

Whether investment climate interventions should explicitly target specific subgroups of the population rather than promoting reforms aimed at improving the general business environment of a country is a question without a straightforward answer. On the one hand, by their very nature reforms are supposed to be general, and any specific provision could be perceived as

TABLE 1.9 Specific Targeting in Design, by Region (percent)

Region	Gender	Formality Status
AFR	9.3	11.3
EAP	9.4	4.7
ECA	4.7	4.0
LAC	3.2	5.6
MNA	17.5	19.0
SAR	5.1	6.3
World	13.8	5.2

SOURCE: IEG portfolio review.
NOTE: Regions: AFR = Africa; EAP = East Asia and Pacific; ECA = Europe and Central Asia; LAC = Latin America and the Caribbean; MNA = Middle East and North Africa; SAR = South Asia.

TABLE 1.10 Specific Targeting in Design, by Network (percent)

Network	Gender	Age	Formality Status	Industry
IFC	9.9	0.0	11.7	12.2
FPD	12.9	3.2	17.7	11.3
HDN	7.1	14.3	14.3	0.0
PREM	4.1	2.3	2.3	3.6
SDN	8.0	2.1	4.3	4.3

SOURCE: IEG portfolio review.
NOTE: IFC = International Finance Corporation. **Networks**: FPD = Finance and Private Sector Development; HDN = Human Development; PREM = Poverty Reduction and Economic Management; SDN = Social Development.

a politically unpalatable affirmative action. On the other hand, normally the playing field is not leveled for everybody, and certain entrepreneurs or firms, current or potential, experience obstacles that are specific to their group and, if not addressed, not only raise issues of fairness and equity, but can also hinder the growth potential of the whole economy.

The disadvantageous position of women in entrepreneurship has been widely documented. Gender-specific obstacles make it harder for women than for men to start and grow enterprises. Fewer women than men own and manage businesses worldwide (Kelley and others 2012). Also, in all regions of the world, including in developed economies, female-owned enterprises are substantially and significantly smaller (Bardasi, Sabarwal, and Terrell 2011; Minniti 2010), partly because women are more likely to operate in industries where firms are smaller and less efficient, but also because women face disproportionate obstacles in obtaining licenses and permits (because of limited mobility, time constraints, and sometimes discrimination and higher exposure to bribes and sexual harassment) and in accessing a number of things: finance, markets, courts and dispute resolution systems, networks, and assets and property.

In addition to de facto constraints such as those highlighted above, in some countries women also suffer legal discrimination, as has been documented in the World Bank Group report *Women, Business, and the Law*. In several countries women have lower legal status and fewer property rights than men; they may be subject to travel restrictions; or they may be forbidden from pursuing certain trades or professions in the same way as men (World Bank 2014). Reforms that neglect to consider de facto or legal constraints that limit women's opportunities could have unintended consequences—the assumption may be that the intervention is "gender neutral" although in fact only some are able to benefit. Investment climate reforms could address existing constraints that limit women's business opportunities, thus leveling the playing field and enhancing the project efficacy.

On the basis of the existing literature and *Women, Business, and the Law* (World Bank 2014), IEG identified four types of constraints as directly impacting the ability of women to operate in the business environment: unequal ownership rights to property; inability to sign a contract in the same way as a man; inability to register a business in the same way as a man; and inability to open a Bank account in the same way as a man. Typically, these limitations apply only to married women. Four possible combinations can be observed (Table 1.11). Investment climate reforms may be designed with knowledge of legal or de facto constraints and explicitly aim to address those constraints to ensure inclusion. Alternatively, investment climate reforms may claim to be gender neutral, although they might be implemented in environments where specific gender constraints exist.

IEG's review of the investment climate portfolio shows that in 89 percent of interventions targeting is, in principle, done correctly. More specifically, in 81 percent of interventions, investment climate reforms do not include gender targeting when there are no gender-specific legal constraints (although other relevant constraints may exist), and in 8 percent of interventions investment climate reforms target businesswomen because of other nonlegal constraints.

TABLE 1.11 Intervention Targeting Gender and Existence of Legal/Other Constraints

	Existence of Legal Constraints	No Legal Constraints (but de facto constraints may exist)
Investment climate reforms that target women	(i) Investment climate reforms may address the existing legal constraints and help level the playing field (at least on paper). (ii) Investment climate reforms may include gender-relevant activities that are unrelated to existing constraints, with the intent of "bypassing" them or implement other relevant gender activities. (iii) Investment climate reforms may be based on poor gender analysis and contradict existing legal constraints. Their efficacy for women may be undermined. **1.4%**	Investment climate reforms may be targeting women to address de facto constraints and to facilitate the inclusion of women among the pool of beneficiaries. **7.7%**
Investment climate reforms that do not target women	Investment climate reforms are "technically" gender neutral, but in reality they may not benefit women. **9.8%**	From a legal point of view, men and women have the same rights. There may still be important constraints arising either from customary laws or from uneven access to resources based on gender, so that in reality investment climate reforms may not deliver the same results for men and women. **81.1%**

SOURCE: IEG portfolio review.
NOTE: The percentage in each cell refers to investment climate interventions (in client countries included in the database) for each case. The legal constraints considered four types of restrictions, based on the Women, Business, and the Law database: unequal ownership rights to property; inability to sign a contract in the same way as a man; inability to register a business in the same way as a man; and inability of opening a Bank account in the same way as a man.

However, in 10 percent of interventions there was no targeting. That is, investment climate reforms do not target women when there are legal constraints that would make such reforms not gender neutral.[29]

Few countries in the world have either one of these limitations, yet 12 countries in the investment climate portfolio have at least one of the above constraints (Table 1.12). Four of these countries (Côte d'Ivoire, Democratic Republic of Congo, Pakistan, and the Philippines) have at least one

TABLE 1.12 Gender Targeting and Existence of Legal/Other Constraints

Countries with Gender Obstacles	Total Number of Investment Climate Interventions	Total Number of Woman-Friendly Interventions	Existence of at Least One Project Targeting Women in PAD
Cameroon	11	6	
Chile	5	1	
Congo, Dem. Rep. of	12	2	√
Congo, Rep. of	5	1	
Côte d'Ivoire	9	4	√
Ecuador	9	1	
Gabon	0	0	
Haiti	3	0	
Mauritania	3	1	
Niger	11	3	
Pakistan	25	9	√
Philippines	10	5	√

SOURCE: IEG.
NOTE: PAD = Project Appraisal Document.

investment climate project targeting women. Moreover, several of these countries implement interventions that tend to be woman friendly, even if there is no explicit gender targeting. These are examples where targeting may not have been correctly done, as obstacles for businesswomen were not in the regulatory environment for businesses but in the discriminatory legal framework.

IEG found one example of proper targeting. In Côte d'Ivoire, one IFC project includes a gender component that is explicitly based on the results of the Women, Business, and the Law database. The intervention (ongoing) aims to give married women the same economic opportunities that men have (activities include support for legal reforms, communication along the reform process, and development of evaluation tool for measuring their effective impacts). According to the Project Appraisal Document, this will result in an improvement of the economic situation of women, measured by the increase in the number of individual enterprises owned by women. In general, however, projects that target women deliver training and capacity-building activities that, although they may increase women's awareness of their disadvantaged situation, do not directly tackle existing legal constraints.

INVESTMENT CLIMATE PORTFOLIO: FCS

Overall, 15 percent of investment climate projects are implemented in FCS countries. IFC shows a slightly higher share of investment climate projects in FCS countries than the World Bank. However, in absolute terms, both institutions have approximately the same number of investment climate projects. Over time, the number of investment climate projects has held steady at around 12 per year, with both institutions having seen a drop in the number of projects in FCS countries over the last few years (Figure 1.8).

In terms of interventions, the most common interventions in FCS countries (accounting for over 50 percent of all) are regulation, investment promotion, trade, and public-private dialogue.

INVESTMENT CLIMATE PORTFOLIO: INDUSTRY-SPECIFIC SECTORS

Recent FIAS strategies identified two sectors for specific investment climate interventions: agribusiness and tourism. The agriculture sector accounts for a substantial share of

FIGURE 1.8 Number of Investment Climate Projects in FCS and Non-FCS Countries, by Approval Year

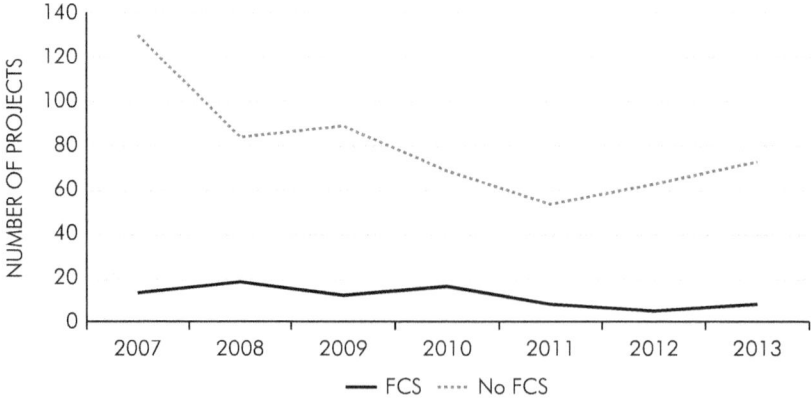

SOURCE: IEG portfolio review.
NOTE: FCS = fragile and conflict-affected situation.

developing countries' economies, growing at a rate of more than 5 percent every year and providing income for more than half of the countries' workers. Moreover, most of the population in developing countries lives in rural areas and depends on agriculture for its livelihood. Inefficient market for inputs, overregulation, and costly trade logistics in turn make domestic products uncompetitive. Given the importance of the agribusiness sector to the economy, governments have identified it as a priority, aligning World Bank interventions to countries' own national strategies in, for example, Bangladesh, Ghana, Honduras, India, Mali, the Philippines, and Ukraine.

Tourism represents approximately 70 percent of export services for the world's least developed countries (compared to the world average of 35 percent).[30] Tourism dominates the service sector in most client countries, which identify it as a key economic sector in the national strategies of, for instance, India, Peru, Saint Lucia, and Sierra Leone. It is second to agriculture in terms of employment generation per unit of investment and is a valuable source of foreign exchange. However, a range of impediments continues to inhibit investment, including complicated and nontransparent approval processes for tourism licenses; ineffective institutional structures of public or private sector agencies responsible for tourism development; weak institutional capacity to develop appropriate policy, plans, and processes for tourism investments; accessibility; complex land issues/limited availability of land for tourism development; ineffective aviation policies; and lack of access to finance.

The relevant portfolio includes both projects mapped under the Investment Climate for Industry practice and those not mapped to it but that cover sector-specific sector reforms in agriculture and industry, including regulatory reforms. To characterize and evaluate this portfolio of activities, IEG took two approaches. First, as part of the broad review of all investment climate projects, the portfolio analysis identified projects within the investment climate portfolio that (i) promoted sector-specific reforms in agribusiness or tourism; (ii) identified agribusiness or tourism as industries of interest; and (iii) had components and/or project development objectives that mentioned developing the agribusiness and tourism sectors.[31]

In addition, IEG reviewed a list of relevant projects provided by the Investment Climate for Industry practice and added those projects not already identified in the portfolio review that were deemed to meet both the general criteria for belonging in the investment climate portfolio and the criteria for being sectorally relevant to agriculture or tourism. Second, the team reviewed evidence from 19 completed case studies to consider if country strategy identified these sectors as development priorities and if specific interventions promoted Investment Climate for Industry in these two sectors. IEG then further considered case studies that met both criteria.

Investment climate projects with components focused on agribusiness and/or tourism constitute a significant part of the overall investment climate portfolio, including about 18 percent of World Bank investment climate investment projects and 16 percent of IFC investment climate advisory projects (Appendix Figure B.1). By commitment value of relevant components, again 18 percent of the World Bank investment climate portfolio and 16 percent of the IFC investment climate portfolio involve investment climate for agribusiness or tourism elements. Although the number and value of investment projects on the World Bank side do not show a clear trend since the creation of a practice group, the IFC advisory portfolio has expanded in recent years.

Regionally, more than half of the World Bank's projects are in Africa (Appendix Figure B.2) and a further quarter in Eastern Europe and Central Asia; IFC has its largest share (305) in Africa but a more even distribution across other regions. Thirteen percent of its investment climate industry advisory projects are not in any one region, but are global in focus. However, in terms of commitment value of components, the IFC and the World Bank each has just under half the portfolio value in Africa. Further, the World Bank has nearly a third of its component commitment value in Europe and Central Asia, whereas IFC has 17 percent of commitment value there. Comparing the investment climate industry portfolio to the investment climate portfolio in energy sector projects, the latter is considerably more concentrated in Europe and Central Asia for the World Bank and in the Middle East and North Africa, Europe and Central Asia, Latin America and the Caribbean, and "world" for IFC.

Finally, by income level, although it appears that by number the World Bank is more focused on lower-income countries and IFC advisory on lower-middle-income countries, component commitment levels suggest much more of a balance between the two institutions (Appendix Figure B.3.B). The Bank and IFC each have around half of their portfolios in lower-income countries and most of the balance in lower-middle-income countries, suggesting a serious focus on countries with large numbers of poor people and development challenges.

Many of the activities supported under investment climate for industry do not fit strictly within the confines of the legal and regulatory focus of the investment climate portfolio. Instead, sectoral studies often identify a much broader variety of constraints, opportunities, and challenges and often map out relevant value chains or supply chains. World Bank investments often have financing components, whereas IFC projects often incorporate "stakeholder engagement and outreach." There are elements of investment and sectoral promotion, training, capacity building, technological upgrading, and even physical infrastructure improvement in some of the projects (Appendix Table B.1). Box 1.1 provides examples of industry-specific projects. In fact, both the investment climate for industry and the competitive industries practices often employ value chain approaches to promote sectoral development and increased sectoral competitiveness.

In **agribusiness**, specific interventions either are trade reforms or are aimed at restructuring the agricultural industry per se. When it comes to **agricultural trade**, specific interventions are aimed at reducing compliance, transport, and transaction costs for agribusiness products and related inputs that can result in a more efficient and competitive trade and transport environment. This is mainly done in three ways: (i) simplification of regulatory instruments and requirements for trade facilitation and logistics; (ii) reforms in the shipping methods to remove anticompetitive regulations and promote competition, such as shipping association certification for chartering of foreign vessels for deployment in domestic routes; and (iii) a project agenda usually being facilitated through a focused public-private dialogue platform on agribusiness trade logistics, and transport, which is a structured stakeholders' dialogue to improve policy design, increase ownership and sustainability of reforms, and, ultimately, reform effectiveness. The 2011 Philippines Agribusiness Trade Competitiveness and the Honduras Agribusiness Trade Logistics Projects are examples of this.

When a project is aimed at improving the **agricultural industry** per se, reforms address the main regulatory and policy constraints hindering priority commodities (national produces) that aim to improve input market and storage capacity and modernize food safety, roads, and agricultural infrastructures (such as irrigation) and product certification system to facilitate investments in the sector. Another approach is to simplify procedures related to agriwaste processing and production of renewable energy, as in the Ukraine Investment Climate: Agribusiness and Cleaner Production Project. The interventions also support individual producers, community groups, and agricultural processors; they help test and develop technology appropriate to identified market opportunities and facilitate access for individual small and medium-size farmers to finance for small capital improvements and working capital through existing eligible microcredit organizations. An example of this is the Small-Scale Commercial Agriculture Development Project in Bosnia and Herzegovina.

In **tourism**, interventions are typically less specific and coincide with the creation of a diagnostic tool such as a database, interpretation and presentation of findings and scores on the preparedness for sustainable development of the tourism sector, or benchmarking of destinations. This is the case of the Tourism Investment and Development Advisory Services Global Project. Sometimes, the interventions become more explicit and entail assisting the government in structuring hotel deals, attracting foreign investors, and updating the land legislation. Other reforms deal with operation licenses and renewals for hotels and other SMEs involved in tourism, or the upgrading of the public transport system and museums. More explicit interventions are, for example, the Investment Climate Reform Project in Mali and the Bihar Investment Climate Reform Phase II Project.

SOURCE: IEG review.

Given the focus on sectoral promotion and value chain deepening in agriculture and tourism, many of the activities supported under investment climate for industry go well beyond the confines of the legal and regulatory focus of the investment climate portfolio.

Notes

[1] See Sinha, Holmberg, and Thomas (2013) and World Bank (2004b) for surveys of the literature on this issue.

[2] Levine and Renelt (1992)use a version of Leamer's (1983) extreme bound analysis.

[3] Sala-i-Martin (1997) uses a slightly less restrictive definition of robust than Levine and Renelt (1992).

[4] See, for example, Cai, Fang, and Xu (2011), Dinh and Clarke (2012), Dollar, Hallward-Driemeier, and Mangistae (2005), Fernandes (2008), Gatti and Love (2008), Hallward-Driemeier, Wallsten, and Xu (2006), Li, Mengistae, and Xu (2011), and Harrison, Lin, and Xu (2013). Xu (2011) summarizes this literature. Similarly, different types of firms are likely to be affected differently by the business environment. Many studies have found that small, medium-size and large firms face very different constraints within the same country (Clarke 2011; Gelb and others 2006; Hallward-Driemeier and Aterido 2009).

[5] This section of the report focuses only on the role of PSD in FCS and the debate on the sequencing of investment climate reforms. The broader debate on determinants of economic growth is beyond the scope of this evaluation.

[6] The estimate of 1.5 billion refers to people living in fragile and conflict-affected states or in countries with very high levels of criminal violence.

[7] http://go.worldbank.org/SGSH2VXZC0.

[8] The Sierra Leone case on which the paper is based set the following legal issues to attract investment: move from a traditional legal code to current international best practices, develop a regulatory framework for labor, privatization, and corruption, and a free and fair judiciary system (IFC 2004).

[9] "To the extent that the government was a party to the conflict, it may have reduced legitimacy and/or effectiveness in dealing with private sector regulation and governance reform" (http://go.worldbank.org/SGSH2VXZC0).

[10] See the DCED's useful bibliography on different direct intervention approaches: http://www.enterprise-development.org/page/direct-intervention-approaches.

[11] http://go.worldbank.org/SGSH2VXZC0.

[12] The report also importantly cautions that reforms not come too quickly, so as not to reignite violence and entrench social division (Masinde and Harwit 2014, p. 4).

[13] See also a DCED report by Curtis and others (2010) covering seven established PSD tools used in fragile and conflict-affected settings. The purpose and benefits of each tool is explained and applied to different phases of conflict, along with a discussion on the drawbacks of the approaches.

[14] Investment climate for industry strategy note and Investment Climate for Industry webpage. http://fpdweb.worldbank.org/units/fpdvp/ficdr/cicin/Pages/en/default.aspx.

[15] This is the only World Development Report to specifically focus on the investment climate. The 2002 World Development Report (World Bank 2001) focused on institutions and overlapped with the 2005 World Development Report. In particular, the report had chapters on courts, finance, and infrastructure. The 2002 report, however, did not focus on investment and did not rely primarily on firm-level evidence.

[16] In addition to FIAS, the CIC also included the Monitoring and Analysis Group that created the Doing Business report and Investment Climate Unit that oversaw Investment Climate Assessments (World Bank 2004a).

[17] Forty percent of MIGA's technical assistance interventions were overlapping with FIAS technical assistance operations, because of an explicit shift in MIGA strategy in 2003 that called for greater alignment with investment climate work across the institutions (World Bank 2006).

[18] The Doing Business law library is a comprehensive online collection of business laws and regulations. The coverage of the laws is not limited to Doing Business indicators. It links to official government sources (that is civil laws, commercial laws, and so forth) when possible.

[19] Starting from 1995 till the mid-2000s, FIAS produced diagnostic reports on administrative barriers. FIAS conducted business surveys and templates to provide more detail and data to its general diagnostics. Starting from the 2000s, FIAS moved from stand-alone diagnostics to projects that focus on solution design and implementation. In FY07, less than 20 percent of completed projects were stand-alone diagnostics.

[20] See Appendix A for a detailed description of the portfolio methodology.

[21] The number of projects includes World Bank projects that were open in FY07 even if approved as early as FY03.

[22] All values for the World Bank are estimated and refer only to investment climate interventions (not to the whole project value). Further, this estimate excludes the value of sector specific interventions, estimated at $61 million for IFC and $2,649 million for the World Bank. See Appendix B for more details on portfolio characteristics.

[23] Relative to the total network portfolio.

[24] The intervention classification is based on the classification reported in the project documents. Consequently the classification "DB indicators" appears as reported in project documents.

[25] Intervention is the specific regulatory reform being achieved.

[26] The design of the project was informed by the 2011 Nepal Investment Climate Assessment report, based on the Nepal Enterprise Survey of 2009.

[27] Women are typically the targeted group.

[28] Probit regressions have been estimated for the probability of including a specific targeting in design, controlling simultaneously for fiscal year, region, network, and country income classification.

[29] In the remaining 1 percent of cases it is not possible to assess whether there was targeting because of multiplicity of situations that can occur.

[30] IFC-Tourism Sector Diagnostic Benchmarking database.

[31] This was not always evident from the coding. For example, several World Bank and IFC projects coded "trade facilitation" contained specific language about the agribusiness supply chain.

References

Athreya, K. B. 2013. *Big Ideas in Macroeconomics: A Nontechnical View.* Cambrtidge, MA: The MIT Press.

Bagwitz, D., S. Becker, R. Elges, H. Grossman, G. Kruk, and A. Mierk. 2008. "Private Sector Development in (Post-) Conflict Situations." GTZ, Berlin, Germany.

Bardasi, E., S. Sabarwal, and K. Terrell. 2011. "How Do Female Entrepreneurs Perform? Evidence from Three Developing Regions." *Small Business Economics* 37: 417–41.

Cai, H., H. Fang, and L. Xu. C. 2011. "Eat, Drink, Firms, Government: An Investigation of Corruption from Entertainment and Travel Costs of Chinese Firms." *Journal of Law and Economics* 54: 55–78.

Clarke, G. R. G. 2011. "Are Managers' Perceptions About Constraints Reliable? Evidence from a Natural Experiment in South Africa." *Journal of Globalization and Development* 2: 1–28.

Collier, P., and A. Hoeffler. 2000. "Greed and Grievance in Civil War." *Oxford Economic Papers* 56: 563–95.

———. 2002. "Aid, Policy and Growth in Post-Conflict Societies." World Bank Policy Research Working Paper 2902, Washington, DC.

Cramer, C. 2009. "Trajectories of Accumulation Through War and Peace." In *The Dilemmas of Statebuilding: Confronting the Contradictions of Postwar Peace Operations*, eds. R. Paris, T. D. Sisk, London: Routledge.

Curtis, L., P. Davis, C. Gündüz, A. Ockenden, T. Pedrick, and T. Vaux. 2010. *Private Sector Development in Conflict-Affected Environments*. Cambridge, UK: DCED.

del Castillo, G. 2001. "Post-Conflict Reconstruction and the Challenge to International Organizations: The Case of El Salvador." *World Development* 29 (12).

———. 2008. *Rebuilding War-Torn States: The Challenge of Post-Conflict Economic Reconstruction*. Oxford, UK: Oxford University Press.

Devarajan, S., W. R. Easterly, and H. Pack. 2003. "Low Investment Is Not the Constraint on African Development." *Economic Development and Cultural Change* 51: 547–71.

Dinh, H. T., and G. R. Clarke. 2012. *Performance of Manufacturing Firms in Africa: An Empirical Analysis*. Washington, DC: World Bank.

Dollar, D., M. Hallward-Driemeier, and T. Mengistae. 2005. "Investment Climate and Firm Performance in Developing Countries." *Economic Development and Cultural Change* 54: 1–31.

Dudwick, N. R., J. Srinivasan, J. Cuesta, and D. Madani. 2013. *Creating Jobs in Africa's Fragile States: Are Value Chains an Answer?* Washington, DC: World Bank.

Euser, S. 2011. "What Is the Role of Foreign Companies in Private Sector Development in Post-Conflict Situations?" Maastricht School of Management dissertation.

Fernandes, A. M. 2008. "Firm Productivity in Bangladesh Manufacturing Industries." *World Development* 36: 1725–2008.

Gatti, R., and I. Love. 2008. "Does Access to Credit Improve Productivity? Evidence from Bulgaria." *Economics of Transition* 16: 445–65.

Gelb, A., V. Ramachandran, M. K. Shah, and G. Turner. 2006. *What Matters to African Firms? The Relevance of Perceptions Data*. Washington, DC: World Bank.

Hallward-Driemeier, M., and R. Aterido. 2009. "Comparing Apples with...Apples: How to Make (More) Sense of Subjective Rankings of Constraints to Business." World Bank Policy Research Working Paper 5054, Washington, DC.

Hallward-Driemeier, M., S. J. Wallsten, and L. C. Xu. 2006. "Ownership, Investment Climate and Firm Performance." *Economics of Transition* 14: 629–47.

Hameed, S. 2013. "Private Sector Development in Fragile, Conflict-Affected and Violent Countries. A Research Project on U.S. Leadership in Development and the Program on Crisis, Conflict, and Cooperation." CSIS, Washington, DC.

Harrison, A. E., J. Y. Lin, and L. C. Xu. 2013. "Explaining Africa's (Dis)advantage." *World Development*.

IFC (International Finance Corporation). 2004. *Sierra Leone: Diagnostic Study of the Investment Climate and the Investment Code. Foreign Investment Advisory Service*. Washington: IFC.

Kelley, D. J., C. G. Brush, P. G. Greene, Y. Litovsk, and GERA (Global Entrepreneurship Research Association). 2012. *Global Entrepreneurship Monitor 2012 Women's Report*. Wellesley, MA.

Kusago, T. 2005. "Post-Conflict Pro-Poor Private-Sector Development: The Case of Timor-Leste." *Development in Practice* 15 (3–4).

Leamer, E. E. 1983. "Let's Take the Con Out of Econometrics." *American Economic Review* 73.

Levine, R., and D. Renelt. 1992. "A Sensitivity Analysis of Cross-Country Growth Regressions." *American Economic Review* 82: 942–63.

Li, W., T. Mengistae, and L. C. Xu. 2011. "Diagnosing Development Bottlenecks: China and India." *Oxford Bulletin of Economics and Statistics* 73: 722–52.

MacSweeney, N. 2008. *Private Sector Development in Conflict-Affected Environments: A Review of Current Literature and Practice*. Cambridge, UK: DCED.

Masinde, C. K., and E. Harwit. 2014. "Improving the Investment Climate in Fragile and Conflict Situations: Lessons from IFC Projects for Operationalizing the World Development Report 2011." World Bank Policy Research Working Paper, Washington, DC.

Mills, R., and Q. Fan. 2006. *The Investment Climate in Post-Conflict Situations*. Washington, DC: World Bank.

Minniti, M. 2010. "Female Entrepreneurship and Economic Activity." *European Journal of Development Research* 22: 294–312.

Paris, R. 2004. *At War's End: Building Peace after Civil Conflict*. Cambridge, UK: Cambridge University Press.

Peschka, M. P. 2010 (updated April 2011). "The Role of the Private Sector in Fragile and Conflict-Affected States." World Bank World Development Report Background Paper, Washington, DC.

Phetsavong, K., and M. IchiHashi. 2012. *The Impact of Public and Private Investment on Economic Growth*. Hiroshima, Japan: Hiroshima University.

Piffaretti, N. 2010. "From Rent-Seeking to Profit Creation: Private Sector Development and Economic Turnaround in Fragile States." Munich Personal RePEc Archive.

Sala-i-Martin, X. 1997. "I Just Ran Two Million Regressions." *American Economic Review* 87: 178–83.

Sala-i-Martin X., and E. V. Artadi. 2002. "Economic Growth and Investment in the Arab World." Columbia University Department of Economics Discussion Paper Series 0203-08, New York.

Schoof, U. 2006. *Stimulating Youth Entrepreneurship: Barriers and Incentives to Enterprise Start-Ups by Young People*. Geneva: International Labour Office.

Simavi, S., C. Manuel, and M. Blackden. 2010. *Gender Dimensions of Investment Climate Reform: A Guide for Policy Makers and Practitioners*. World Bank, Washington, DC.

Sinha, S., J. Holmberg, and M. Thomas. 2013. "What Works for Market Development: A Review of the Evidence." Swedish International Devlopment Cooperation Agency UTH Working Paper 2103:1, Stockholm, Sweden.

UNIDO-GTZ. 2008. *Creating an Enabling Environment for Private Sector Development in Sub-Saharan Africa*. Vienna: UNIDO.

Veljanovski, C. 2010. "Economic Approaches to Regulation." In *The Oxford Handbook of Regulation*, eds. R. Baldwin, M. Cave, and M. Lodge. Oxford: Oxford University Press.

World Bank. 2001. *World Development Report 2002: Building Institutions for Markets*. Washington, DC: World Bank.

———. 2003. *Doing Business 2004*. Washington, DC: World Bank.

———. 2004a. *Doing Business 2005*. Washington, DC: World Bank.

———. 2004b. *World Development Report 2005: A Better Investment Climate for Everyone*. Washington, DC: World Bank.

———. 2006. *Investment Promotion Agency. Performance Review 2006*. Washington, DC: World Bank.

———. 2009. *Sector Licensing Studies. Mining Sector*. Washington, DC: World Bank.

———. 2010. *World Development Report 2011: Conflict, Security and Development*. Washington, DC: World Bank.

———. 2011. *Investment Climate in Practice*. Washington, DC: World Bank.

———. 2013. *Doing Business 2014: Understanding Regulations for Small and Medium-Size Enterprises*. Washington, DC: World Bank.

———. 2014. *Women, Business and the Law 2014: Removing Restrictions to Enhance Gender Equality*. Washington: World Bank. http://www.enterprisesurveys.org/~/media/FPDKM/EnterpriseSurveys/Documents/Misc/Indicator-Descriptions.pdf.

Xu L. C. 2011. "The Effects of Business Environments on Development: Surveying New Firm-Level Evidence." *World Bank Research Observer* 26: 310–340.

2 Relevance of World Bank Group Investment Climate Interventions

HIGHLIGHTS

- At the corporate and network level, strategies have identified improving the business environment as one of the strategic pillars of the institutions' agenda under PSD.

- At the country level, nearly all World Bank Group country partnership and assistance strategies identify enhancing the investment climate as a main objective. The main constraints are lack of competition, barriers to establish and operate businesses, costs of doing business, and regulatory burdens.

- Virtually all regulatory areas for a business-friendly regulatory environment are covered by World Bank Group interventions, and interventions are properly prioritized in client countries.

- Two diagnostic tools most commonly used to identify regulatory reforms, Doing Business and Enterprise Surveys, are only partially relevant in helping the World Bank Group identify appropriate areas of intervention.

- The consultation process and diagnostic analysis rarely cover a set of stakeholders in society beyond government and businesses.

This chapter presents evidence on the extent to which support for regulatory reforms has been a strategic priority for the World Bank Group and whether it has been relevant to client countries. IEG provides evidence at three levels: (i) Strategic level—do corporate and country strategies identify investment climate reforms as a priority? (ii) Interventions level—is the World Bank Group offering the right set of investment climate reforms in the right countries? and (iii) Analytical level—do diagnostic tools adequately inform investment climate reforms supported by the Bank Group?

Between 2007 and 2013, the Bank Group supported regulatory reforms in 119 countries through nearly 15 types of interventions. These countries significantly varied in terms of their development levels and challenges, but they all pursued investment climate reforms with the goal of improving the regulatory environment for private sector development.

Overall, World Bank Group strategies intend to enhance competition, foster enterprise creation and growth, facilitate international trade and investment, and unlock sustainable investment opportunities in key sectors, such as agribusiness and tourism (World Bank 2002, 2013). They pursue these objectives by reducing time, costs, and procedures and by simplifying regulations. For example, the FIAS strategy (2012–16) indicates that more firms enter the market and grow when start-up time and cost are cut, operating licenses and fees preventing entry to specific markets are removed, tax distortions are eliminated, and tax procedures are simplified.

In general, these strategies focus on creating favorable market conditions for enterprises and do not explicitly take into account other stakeholders in society; the earlier 2002 PSD strategy indicates that consultations for reforms should fit with what is achievable in a given economic, political, and social context. Basically, these reforms assume that what is good for firms is also good for society, although some (de)regulations may have significant consequences for different stakeholders in society.

Relevance of Investment Climate at the Corporate and Country Strategic Levels

At the corporate level, the most recent World Bank Group Strategy (2013) acknowledges that improving business environment is a key to stimulating private sector investment and jobs and achieving the twin goals of ending extreme poverty and promoting shared prosperity. Similarly, earlier World Bank and IFC corporate strategies made improving the investment climate one of the strategic pillars of the institutions' agenda for PSD (World Bank 2009–10, IFC 2007–13).

The World Bank strategy commits the institution to promoting reforms aimed at improving the environment for business, with the objective of promoting a robust and competitive private sector. Similarly, IFC's corporate strategy commits the institution to promote open and competitive markets in developing countries through, among other initiatives, reforms of the business enabling environment (IFC 2013). The latest World Bank Group strategy renews the commitment of the Bank Group to help countries improve their business environment through institutions and regulations that support PSD, policy dialogue, and advisory and knowledge work.

Although corporate strategies do not touch on the contextual factors in the delivery of investment climate interventions, the most recent FIAS strategy prioritizes IDA-eligible countries, Sub-Saharan Africa, FCS, and sectoral interventions (for example, agribusiness and tourism). In IDA countries, investment climate reforms aim to provide a signaling effect for both domestic and foreign investors. Fostering employment and competitiveness, reducing vulnerability, and strengthening resilience are themes in the Bank's Africa regional strategy, and investment climate strategic priorities are aligned with these. In FCS, the World Bank Group aims to support the implementation of integrated programs that draw on products and expertise that have been particularly useful to them, such as business entry, licensing, tax reforms, SEZs, trade logistics, and industry-specific investment climate work with related investment facilitation activities.

Finally, the World Bank Group puts a special focus on investment climate reform in two sectors that have broad relevance to development in many low-income countries: agribusiness and tourism. These two sectors are major sources of employment. Agriculture is the most important sector in most developing countries. Therefore, identifying and removing industry-specific barriers that hinder competition and improving the regulatory and institutional framework for accessing finance in agriculture are important. Similarly, tourism is in some cases the most significant service sector for many IDA countries, second to agriculture only in terms of employment generation per unit of investment (World Bank 2011a).

At the network level, a number of sectors have equally identified the improvement of the regulatory environment as a key aspect of their strategy. The most obvious is FPD. Investment climate, under different names (that is, business environment, enabling environment), has been part of the World Bank's PSD strategies since the late 1980s. The 1980s witnessed increased attention to the promotion of foreign investments with the establishment of FIAS by IFC in 1985 and, soon after that, the creation of MIGA, with the mandate to facilitate foreign direct investment.

The World Bank Group PSD strategy (2002) remains the strategy with the most emphasis on investment climate activities. It defines a good investment climate as a sensible governance system that allows firms and farms to pursue productive activity, with contracts and property rights respected and with reduced corruption. Overall, enhancing the investment climate is seen as a strong public policy for the private sector, including the required supporting institutions. The strategy identifies three main sets of activities to improve investment climate in client countries: (i) indicators and benchmarking country performance; (ii) responsive advisory services that equip governments with the tools to implement reforms and measure results; and (iii) policy and investment loans to support requests based on these reforms. The strategy promotes systematic Enterprise Surveys and Investment Climate Assessments to identify features of the investment climate that matter most for productivity, as well tracking changes over time in the investment climate within and across countries. The lending or technical assistance of the Bank Group would build on these assessments. The 2009 update to the PSD strategy reiterated the importance of enhancing investment climate. Its focus is on improving regulatory quality and systemic capacities to develop new regulation.

Other networks' strategies have devoted attention to the policy and regulatory environment. For example, one of the priorities of the Bank trade strategy is to support regulatory reform and cooperation. The Bank Group trade strategy (2011) proposes a continuation of the current lending trend, but with a stronger focus on the regulatory dimensions of transport and facilitation projects. The strategy emphasizes the need to help countries mainstream trade into statistical development strategies at national and regional levels so that barriers to trade (including regulatory) can be assessed and benchmark indicators can be developed to assess performance. The International Trade Department is developing a toolkit for trade-impact assessment tailored to the needs of developing countries based on the principles of Regulatory Impact Assessment. The development of the trade barriers database by the Development Economics Vice Presidency has been particularly useful in identifying these barriers (World Bank 2011b).

The most recent Agriculture and Rural Development Strategy plans to expand the Bank's role in the regulatory reform area. For many years the network has been supporting analytical work to guide dialogue with client countries on improving the policy and legal environment for agriculture including developing methods and country case studies of the rural investment climate. With its new agriculture strategy (FY13–15) the World Bank intends to continue to support analytical work, whereas IFC focuses on regulatory reform, warehouse system regulation, competition policy, and tax and incentive reform in the sector. In addition, the World Bank Group is developing the Benchmarking the Business of Agriculture program which will identify and monitor policies and regulations that limit market access for small to medium-size producers, providing policy makers with a tool that can be used to strengthen the investment climate for local and regional agribusiness.[1]

Similarly, the most recent energy strategy (2013), environment sector strategy (2012–22), and infrastructure sector strategy (FY12–15) emphasize the importance of strong institutions, legislation, regulation, and enforcement. They recognize that a clear, predictable regulatory framework is needed to facilitate private sector participation. In particular, the Infrastructure Strategy (2012) commits the World Bank to support reforms of labor and land regulation, as well as to deploy new approaches to improve the business environment, such as the regulatory "guillotine," which, combined with regulatory impact assessment, will help reduce the amount of business regulations.

In parallel to corporate and sector strategies, regional strategies identify improving the regulatory environment as one of the areas to support. For example, one of the three strategic pillars of the 2004 Strategic Initiative for Africa is to improve the investment climate. The recent Africa strategy continues to focus on business environment. It identifies business environment as the second priority after infrastructure. Building on the Arab Spring, one of the strategic directions of the World Bank Group in the Middle East and North Africa Region is to create jobs by providing an enabling environment for opportunity, competition, innovation, and entrepreneurship (World Bank 2013).

IEG undertook 25 country case studies to assess whether World Bank Group support for regulatory reforms has been relevant to client countries. The review covered Country Assistance Strategies (CASs) and CASCR Reviews produced during the evaluation period, as well as client countries' development strategies.

At the country level, nearly all World Bank Group country partnership and assistance strategies identify enhancing the business environment as a main objective (see Box 2.1). Not surprisingly, the definition of business environment in these strategies is generally broad, including, along with regulatory reforms, infrastructure, labor skills, access to finance, corruption, governance, and so forth. For example, the Philippines CAS for FY10–12 focused on enabling the business environment to promote competitiveness, productivity, and employment, with three intended outcomes: enhanced institutional capacity for investment, service delivery, and trade; increased investment; and increased employment.

FCS country strategies prepared right after post-conflict periods were an exception. They did not focus on enhancing business environment (for example, Nepal ISN 2007–09), but focused instead on postconflict economic programs.[2] In line with the literature that links a good business environment to growth and poverty reduction, most investment climate focus falls either under the growth pillar or the PSD pillar of country strategies. For example, the Cambodia CAS points out that a weak business environment resulted in very narrow growth, high levels of informality, and a drop in FDI.

Although most country strategies that IEG reviewed acknowledge the importance of and support improvements to the business environment, most of them do not articulate which specific reform to support. In a few countries, regulatory reforms were specifically identified as an important part of the country development strategy. Lack of competition, barriers to establish and operate businesses, costs of doing business, and regulatory burdens are the

The Jordan FY06–11 CAS had as strategic pillar strengthening the investment environment and building human resources for a value-added, skill-intensive, and knowledge-based economy. During this period, the country initiated an investment climate reform process with World Bank Group support. Key reforms included the reduction of the minimum capital required to establish a limited liability company, lowering property taxes, establishing a single reception service for company registration, and improving the resolution of business dispute. World Bank support included lending through the Recovery Under a Global Uncertainty Development Policy Loan, which focused on taxation and business entry; and analytic and advisory activities in the form of an Investment Climate Analysis (2007), Doing Business (various years), Quick Response Surveys (November 2008 and April 2009), and programmatic technical assistance.

In Vietnam, enhancing the business environment was one of the pillars of the CAS for FY07–10. Improving the business climate and strengthening competitiveness was a key objective. IBRD/IDA assistance supported this objective with credits and analytic and advisory activities on World Trade Organization accession, Vietnam Development Results 2007, competitiveness and innovation, and a report on the observance of standards and codes. IFC advisory services supported simplification of business-related procedures.

SOURCE: IEG review.

main constraints mentioned. Few strategies identify even the specific areas of intervention aimed at reducing regulatory burdens for businesses. For example, the Georgia CPS for FY06–09 focused on reducing barriers to establishing and operating businesses so aimed at supporting inspection processes, permits, and licensing requirements; customs border processing; and standardization. Similarly, Rwanda's FY09–12 CAS identified commercial law reform, capacity building of the Rwanda Investment Promotion Agency, public-private dialogue, and the government's Doing Business reform action plan as key intervention areas. Analytical work on investment climate also was a priority in a number of countries with the expected completion of Investment Climate Assessments.

In Cambodia, the focus was on the basic regulatory reform elements for trade-related business operations, such as the time and cost of administering exports and imports, investment promotion, and trade-supporting networks. Finally, in a few countries the World Bank Group has had a long-term and programmatic engagement in the investment climate area, whereas in most countries the engagement focused on specific areas. Bangladesh is a good example, with the Bank Group supporting regulatory reforms since early the 2000s with a comprehensive reform agenda.

Contrary to the evident emphasis shown at the network level, only a few country strategies emphasized the importance of sector-specific regulatory reforms (that is, Georgia, Guinea, and so forth). For example, in the Guinea Interim Strategy Note, the government stresses the improvement of the investment climate, in particular in agriculture and the mining sector.

Although World Bank Group CASs put a significant emphasis on improving the business environment, and at times the regulatory environment specifically, client countries' own development strategies assign much less weight to enhancing the investment climate. Most of the countries reviewed in the case studies have their own country development strategy (that is, Vision 2030 for Kenya, Vision 2021 for Rwanda). These strategies place an important role on PSD, but they do not emphasize as much the support to the business environment or to the regulatory environment, as is done in Bank Group country strategies. Such cases include Georgia and Kenya. The Georgia 2003 Economic Development and Poverty Reduction Program prioritized improving several business environment areas with the goal of economic development and poverty reduction. Kenya's Vision 2030 aimed to transform Kenya into a globally competitive middle-income country by 2030. In 2011, the government released a specific regulatory reform strategy (June 2011–June 2014) to ensure improvement in the business regulatory environment in areas such as licensing, Doing Business indicators, inspections and enforcement, regulatory impact assessment, and regulatory streamlining.

Consistent with that, evidence shows that prioritizing business environment in the country partnership and countries' own development strategies does not always translate into strong commitment at the project level. Table 2.1 presents six country-owned development strategies that focus on improving business regulatory environments. It also presents the relevant World Bank Group interventions in response to the governments' priorities. IEGs' analysis shows that, notwithstanding a government commitment at the strategic level, in three of six cases the projects faced political commitment problems during implementation. This highlights the importance of proper engagement and shows that having commitment at the strategy level is not enough.

Relevance of Interventions

One condition for the World Bank Group to be relevant in investment climate reforms is that it diagnose and offer a comprehensive set of regulatory interventions that can be adjusted to country needs. At the same time comprehensiveness does not automatically imply relevance, from the perspective of the World Bank Group, as the Bank Group might deliberately decide not to support all possible areas of the regulatory environment. However, from the client perspective, comprehensiveness ensures that any regulatory reform supported by the Bank Group is relevant to the client countries priorities. In this section IEG presents evidence on whether the Bank Group is offering a comprehensive set of regulatory reforms to its client countries.

TABLE 2.1 Government-Owned Strategies and Relevant World Bank Group Interventions

Country	Country's Own Development Strategy/Vision	World Bank Group Interventions	Issues Regarding Government Commitment
Cambodia	Strengthening the legal framework for enterprises, including laws, regulations, and institutional capacity that facilitate business, trade and private investment in a climate of fair competition, transparency, accountability, and predictability. Operating a "single window" as a speedy facilitating mechanism for trade and all private investor requirements from the government. Dialogue with the private sector through the Private Sector Forum and the Steering Committee for Private Sector Development to address concerns of the private sector.	Trade-export markets, WTO entry ADR, special economic zones. Sector reform-agribusiness. Trade and investment-related processes and procedures Improve legal and investment process transparency Electricity sector regulatory framework for commercialization and privatization	The IFC Advisory Services Cambodia SEZ Legal and Institutional Framework encountered problems. The client was mainly interested in getting a draft law but was not prepared to begin the inter-ministerial consultation process during the project In the World Bank Cambodia Trade Facilitation and Competitiveness, the impact of the global financial crisis in 2009 and lack of government commitment led to negligible progress in introducing legal and investment process transparency. In addition there was a safeguards dispute between the World Bank and the government that put the World Bank program on hold.
Georgia	Objective of the strategy was economic development and poverty reduction. The specific interventions focus on customs, tax, financial control, better business licensing (entry), standardization, metrology, accreditation, and market supervision systems. Sectors targeted for specific interventions are: tourism, agriculture, and agro-processing.	Tax, Sector reform, Trade logistics Property Rights, Regulation, licensing	No serious issues were raised.

Country	Country's Own Development Strategy/Vision	World Bank Group Interventions	Issues Regarding Government Commitment
Kenya	GoK Vision 2030 initiatives aim to improve the regulatory environment for various sectors in the economy. In 2011, the GoK released a specific Regulatory Reform Strategy (June 2011–June 2014) to ensure improvement in the business regulatory environment.	**World Bank**: ADR, Tax **IFC**: Doing Business Indicators Registration Regulation Special economic zones Trade and Logistics Licensing Sector reform Competition policy	Civil unrest led to a freeze of all World Bank Group activities in Kenya. Political movements affected government commitment toward the reform process; certain components of the project had higher government priority than others. The business law reform process was largely affected by the Constitution making process that prioritized enabling laws in preparation for the advent of Devolution and the Presidential and Parliamentary elections. The tax component of the World Bank project was dropped because that specific intervention was no longer a government priority. The government focused on large taxpayers instead.
Liberia	Enhanced economic competitiveness and diversification. Improved administrative and policy environment. Issues in the regulatory environment include both	**World Bank**: investment policy and promotion Property rights Sector reform Property rights Trade logistics Sector reform	Most projects noted the strong government commitment to the reform effort.

continued on page 56

Country	Country's Own Development Strategy/Vision	World Bank Group Interventions	Issues Regarding Government Commitment
	rules for entering the formal sector and implementation of regulations for firms in the formal sector. Specific highlighted outcomes include improvements in Doing Business and other international ratings of Liberia's business climate.	**IFC:** Investment policy PPD Registration Regulation Sector reform Trade logistics Tax	
Rwanda	Competitiveness and entrepreneurship. Comprehensive privatization policy to reduce costs and prices and widen consumer choice • Development of the informal sector • Encouraging foreign direct investment • Legal frameworks are geared toward stimulating economic activity andprivate investment • Promotion of local business through the introduction of export processing zones	**World Bank and IFC:** Regulation Investment Policy and Promotion Property Rights: Registering property Sector Reform: Agriculture Trade Logistics Sector Reform: Energy Property Rights: Land administration Competition policy Public-private dialogue Tax Contract Enforcement Labor Licensing Special economic zones	High government commitment
Yemen, Rep.	Objectives of Yemen, Rep. Strategic Vision 2025: Foster competitiveness and the participation and the empowerment of the local	Sector reform Registration Tax Doing Business indicators Licensing and regulation	The civil conflict diverted government attention from reform. Corruption and weak administrative capacity limited government reform credibility.

Country	Country's Own Development Strategy/Vision	World Bank Group Interventions	Issues Regarding Government Commitment
	and foreign private sector; develop and rationalize agriculture, balanced exploitation of fisheries, exploit the potentials in tourism and in exports, modernize the public administration. Broaden the base for small investments, in order to enable all social groups to set up their own businesses or to provide job opportunities for such categories (business entry).	World Bank: Business operations: IPP Business operations: Sector reform Business operations: IPP	

SOURCE: IEG.
NOTE: ADR = Alternative Dispute Resolution; IPP = Investment Policy/Promotion; IRPC =Corporate Income Tax Code; PPD = Public Private Dialogue; SEZ = special economic zone; WTO = World Trade Organization.

Using the good practice standards presented in Chapter 1, IEG mapped the 1,499 interventions supported by the Bank Group over the period 2007–13 (as seen in Table 1.4) to this list. The aim of this test was to demonstrate how extensive the menu of interventions offered by the World Bank Group is. The results, presented in Table 2.2, show that the Bank Group has provided support in nearly all regulatory reform topics, except a few—environmental laws and consumer protection. It is important to note, however, that this mapping exercise excludes sector-specific reforms. IEG characterized the industry-specific regulations separately, as they are specific to a certain industry or sectors and cover multiple areas of intervention. Consequently, environmental regulations are not included in the above mapping, as they are sector specific. Furthermore, recent CIC interventions have covered environmental areas, such as green building regulations. Thus, only consumer protection has not been covered, although the financial aspect of consumer protection has been covered by the corresponding sector.

In sum, virtually all regulatory areas for a business-friendly regulatory environment are covered by World Bank Group interventions. Two-thirds of interventions are concentrated in one-third of reform areas. Interventions are mostly concentrated in business registration, licensing, and inspections, followed by trade and logistics, investment policy/promotion, and taxation. At the same time, some areas have only a handful of World Bank Group interventions, such as bankruptcy (1 percent), competition policy (2 percent), ADR (3 percent), debt resolution and insolvency (3 percent), labor laws (3 percent), contract enforcement (3 percent), property (4 percent), and land registration (5 percent).

TABLE 2.2 Comprehensive Menu of Regulatory Areas

	Regulatory Areas		No. of Interventions	% of Interventions
Entry	Commercial laws		59	6
		Business regulation	51	5
		Business licensing	8	1
Operations	Commercial laws		274	26
	Accounting and auditing		—	
	Registration		25	2
	Business licensing/permits		65	6
	Company laws (business regulations, inspections)		184	17
	Contract laws		—	
	Competition policy		26	2
	Consumer protection		—	
	Courts and proceedings (contract enforcement)		36	3
	Environmental laws		—	
	Property rights		52	5
		Property law		
		Intellectual property and other goods		
		Protection (privacy laws, copyrights, patents/ trademarks, unfair business practices acts)		

Regulatory Areas			No. of Interventions	% of Interventions
Investment policy/promotion			159	14
Labor laws			31	3
	Employment law			
	Labor protection			
	Apprentices and training			
	Labor safety and health			
Land regulations			61	6
Taxation			104	10
Trade and logistics			172	16
Special economic zones			17	2
Exit Bankruptcy			7	1
Debt resolution and insolvency			35	3
Alternative dispute resolution			31	3

SOURCES: IEG review based on IFC Law Library and country Web pages on regulations and World Bank Group database.

The mapping exercise provides evidence that the World Bank Group generally offers interventions in relevant areas, that is, in the whole set of regulatory areas of a hypothetical country with a business-friendly environment.

Apart from offering a complete menu of reforms, is the Bank Group supporting the right regulatory reforms in the right countries? To answer this question, IEG conducted two tests: one to establish if, across interventions, the Bank Group supports the reforms most needed by client countries; and another to establish if, among interventions, the Bank Group supports regulatory interventions in those countries that need those most.

For the first test IEG used Enterprise Survey data on firm obstacles to operations from more than 60,000 firms in 113 countries during the period 2007–13.[3] Unfortunately, the survey does not cover all regulatory aspects listed in Table 2.2. Nevertheless, five questions are directly relevant and refer to tax rates and tax administration, business licensing and permits, access to land, and labor regulations. For each survey question, IEG calculated the share of firms that considered it a major constraint in each country and took the average across countries.[4] The average value was then used to establish an order of priority among these five regulatory areas.

According to this estimate, tax is the most important regulatory constraint, with 28 percent of firms on average considering it a major obstacle, followed by land (20 percent), customs (19 percent), licensing and permits (15 percent), and labor regulations (13 percent) (Table 2.3). Then IEG mapped the share of interventions identified in the portfolio corresponding to these five regulatory areas (Table 2.3). To establish if the World Bank Group properly prioritizes interventions, IEG estimated the rank correlation among the series of perceived obstacles and the amount of interventions. Spearman's rank correlation is +0.5, indicating that priorities perceived by managers are in line with interventions by the Bank Group with a good degree the association.

Finally, IEG collected 39 regulatory environment indicators from different sources, such as the Doing Business, WEF, and Logistics Performance Index, covering almost all interventions in entry, operation, and exit. For each indicator IEG estimated the average value in countries with and without Bank Group projects. For a regulatory intervention to be relevant, the expected average value of an indicator in countries with Bank Group–supported reforms would be worse than its value in countries without a Bank Group–supported project. Figures 2.1 and 2.2 show some of the results of this test.[5]

TABLE 2.3 Enterprise Survey Regulatory Reform-Related Obstacles and World Bank Group Interventions

Regulatory Topics	% of Firms That Perceive as Obstacle	Order Ranking % of Firms Perceive as Obstacle	Share of World Bank Group Interventions	Order Ranking % of World Bank Group Intervention
Tax (tax rates and administration)	28	1	9	2
Land (access to land and zoning restrictions)	20	2	5	4
Customs and trade	19	3	15	1
Licensing and permits	15	4	6	3
Labor regulations	13	5	3	5

SOURCES: IEG calculations from Enterprise Survey data and investment climate portfolio analysis.
NOTE: Table reports the number of observations.

FIGURE 2.1 Regulatory Reform–Related Obstacles in Countries With and Without a World Bank Group Intervention—1

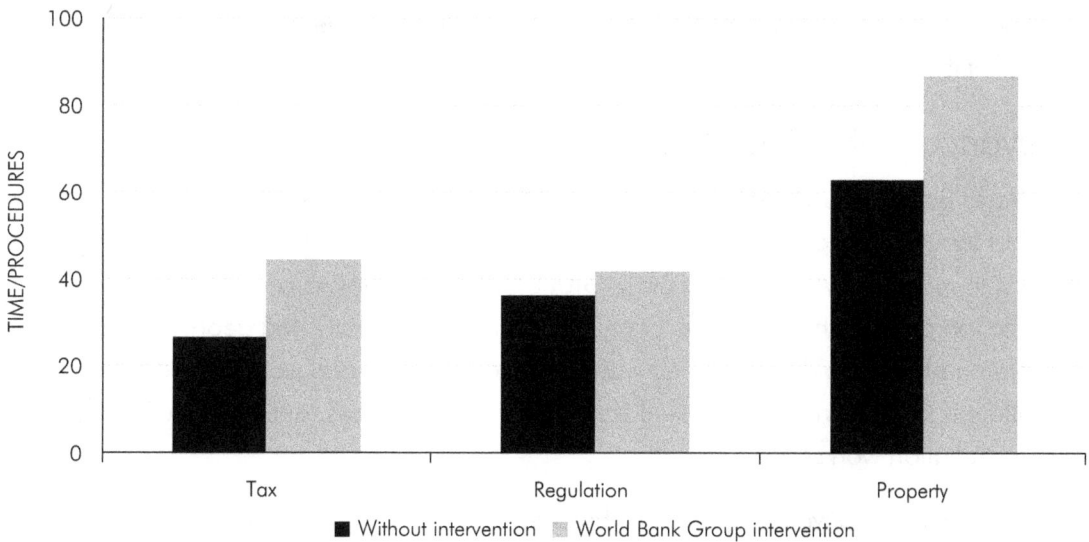

SOURCE: IEG calculations using Doing Business data.
NOTE: Differences are statistically significant.

FIGURE 2.2 Regulatory Reform–Related Obstacles in Countries With and Without a World Bank Group Intervention—2

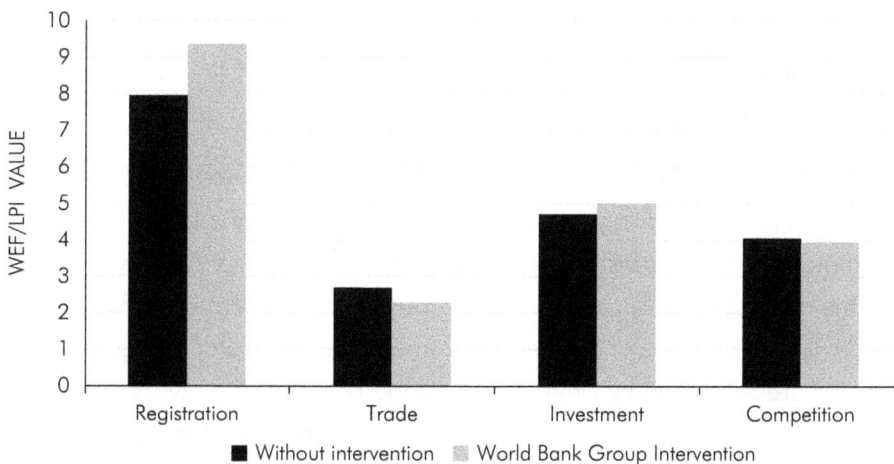

SOURCE: IEG calculations of WEF and LPI data.
NOTE: Differences are statistically significant for registration and trade only. LPI = Logistics Performance Index; WEF = World Economic Forum.

In all but two areas, the World Bank Group is targeting the right countries, as, prior to the intervention, at least one of its indicators is significantly worse in countries with Bank Group–supported projects compared to countries without. For example, Doing Business indicators of processes and cost were significantly higher in Bank Group–supported countries than the rest. The only two interventions with nonsignificant results are investment promotion and competition. That implies that, according to the WEF indicator, countries with Bank Group investment promotion activities had a more favorable FDI environment before the intervention than countries without.

Relevance at the Analytical Level

The World Bank Group identifies regulatory reforms to support on the basis of stakeholder consultations and diagnostic analysis. IEG's review of 25 country strategies showed that, at the CAS level, the Bank Group generally employs an extensive consultation process. For example, in India, given the multiplicity and geographical distribution of stakeholders and their wide range of priorities and points of view, the consultation process included a client survey, targeted meetings, online consultations, and consultation workshops.

Furthermore, public private dialogue has become an important instrument to engage a broad set of constituencies. In the recent years, it has been used as a cross-cutting tool. Almost all CASs in the 25 countries used at least one type of diagnostic tool. For example, the diagnostic tools used in Jordan CAS for FY06–10 were the poverty assessment jointly prepared by the government and the World Bank; comparative international indicators; research carried out for the Middle East and North Africa Governance Report, the Jordan Public Expenditure Review, and creditor rights report on the Observance of Standards and Codes. The recent Jordan CAS (FY12–15) utilized the Investment Climate Assessment that was prepared during the previous CAS period.

IEG reviewed evidence of the extent to which diagnostic tools are relevant to identify World Bank Group activities in regulatory reforms. The Doing Business and Enterprise surveys are the most commonly used diagnostic tools in the World Bank Group. As noted in Chapter 1, although the most commonly used diagnostic tools are rich in terms of information and detail, they are limited in scope and cover only some of the good practice regulatory issues. Interestingly, the areas covered by Doing Business and Enterprise Surveys are those where the Bank Group supports client countries heavily, such as business registration, taxation, trade, and so forth.

This implies that these two diagnostic tools are only partially relevant in helping the Bank Group identify appropriate areas of intervention. In recent years the World Bank Group has developed new diagnostic instruments for specific areas of the investment climate. For instance, PREM Trade has been investing on a series of tools (trade competitiveness diagnostic, the non-tariff measures toolkit, the trade in services toolkit, Tax Compliance Cost Survey, Women Business and the Law, Investing Across Borders, and so forth).

These tools focus on a specific area of regulatory reforms and they are not integrated into a broad diagnostic tool such as Doing Business or Enterprise Surveys to allow comparability among indicators.

This conclusion is confirmed by data from the portfolio review. Of all the projects in the portfolio, 60 percent have used at least one type of diagnostic analysis, such as Investment Climate Assessment, memos, Country Economic Memoranda, working papers, or academic papers, when deciding on investment climate–related interventions (Table 2.4). At the project level, the use of diagnostic tools was more common in the World Bank (68 percent); IFC advisory projects relied on diagnostics tools in 47 percent of the projects and more on government request or stakeholder consultations.[6] Historically, some of IFC's investment climate projects have relied on FIAS's administrative barriers to invest diagnostic reports. Over time, Doing Business became a de facto diagnostic tool for IFC. Doing Business does not cover a range of FDI and licensing concerns, but it covers some dimensions

TABLE 2.4 Diagnostic Tool Use in World Bank Group Interventions

Intervention	No	Yes	%
Trade	63	120	66
Regulations	34	40	54
Tax	13	43	77
Construction permit	4	7	64
Competition policy	2	10	83
Property registration	5	11	69
Bankruptcy	2	18	90
Investment promotion	26	10	28
Registration	10	23	70
Judiciary reform	0	4	100
Total (projects)	**335**	**484**	**60**

SOURCE: IEG portfolio review.

that administrative barriers did not include. The Doing Business report has been used as diagnostic tool 62 percent of the time in IFC and only 20 percent of the time in Bank projects.

Investment climate assessment is another analytical tool that interprets Doing Business and Enterprise Survey indicators and, at times, goes beyond their coverage. During the 2007–13 period, Investment Climate Assessments were carried out in about 46 countries in every region of the world. These assessments are comprehensive and often supplemented Enterprise Surveys and Doing Business data with additional analysis of regulatory issues. Libya is an example where a legal expert went beyond standard indicators (Libya was not included in Doing Business) to make recommendations about reform of taxation, property registration, business registration and licensing, bankruptcy, commercial dispute resolution, corporate governance, land registration and transfer, collateral law, and even the labor code.

IEG also found that the diagnostic analysis focuses only on enterprises and generally seems to overlook other stakeholders. Even in the consultation process it is not clear whether all relevant parties are included in the discussion. A review of 25 countries reveals that in only four countries (Cambodia, Georgia, Lao PDR, and Liberia) did the World Bank Group conduct specific analysis for SME and/or informal enterprises and in only three countries (Bangladesh, Cambodia, and the Republic of Yemen) were gender assessments conducted. Nepal stakeholder consultations included government officials as well as private firms, business intermediaries, civil society representatives, trade unions, technical experts, and donors. These discussions led the project team to conclude that labor regulations, trade facilitation, tax policy and administration, licensing and inspections, and barriers to exit are key constraints to private investment. However, this is a rare example of diagnostic tools including the social impact of investment climate reforms.

In sum, the World Bank Group has supported a comprehensive menu of investment climate reforms. IEG's analysis indicates that these reforms were generally supported in the right countries and generally addressed the right areas of the regulatory environment. There is some evidence that the World Bank Group country partnership strategies assign a higher priority to investment climate reforms than client countries' own development strategies do. The Bank Group relies heavily on investment climate diagnostic tools, but its coverage is incomplete.

Notes

[1] Earlier ADR has worked on developing methods and country case studies of the rural investment climate.

[2] In the subsequent Interim Strategy Notes and the new CAS, private sector development and investment climate are part of the growth pillar in the new CPS (2014–17), as well as the growth and connectivity pillar of the 2011–13 Interim Strategy Note. Both strategies emphasized the importance of the World Bank Group working on improving the enabling environment for private sector growth. Both strategies used the analytical work undertaken under the Nepal Investment Climate Assessment in 2011 to inform these recommendations.

[3] IEG acknowledges that enterprises respond to questions about their constraints based on their subjective opinion, which may or may not be aligned with the public interest. Lower taxes, cheaper credit, and less competition are favored by almost all firms. It should also be noted that these views expressed are those of current entrepreneurs and not of potential entrepreneurs who have not yet entered to market. Regardless, these survey questions are widely used and provide strong insights on areas where businesses perceive bottlenecks. For the purpose of this test, these questions provide a comparable way to establish an order of priority among different bottlenecks.

[4] An alternative approach would be to perform the same rank correlations at the country level. Such a test, however, would be biased by a small sample size because the World Bank Group did not support interventions in each of the five regulatory areas in each country.

[5] See Appendix C for full set of results.

[6] The results are based on references provided in the World Bank and IFC project documents.

References

IFC (International Finance Corporation). 2013. *International Finance Corporation. Road Map*. Washington, DC: World Bank.

World Bank. 2002. *World Development Report*. Washington, DC: World Bank.

———. 2011a. *Lessons from the World Bank Group's Investment Climate interventions*. Washington, DC: World Bank.

———. 2011b. *Trade Strategy*. Washington, DC: World Bank.

———. 2013. *Doing Business 2014: Understanding Regulations for Small and Medium-Size Enterprises*. Washington, DC: World Bank.

3

Effectiveness of World Bank Group Support to Investment Climate Reforms

HIGHLIGHTS

- Investment climate projects are rated just as successful as non-investment climate projects in both the World Bank and IFC. At the same time, there is a significant degree of variability in the success rate of different interventions.

- The method of analysis used—before and after versus difference in differences—matters for the assessment of World Bank Group effectiveness (80 percent versus 60 percent, respectively).

- Within the limits of the Doing Business indicators, most investment climate interventions produce positive intermediate outcomes in terms of improvement in time, number of procedures, and cost.

- The impact on regulatory reforms on growth, investment, jobs, and entry is, however, unclear because of methodological problems with available data, mixed results from the relevant literature, IEG's case studies findings, and the absence of a proper valuation of social benefits (and costs).

A wide range of interventions has been developed by the World Bank Group to help client countries improve their regulatory environment. They range from licensing and registration procedures, to property rights and competition policy, to bankruptcy law and dispute resolution mechanisms. They all aim to enhance the regulatory environment in which business operates in order to facilitate entry, promote competition, and ensure the efficient redeployment of assets within the economy. Many also aim to enhance fairness and expand opportunity through a level playing field. As shown in Table 3.1, each intervention aims at specific objectives, from reducing barriers to economic activities, to facilitating access to markets, to reducing risks.

TABLE 3.1 Objectives of the World Bank Group Interventions

Intervention	Objectives
Licensing	Reforms of licensing procedures remove regulatory compliance burdens that can restrict healthy competition and impose significant and unnecessary entry barriers to particular economic activities and markets, while maintaining adequate requirements to achieve important economic, social, safety, security, or environmental outcomes.
Registration	These interventions aim to simplify and reduce the procedures, bottlenecks, and hurdles needed to register a formal business. This is done through capacity building for business registries; establishment and automation of one-stop shops for registration, review, and re-engineering of existing processes; and regulation of timetables for completing registration procedures.
Competition policy	Competition policies aim at increasing or sustaining competition within sectors and across economies. These reforms intend to open markets and remove anticompetitive regulation—such as price controls, statutory monopolies, restrictions on the number of firms, and discriminatory treatment of certain firms.
Contract enforcement	A country's contract enforcement and dispute resolution system (that is, contract law and supporting legal institutions) ensures that the business commitments between transacting parties take place and are enforced at a reasonable cost. Reforms in this area are designed to increase the efficiency of the enforcement system through the introduction or expansion of specialized courts to deal with commercial cases, the overhaul of judicial case management that deals with commercial dispute resolution, and the approval of laws designed to increase the efficiency of enforcement.

Intervention	Objectives
Doing Business indicators	Doing Business indicator work plays the role of an entry point for investment climate programs by responding to specific client requests generated by the Doing Business Report (global and subnational) and other datasets. Recommended actions serve to (i) identify key areas where the impact of reforms could be substantial and where government intervention is most likely to succeed in the short to medium term; (ii) propose reforms in these areas and the feasibility of their implementation; and (iii) identify needs for further first response technical assistance in areas related to Doing Business.
Investment policy and promotion	Investment policy reforms help developing economies better integrate their private sectors with global value chains. These reforms address the legal, regulatory, and administrative impediments to attracting and retaining FDI. They also promote steps to maximize the potential benefits of FDI and its interaction with the domestic economy to foster sustainable development.
Labor	This type of intervention aims to revise the legal framework governing the labor market to improve labor market flexibility, improve employment relations and compensation schemes, reform pension systems, and make the hiring of foreign labor more flexible. This is done through new or amended labor laws, addressing wage setting mechanisms and hiring quotas, and revising residency permits for foreign skilled workers.
Property rights	Interventions in this area aim to make it easier for businesses to register property by reducing the time, procedures, and costs through combining procedures, increasing administrative efficiency, computerizing registries, and lowering property transfer taxes.
Public-private dialogue	These interventions aim to establish forums for effective dialogue between stakeholders from the public and private sectors and civil society. This is achieved through communications and outreach, formation of steering committees, membership organization support, and development of online tools for sustained dialogue.
Special economic zones	Policies that enable SEZs can be a useful tool to enhance industry competitiveness and attract FDI. Interventions on SEZs help a country develop and diversity exports, support local industry and clusters, create jobs, and pilot new policies and approaches in, for example, financial, legal, labor, and pricing aspects. SEZs may allow for more efficient government regulation of enterprises, provision of off-site infrastructure, and environmental controls.

continued on page 70

Intervention	Objectives
Business taxation	Reforms in business taxation help foster transparent and predictable tax systems that are equally applied to all; to widen participation in the tax system at all levels, with particular focus on micro, small, and medium-sized enterprises; and to enhance the ability to raise revenues in the long run through more effective tax administration and tax base expansion. They also promote good governance through transparent systems, procedures, and effective audit, and assist countries in adopting internationally accepted norms and standards. Finally, these interventions also serve to foster investment through reviews of the tax code and implementation of tax incentives.
Trade logistics	This type of intervention aims to streamline and harmonize procedures for trading across borders. This includes implementation of single window systems, one-stop border posts, and customs risk management systems to rationalize inspections. Custom agencies receive training and capacity building to enhance their ability to facilitate trade and reduce border clearance times.
Alternative dispute resolution	ADR interventions aim at providing faster and cheaper resolution of commercial disputes, reducing formality through simplified and accessible processes, allowing a more efficient dispute resolution in highly technical specialized areas, and reducing the backlog of court cases.
Bankruptcy, debt resolution/ insolvency	Debt resolution and business exit work stimulates enterprise growth by improving access to credit, increasing firm dynamism through streamlined exit procedures, ensuring the efficient redeployment of assets and capital from failed businesses to viable ones, and mitigating investor risk by providing efficient commercial dispute resolution mechanisms.

SOURCE: IFC and World Bank documents.

NOTE: ADR = Alternative Dispute Resolution; FDI = foreign direct investment; SEZ = special economic zone.

Effectiveness of World Bank Group–Supported Investment Climate Reforms

In this section IEG assesses whether regulatory reforms supported by the World Bank Group have achieved the policy objective of improving the regulatory environment in which business operates. IEG presents evidence on the effectiveness of the World Bank Group support to investment climate reforms, first in terms of reaching the project development objectives, and second in terms of achieving specific outcomes.

PROJECT RATING

In assessing effectiveness in terms of achievement of development objectives, IEG includes only ratings that have been validated and that are directly assigned to investment climate components. That reduces the sample of projects to 47 projects for IFC and 147 for the World Bank.

Within each institution, IEG observes that investment climate projects are about as successful as the rest of the portfolio.[1] In the World Bank three of four investment climate projects achieve their development objective, and in IFC over half of them (55 percent) do so.[2]

The data show different patterns of effectiveness in reference to income level of client countries. For the World Bank the proportion of successful investment climate projects increases with the level of income, but for IFC the success rate is significantly lower in lower-middle-income countries (Figure 3.1).

FIGURE 3.1 Distribution of Successful Investment Climate Projects by Level of Income

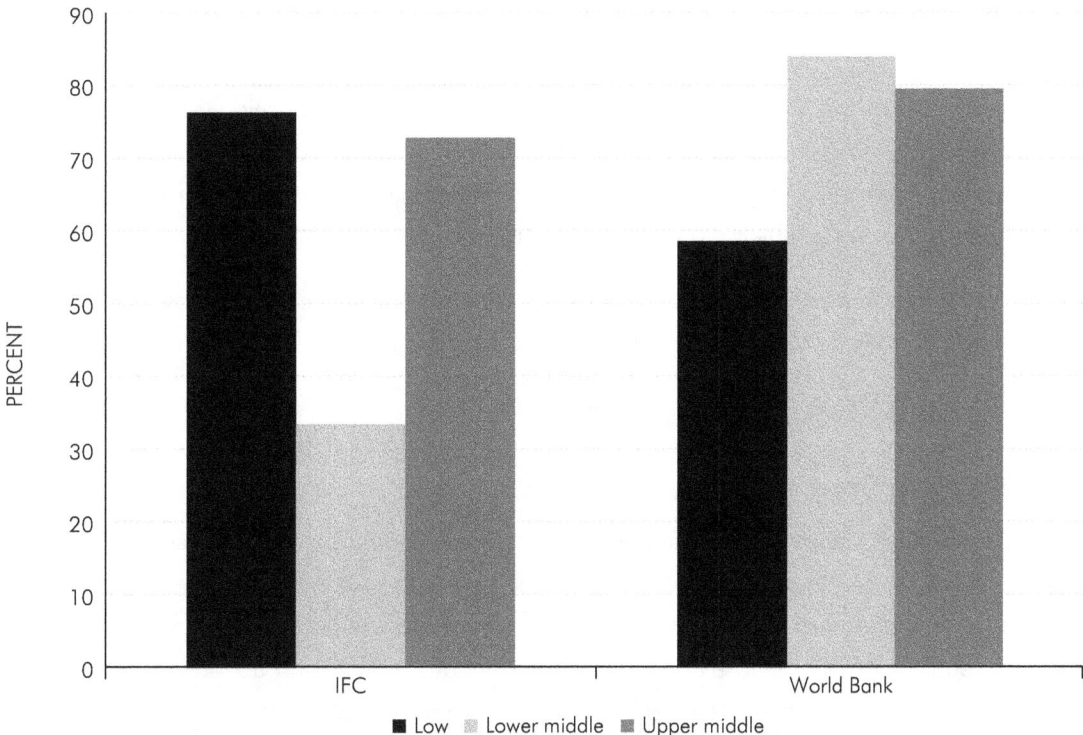

SOURCE: IEG portfolio review.

FIGURE 3.2 Distribution of Successful Interventions, by Region

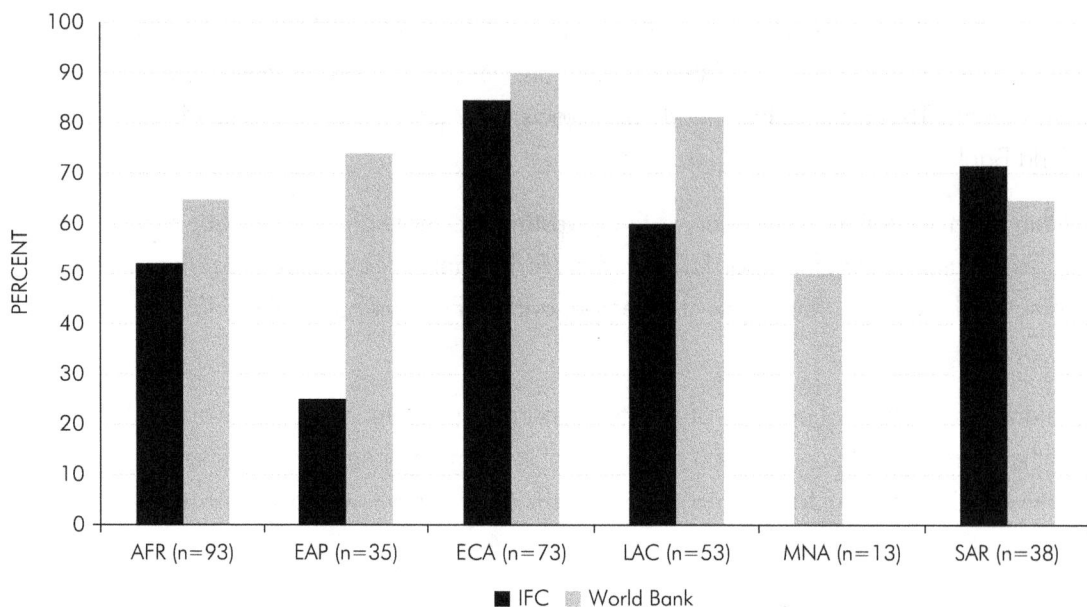

FIGURE 3.2 Distribution of Successful Interventions, by Region

SOURCE: IEG portfolio review.
NOTE: AFR = Africa Region; EAP = East Asia and Pacific Region; ECA = Europe and Central Asia Region; LAC = Latin America and the Caribbean Region; MNA = Middle East and North Africa Region; SAR = South Asia Region.

This is explained by the pattern of interventions—the fact that in lower-middle-income countries IFC implements fewer interventions on trade, licensing, and administrative barriers that tend to have relatively higher ratings and more interventions on tax, property, and investments promotions, which tend to have lower rates of success.

Figure 3.2 shows that across regions, Europe and Central Asia is the most successful region for both IFC and World Bank, and the variability of success is much higher for IFC than the World Bank.

Effectiveness in Gender

As discussed in the first chapter, some general ("untargeted") reforms may be disproportionately beneficial to female entrepreneurs—and needed in countries where the obstacles for businesswomen are greater. According to the literature (Simavi, Manuel, and Blackden 2010), gender-friendly reforms are those dealing with registering property, land administration, permits, tax regulations, agriculture, licensing, access to land, property rights, and regulation more generally. Hence, to establish whether proper targeting is taking place in investment climate projects, IEG identified and classified 19 investment climate projects as disproportionately "woman friendly," that is, as having the potential to address constraints that are especially binding for female entrepreneurs, according to the type of interventions they promote. These interventions—labeled "woman friendly" in Table 3.2 —have been compared to the rest of the portfolio—for example, projects regarding investment policy and promotion, competition policy, construction permits, and so forth—which has a less immediate relationship with gender disparities in entrepreneurship.

The overall WEF score of the Gender Global Gap and the score for the subindex on economic participation have then been used to compare countries with no reforms, woman-friendly interventions, and other types of interventions.[3] This evidence, presented in Table 3.2 , shows that countries that implement interventions that may be disproportionately beneficial to female entrepreneurs are not those where the gender gaps are larger.[4] The low prevalence of gender targeting and the lack of correlation between type of intervention and the WEF Global Gender Gap score (as well as the economic participation score) suggest that the existence of gender gaps in economic opportunities (as captured by indices such as the WEF Global Gender Gap) is not necessarily followed by investment climate interventions aimed to address those gaps.

It is important to note, however, that the type of reforms that could benefit women entrepreneurs may not be, strictly speaking, investment climate reforms as defined in this evaluation. As *Women, Business, and the Law*[5] has well documented, in several countries women have lower legal status and fewer property rights than men; they may be subject to

TABLE 3.2 Relationship between World Economic Forum Global Gender Gap Scores and World Bank Group Investment Climate Interventions

Intervention	WEF GGG Gender Score		WEF GGG Econ. Part. Score	
	Mean	S.D.	Mean	S.D.
None	0.684	0.059	0.633	0.113
"Woman friendly"	0.653	0.053	0.610	0.133
Other	0.651	0.05	0.605	0.127

SOURCE: IEG portfolio review.
NOTE: "woman friendly" interventions have been defined as those relating to access to land, administrative barriers, agriculture, alternate dispute resolution, business taxation, competition policy, contract enforcement, licensing, mediation, permits, property rights, registering property, registration, regulation, tax, tax administration, tax reform, as well as three activities explicitly aimed at women, such as the toolkit to include women in investment climate reform, advocacy and media skills for women in the private sector, and gender outreach. GGG = Global Gender Gap; S.D. = standard deviation; WEF = World Economic Forum.

travel restrictions; or they may be forbidden from pursuing certain trades or professions in the same way as men (World Bank 2014). Moreover, in various countries, notably Sub-Saharan Africa, customary laws overlap and often overrule legal systems (Hallward-Driemeier 2013). Family laws (governing marriage, divorce, and inheritance) also have important consequences for women's access to assets and therefore women's access to start-up capital and their ability to use collateral to access credit. In other words, the barriers that women face as entrepreneurs and business owners may be best addressed by interventions that are outside the realm of investment climate reforms.

Documenting results for specific categories of beneficiaries is challenging, given that not only is explicit targeting extremely limited in the portfolio, but (as shown in Table 1.7) even projects that target specific groups do not necessarily report results for the group that was targeted. Of 29 closed projects targeting gender in their design, only 11 report results by gender, and only 14 of 42 targeting specific industries report results for those industries. The number for the other categories is much lower, in the low single digits.

For gender, the previous section discussed how specific reforms may disproportionately benefit women even in absence of explicit targeting. Unfortunately, projects that promote those interventions do not collect gender-disaggregated data. Because of these limitations, the following considerations have been derived from the analysis of the implementation completion reports of the projects discussing gender issues in their results.

The majority of projects reporting gender results intended to directly benefit women entrepreneurs and business owners. For example, an IFC advisory project in the East Asia and Pacific Region analyzed gender-based barriers across the business enabling environment, including identification of legal, policy, administrative, and institutional constraints for women to start a business, deal with licenses, access and enforce rights over registered land, and access justice including ADR; the project identified 18 different solutions that could be mainstreamed into existing investment climate projects, and interviews were conducted with female entrepreneurs and documented in a report "economic opportunities for women." A few projects focused uniquely on "soft" activities (such as training, workshops, awareness raising), that is, activities complementing the main goal of the project, but not representing the core interventions meant to directly affect women-owned firms and female entrepreneurs in the short term.

For example, the Africa GEM (Global Entrepreneurship Monitor) regional training project supported advocacy and media skills for key stakeholders (women's business associations, government, civil society organizations, lawyers, and so forth) in Ghana, Tanzania, and Uganda, where IFC GEM, PEP Africa, and the World Bank Africa Region have conducted Gender and Growth Assessments, which identify legal and regulatory obstacles facing women entrepreneurs and make recommendations for reforms. The training aimed to equip the participants with advocacy tools and media strategies for taking forward the recommendations of these assessments, to ensure long-term legislative change occurs, thereby enabling women's greater participation in PSD.

In Morocco, IFC's ADR awareness-raising campaigns and public outreach efforts employed a targeted approach to entice women to ADR. Not only was gender integrated in awareness-raising events, but commercial mediation and its implication on women business owners was the focal point of several events, such as a national conference. Also, IFC was able to train women mediators while at the same time supporting a mediation center.

Nine of 11 projects that IEG reviewed documented positive results for women. These successful projects not only collected gender-disaggregated data, but also incorporated into their design activities specifically meant to support and benefit women entrepreneurs. In other words, none of these projects simply reported gender-disaggregated results without including activities explicitly directed at women.

As the number of investment climate interventions with gender-relevant targeting (and even more the number of "gender-informed" projects) is increasing over time, it may be that future projects will include gender-disaggregated indicators even if they have no gender-relevant activities. This will allow a comparison of gender results achieved by interventions with an explicit gender target (and gender-relevant actions) and those obtained by gender-neutral interventions, but with the potential to disproportionately benefit women. With the data currently available, such a comparison cannot be carried out.[6]

The Uganda Private Sector Competitiveness Project strengthened its gender component at restructuring to reflect the increased World Bank Group attention to gender in M&E. Quite interestingly, this project was able to document very meaningful results for women that may have otherwise remained unobserved.[7] In terms of the gender aspect, no specific goals were articulated, but the ex post assessment does show that women were able to benefit significantly from many interventions, including 40 percent of the beneficiaries of the matching grants scheme. This example indicates that the inclusion of gender in M&E, even at a later stage, can generate very interesting findings to inform future operations (this project included gender at the design stage in a different component).

Four projects (in Ghana, Honduras, Lao PDR, and Uganda) supported land reforms[8] and were able to document some positive results for women, confirming that this is an area of great gender relevance. In all three countries, the number of land titles issued to women increased, sometimes substantially, as a result of interventions aimed to harmonize land policies and regulatory framework. For example, in Ghana, a gender strategy for land rights and land administration was completed. The registration of land ownership by women increased. Regarding effectiveness of gender targeting, although the number of deeds and titles registered each year increased during the project span, the gap between those registered to men and those registered to women (or to both partners) did not narrow substantially. Case study evidence also shows no narrowing of the gap.

A further example is Good Practice Gender Framework for SEZs. The BICF promoted a Good Practice Gender Framework for SEZs, which will be rolled out in all future IFC-sponsored SEZ projects. The project produced a publication, *Global Study on Gender in SEZs* (World Bank 2011b) and implemented a pilot project in Bangladesh focusing on initiatives to increase opportunities for leadership, upward mobility, and financial inclusion for female workers. The project succeeded in implementing some gender-inclusive practices, and as a result, the Facility implemented policy recommendations to ensure that 30 percent of seats in worker welfare associations go to female workers. Female representation in these associations has increased from 10.2 percent at baseline to 18 percent.

Further, to ensure awareness and proper implementation of this initiative, the Facility amended the terms of reference for social counselors to add a responsibility for preparing women workers for worker welfare associations and for supervisory positions. Ninety-two percent of the first batch of women participants of the supervisory training have been promoted to higher ranks and are in positions of leadership, and the second batch of women trainees are currently working as probationary supervisors. The project included collaboration with a private commercial bank that accepted IFC's recommendation and developed the first ever financial product for the mainly female garments workers. This product was piloted in the Dhaka Export Processing Zone but is planned for scale-up countrywide across the entire ready-made garments industry.

Effectiveness in FCS

Assessing effectiveness in FCS is much more challenging because of the extremely small number of projects that meet IEG's inclusion criteria. In fact, since FY07 only six IFC investment climate projects have been completed and evaluated, and only one of them has successfully achieved its development objectives. IFC's success rate for investment climate projects stands at less than 20 percent in FCS countries, compared to 60 percent in non-FCS countries. For the World Bank the only investment climate project completed did not achieve its development objective.

Furthermore, as highlighted in a recent IEG evaluation (IEG 2013), investment climate reforms are necessary but not sufficient conditions for PSD in FCS. Without fragility or conflict assessment and an understanding of the political economy, complementary investments are not likely to be forthcoming.

In light of this, IEG conducted an assessment of effectiveness based on case studies,[9] which showed mixed results. Evidence points to the fact that the World Bank Group effectiveness was contingent on a number of factors. These included the complexity of the interventions and whether the reforms were politically feasible, institutional capacity building and implementation assistance, government ownership of investment climate reform, and the fragile political economy.[10]

Effectiveness of Industry-Specific Projects

Similarly, the number of evaluated investment climate industry projects is very small (7 IFC advisory projects and 41 World Bank investment projects). Consequently, it is hard to draw general lessons. On average, IFC investment climate advisory projects in the agribusiness and tourism sectors are more likely to have positive development outcomes than the general investment climate portfolio (71 percent versus 55 percent, although with such a small number of rated projects, the differences are not statistically significant). By contrast, World Bank investment climate investment projects in agribusiness and tourism are on average less successful than the general investment climate portfolio (71 percent versus 82 percent), but again the difference is not statistically significant.

INTERVENTIONS OUTCOME

IEG looked at the extent to which interventions achieved their development objectives. IEG's portfolio review collected information on ratings of individual components in World Bank investment climate projects and used this information along with the ratings of IFC investment climate projects. The data presented in Figure 3.3 show first that the World Bank has, on average, a higher share of interventions rated as successful. Second, the more successful interventions for the World Bank appear to be bankruptcy, contract enforcement, and competition policy (even though the number of observations is small), and for IFC registration and trade.

As described in Chapter 1, World Bank Group investment climate interventions mostly aimed at developing strategies, enacting laws, and simplifying procedures. Consequently, success was mainly represented by reduction of steps, time, and costs to complete bureaucratic requirements. For example, in Lao PDR a World Bank project prior action included a comprehensive strategy for PSD and trade and the revision of foreign and domestic investment laws. Further, a new Enterprise Law, based on international best practices in

FIGURE 3.3 Share of Interventions That Achieved their Development Outcome

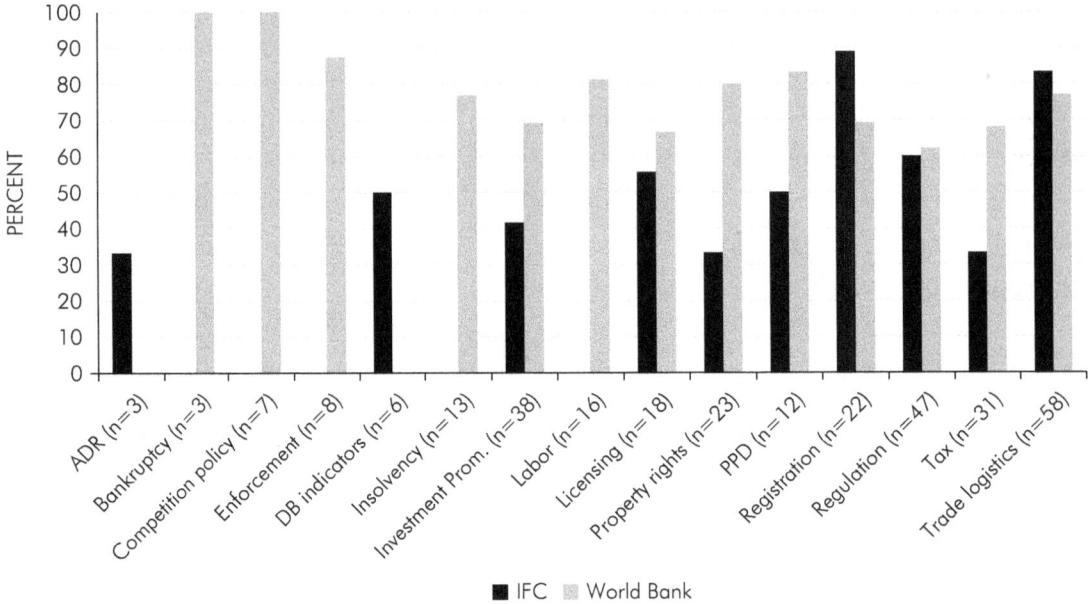

SOURCE: IEG portfolio review.
NOTE: ADR = Alternative Dispute Resolution; DB = Doing Business; PPD = public-private dialogue.

business regulations, was approved by the National Assembly. In Liberia, the Bank Group supported reforms that helped the government reduce the number of steps (from 12 to 6), costs (447.3 percent to 52.9 percent), and time (99 days to 20 days) to register a business.

Along with administrative reforms, the Bank Group supported the design and implementation of a modern business registry. With the completion of the design, the time to register business was fully automated, which allowed registration to be completed within 48 hours. The project enabled the reduction and standardization of 13 key procedures, which eliminated many signatures, paperwork, and stamps for key procedures. The New National Investment Code was submitted to the Parliament in conjunction with the amended Revenue Code in April 2009. The reforms in the investment code, including the elimination of the ad hoc incentives, were enacted in April 2010. They simplified and streamlined nonfiscal incentives for new investments mainly by eliminating any discriminatory and discretionary measures.

Measuring reduction in time, cost, and procedures provides a view of the achievement of the development goals of a project. IEG also tried to determine what impact investment climate projects have had by looking at objective indicators of the business environment related to each intervention. To this end, IEG identified 39 indicators covering almost all interventions for entry, operation, and exit. (Table 3.3) These indicators were gathered from different data sources: Doing Business, the Logistic Performance Indicator, and the WEF's

TABLE 3.3 Description of Indicators Used for Outcome Analysis

Indicator	Source	Description
db_cpipc	Doing Business	Constr. Permit-Cost (% of income per capita)
db_cpproc	Doing Business	Constr. Permit-Procedures (number)
db_cptime	Doing Business	Constr. Permit-Time (days)
db_ptpmts	Doing Business	Paying Taxes-Payments (number per year)
db_pttime	Doing Business	Paying Taxes-Time (hours peryear)
db_pttottax	Doing Business	Paying Taxes-Total tax rate (% profit)
db_ricost	Doing Business	Risolving insolvency-Cost (%of estate)
db_riout	Doing Business	Risolving insolvency-Outcome (0 as piecemeal sale and 1 as going concern)
db_rirec	Doing Business	Risolving insolvency-Recovery rate (cents on the dollar)
db_ritime	Doing Business	Risolving insolvency-Time (years)
db_rpcopv	Doing Business	Registering Property-Cost (% of property value)
db_rpproc	Doing Business	Registering Property-Procedures (number)
db_rptime	Doing Business	Registering Property-Time (days)
db_sbipc	Doing Business	Starting a Business-Cost (% of income per capita)
db_sbimc	Doing Business	Starting a Business-Paid-in Min. Capital (% of income per capita)
db_sbproc	Doing Business	Starting a Business-Procedures (number)
db_sbtime	Doing Business	Starting a Business-Time (days)
db_tabcost	Doing Business	Trading Acr. Boarders-Cost to export ($ per container)
db_tabexpdoc	Doing Business	Trading Acr. Boarders-Documents to export (number)

continued on page 80

Indicator	Source	Description
db_tabexptime	Doing Business	Trading Acr. Boarders-Time to export (days)
db_tabimpcost	Doing Business	Trading Acr. Boarders-Cost to import ($ per container)
db_tabimpdoc	Doing Business	Trading Acr. Boarders-Documents to import (number)
db_tabimptime	Doing Business	Trading Acr. Boarders-Time to import (days)
dbdaysexport	Doing Business	DB export time (customs - term. Handling)
dbdaysimport	Doing Business	DB import time (customs - time term. Handling)
dbexpdocprep	Doing Business	DB export time document preparation
dbimpdocprep	Doing Business	DB import time document preparation
lpi_customs	Logistics Perform. Index	Customs index (1=worst to 5=best)
lpi_score	Logistics Perform. Index	LPI Score (1=worst to 5=best)
Wef_lp0l	World Econ. Forum GCI	Property rights
Wef_lp09	World Econ. Forum GCI	Burden of government regulation
Wef_6p01	World Econ. Forum GCI	Intensity of local competition
wef_6p02	World Econ. Forum GCI	Extent of market dominance
wef 6p03	World Econ. Forum GCI	Effectiveness of anti-monopoly policy
wef_6p09	World Econ. Forum GCI	Prevalence of trade barriers
wef_6pl0	World Econ. Forum GCI	Trade tariffs, % duty
wef_6p11	World Econ. Forum GCI	Prevalence of foreign ownership
wef_6p12	World Econ. Forum GCI	Business impact of rules on FDI
wef_6p13	World Econ. Forum GCI	Burden of customs procedures

SOURCES: World Economic Forum, Doing Business, Logistic Performance Index.
NOTE: GCI = global competitiveness index.

Global Competitiveness Report.[11] These indicators are all independent of project documents. The advantage of this is that they are collected consistently across countries and years. The disadvantage is that, not being linked to the projects, they might not measure exactly what the intervention aims to improve. Hence, although this makes them good outcome indicators, they are not a perfect proxy for investment climate projects.

In assessing the effectiveness of individual interventions,[12] IEG first adopted a before-and-after approach. IEG estimated the value of each indicator for each country before the project and after, and then tested if the distribution of the before-and-after values was significantly different. This analysis showed that investment climate interventions have a significant positive impact on measures of the business environment such as time, cost, number of procedures, index scores, and so forth. Of the indicators for which data could be used, 31 (78 percent) show a significant and positive[13] change[14] (highlighted in Table 3.4 in grey). Only in a handful of cases did the results show a negative impact (blue in the table). Consequently, within the limits of the data used, this method shows that seven of the eight Bank Group interventions displayed a significant outcome in the direction of improvement, the only exception being investment promotion.

However, the before-and-after method has significant methodological shortcomings. IEG therefore verified these results by applying two additional methods of analysis: propensity score match and difference in differences. The results of these methods are significantly different from earlier calculations. Whereas with before-and-after almost 80 percent of the indicators were significant and positive, this share drops noticeably to 30 percent and 60 percent with propensity score and difference in difference, respectively[15] (Table 3.4). Thus, the method of analysis used drives the extent of effectiveness recorded. Simplistic methods such as before-and-after show a much wider impact than more sophisticated approaches.

IEG used the results of the difference-in-difference method, as it was the method with the fewest assumptions.[16] Although the number of statistically significant tests was lower, the difference-in-differences method largely confirmed earlier results. IEG found evidence that all but one intervention—investment promotion[17]—produced positive outcomes. In fact, for almost all interventions, at least one indicator showed a significant change in the right direction, within the limits of the data used. Registration, regulations, and trade showed the strongest results. Interventions in registration and regulations showed an impact on procedures, time, cost, and perception of burden; interventions in trade showed an impact on time, documentation, and perception of custom efficiency; interventions in tax showed reductions in the number of payments; interventions in property registration showed a reduction in procedures and costs. Finally, interventions in bankruptcy and construction permit

TABLE 3.4 Results of Tests on Outcome Indicators, by Method of Analysis

Intervention	Indicator	Source	Before/After	Propensity Score	Difference in Difference	Observations
Registration	wef_1p09	WEF	0.24 **	−0.07	0.28 *	21
	db_sbproc	DB	−2.12 **	−0.37 *	−0.86 *	37
	db_sbtime	DB	−17.07 **	−9.03 **	−11.99 *	37
	db_sbipc	DB	−33.57 **	−10.98 *	−22.36 *	37
	db_sbpimc	DB	−82.62 **	−19.21	−43.92 **	37
Trade	lpi_score	PLI	0.18 **	−0.28 **	0.14 **	31
	lpi_customs	PLI	0.15 **	−0.30 **	0.15 *	31
	db_tabexpdoc	DB	−0.45 **	−0.01	−0.26 **	36
	db_tabexptime	DB	−4.50 **	−2.53 **	−2.85 **	36
	db_tabcost	DB	275 **	−47.60	85.8	36
	db_tabimpdoc	DB	−0.41 **	0.32	−0.13 *	36
	db_tabimptime	DB	−5.49 **	−3.31 **	−3.42 **	36
	db_tabimpcost	DB	353 **	−117.41	119.50	36
	wef_6p09	WEF	−0.17 **	−0.22 **	0.07	21
	wef_6p10	WEF	0.35	0.20	0.30	21
	wef_6p13	WEF	0.36 **	−0.30 **	0.20	21
	dbdaysexport	DB	−0.89 **	−1.01 **	−0.52	36
	dbdaysimport	DB	−1.17 **	−1.37 **	−0.33	36
	dbexpdocprep	DB	−1.86 **	−1.08 *	−1.32 **	36
	dbimpdocprep	DB	−1.95 **	−1.28 *	−0.92 **	36
Tax	db_ptpmts	DB	−12.73 **	7.76 **	−13.50 **	26
	db_pttime	DB	−67.09 **	66.93 **	−60.96	26
	db_pptottax	DB	−18.00 **	10.17 **	−11.69	26

Intervention	Indicator	Source	Before/After		Propensity Score		Difference in Difference		Obser-vations
Regulations	wef_1p09	WEF	0.24	**	−0.07		0.28	*	21
	db_sbproc	DB	−2.12	**	−0.37	*	−0.86	*	37
	db_sbtime	DB	−17.07	**	−9.03	**	−11.99	*	37
	db_sbipc	DB	−33.57	**	−10.98	*	−22.36	*	37
	db_sbpimc	DB	−82.62	**	−19.21		−43.92	**	37
Investment promotion	wef_6p11	WEF	−0.49	**	−0.18		−0.20	**	19
	wef_6p12	WEF	−0.55	**	−0.10		−0.12	*	19
Bankruptcy	db_ritime	DB	−0.09	*			−0.04	**	6
	db_ricost	DB	−0.50				0.04	**	6
	db_riout	DB					−0.05		6
	db_rirec	DB	1.31				−0.12	**	7
Construction permit	db_cpproc	DB	−3.11	**			−2.71	**	9
	db_cptime	DB	−39.02	*			−11.29		9
	db_cpipc	DB	−159	**			−28.13		9
Property registration	db_rpproc	DB	−0.51	**	0.03		−0.18	**	13
	db_rptime	DB	−23.06	**	30.17	**	−23.57		13
	db_rpcopv	DB	−1.18	**	0.47		−0.66	**	13
	wef_1p01	DB	−0.32	**	−0.61	**	0.04		7

SOURCE: IEG calculations.
NOTE: DB = Doing Business; WEF = World Economic Forum. * = significance level 10%; ** = significance level 5%.
a. This refers only to difference in difference and to the number of projects with the respective interventions. The total number of observations of the test is much higher, ranging from 56 to 712.

showed some positive results, but these must be interpreted with caution, given the very small number of observations (Box 3.1).

In contrast, interventions in investment promotions show a consistent negative impact. This might appear in contrast with earlier results with project ratings, where the majority of projects achieved their Development Outcome, but this is not the case. As a matter of fact, for example, in Burundi and Sierra Leone, the objectives of two World Bank projects were simply to enact an investment code law or a guide to investment procedures, incentives, guarantees, and settlement system. The projects did achieve their objectives—enacting the laws and the guide—but no reference was made to any impact indicator such as FDI flows or perception of improvement of the business environment by foreign investors. Furthermore, these results are consistent with the limited literature on the topic, which shows mixed conclusions.

BOX 3.1 Contribution of World Bank Group Support to Investment Climate Reforms around the World

Countries implement regulatory reforms independently of the World Bank Group support. The figure on the next page shows that, over the period 2007–13, more regulatory reforms were implemented in countries without World Bank Group support than in countries with Bank Group projects.[a] On average, countries implement approximately 200 regulatory reforms each year, 40 percent of which are in countries with World Bank Group support. What is the contribution of the World Bank Group to the regulatory reform process around the world? IEG answers this question by testing if the support provided by the Bank Group increases the chances of a country implementing regulatory reforms.

IEG uses a survival model to estimate the impact of lagged Bank Group support to investment climate reforms on the probability of a country implementing regulatory reforms. More specifically, IEG tests if lagged Bank Group investment climate support (in the year 2007 and/or 2008) increases the chances of investment climate reforms in a client country in the following 2009–13 period, compared to countries that do not receive such support.

The results of this test show that Bank Group investment climate projects do not increase the probability of implementing regulatory reforms in countries supported compared to countries not supported. In contrast, countries that receive IFC support for regulatory reforms increase their probability of implementing regulatory reforms by 40 percent.

Furthermore, given that about half of the projects supported by the World Bank Group include in their rationale a reference to the Doing Business ranking, IEG tested whether such rationale increases the probability of regulatory reforms. The results show that projects with a Doing Business ranking in their rationale do not increase the probability of regulatory reforms. In other words, projects that aim to raise the Doing Business ranking do not promote additional regulatory reforms.

Number of Regulatory Reforms With and Without World Bank Group Support

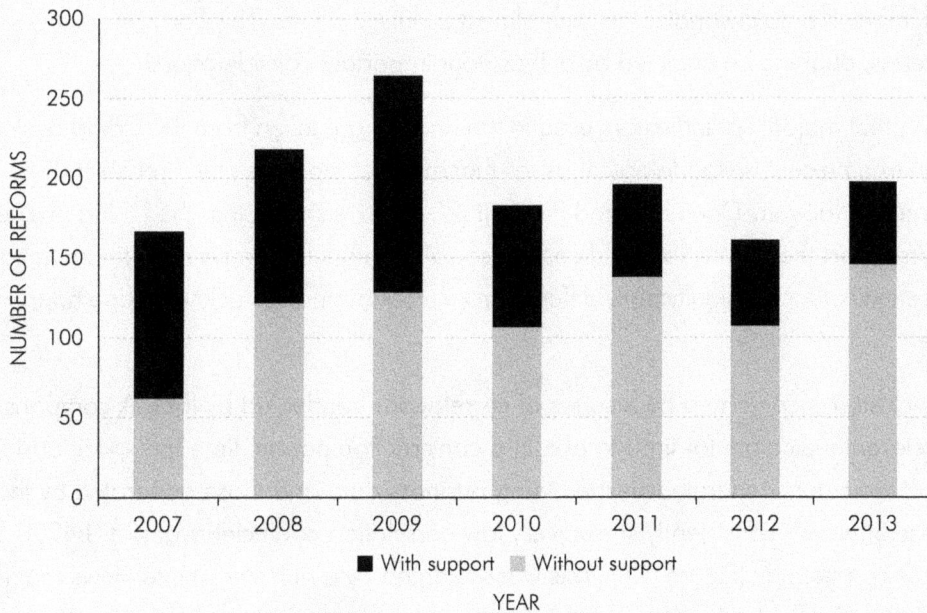

SOURCE: IEG.

a. IEG uses data on regulatory reforms around the world collected by the Doing Business team. According to these data, regulatory reform is represented by a combination of changes in legislation or regulations together with a factual year-to-year change in the outcome variable of at least 10 percent (although the exact definition differs across subindices).

Although some studies support the positive effect of investment promotion activities on FDI inflows (Harding and Javorcik 2011; Bobonis and Shatz 2007; Charlton and Davis 2006), others find no significant impact (Head, Ries, and Swenson 1999), qualified effects (Morisset 2003), or heterogeneous impact (World Bank 2009). Finally, it must be recognized that it is difficult to find appropriate indicators of intermediate outcomes to properly measure the impact of these interventions. IEG could only find two types of indicators, both from the WEF, that measure the prevalence of foreign ownership and the business impact of rules on FDI.

In sum, using difference-in-difference, within the limited perspective of the Doing Business data, IEG was able to identify at least one indicator with a significant impact in the direction of improvement for the majority of interventions. Indicators of time, number of procedures, and cost all show improvement following a World Bank Group–supported investment climate reform. Among them, regulations, registration, and trade appear the most effective.

Limitations of Outcome Measurements

The above evidence shows that, within the limits of the available data, investment climate reforms improve outcome indicators with almost all interventions. This conclusion, nevertheless, ought to be qualified by at least four important considerations.

First, the great majority of indicators used in the analysis are taken from the Doing Business program and present methodological issues that might compromise their reliability.[18] Furthermore, Hallward-Driemeier and Pritchett (2011) have shown that the Doing Business indicators report the formal time and costs associated with fully complying with regulations, but these indicators are significantly different from what businesses acknowledge happens in practice.

This conclusion is confirmed by a series of correlations conducted by IEG. A comparison of the relevant indicators for time to obtain a construction permit, time to export, and time to import indicators generated by the Doing Business data and those generated by the Enterprise Surveys[19] consistently shows very low correlation coefficients of just 0.42, 0.17, and 0.09, respectively (Figure 3.4). This was validated by a number of interviews that IEG conducted in the field, where respondents—some of whom were very familiar with the Doing Business methodology—specifically criticized the rigid structure of the methodology, which does not allow country-specific realities to be accounted for; nor does it measure the whole bureaucratic process beyond cost, time, and procedures (for example, it did not take into account the recourse mechanism in tax disputes). In particular, one respondent inquired, "What is the value of rating a country on the basis of, say, 10 percent corporate rate on profits if tax authorities have full and unchallenged power to estimate you tax liability?"

Second, the literature on the impact of regulatory reforms is extensive but presents mixed and qualified results, suggesting that a good regulatory environment is a necessary but not a sufficient condition to achieve growth, investment, entry, and jobs. Several studies suggest that there might be a correlation between regulation and growth. Growth in countries where the burden of regulation is high appears to have slowed in the period before regulations is measured (Djankov, McLeish, and Ramalho 2006; Hanush 2012). Yet causality is much harder to prove (Eifert 2009), although some impact can be detected in a smaller subset of countries (Dong and Xu 2008, 2009; Ahsan and Pages 2009; Amin 2009) or on small firms (Altenburg and van Drachenfels 2006; Clarke 2014; Gelb and others 2006; Pierre and Scarpetta 2006; Ahsan and Pages 2009; Abidoye, Orazem and Vodopivec 2009). Some studies find a mixed impact of tax regulations on investments (Djankov and others 2010; Sentance 2013; Lawless 2013), GDP per capita growth (Lee and Gordon 2005),

FIGURE 3.4 Days to Obtain a Construction Permit (median value for domestic, SME)

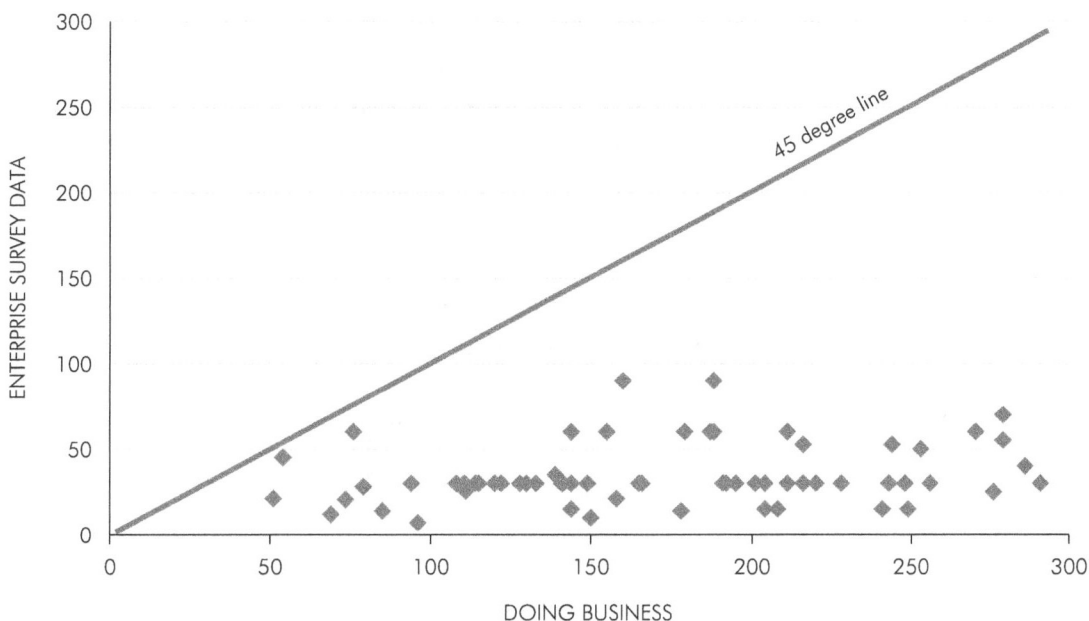

SOURCE: IEG calculations based on Doing Business and Enterprise Survey data.
NOTE: SME = small and medium-size enterprise. Unit of measure is days.

labor productivity (Dall'Olio and others 2013), and total factor productivity (Arnold and Schwellnus 2008).

Other studies concluded that reducing registration requirements might increase business formation or total factor productivity (Bruhn 2013; Kaplan, Piedra, and Seira 2011 in Mexico; Cárdenas and Rozo 2009 in Colombia; Branstetter and others 2010 in Portugal; Aghion and Marinescu 2008). However, these increases in registration might be temporary or even lead to a decrease in entry, depending on other factors of the business environment (Bruhn and McKenzie 2013; Chari 2011; Alcázar, Andrade, and Jaramillo 2011; Economisti Associati 2011). For example, Kaplan, Piedra, and Seira (2011) showed that the increase in registration in Mexico was concentrated in the first 15 months after implementation, with a subsequent decline. Similar results were shown in Peru (IEG 2011), where registration went up significantly after the reform, but by the third year it had tapered off. At the same time, some studies point out that a critical mass of reforms might be needed for an impact on business formation to be seen (Klapper and Love 2014; Kaplan, Piedra, and Seira 2011).

Furthermore, empirical tests of the expectation that reducing the time and cost of registration might affect formalization have found mixed results (Klapper, Amit, and Guillen 2010; Kaplan,

Piedra, and Seira 2011). For example, the World Bank (2008, p. 13) notes that "[after] Madagascar reduced its minimum capital requirement by more than 80 percent in 2006, the rate of new registrations jumped from 13 percent to 26 percent." However, Bruhn (2008, 2013) in Mexico and De Giorgi and Rahman (2013) in Bangladesh found limited indications that formalization took place. Other evidence shows that reforms of tax registration might impact formalization, but only under specific circumstances (McKenzie and Sakho 2010; Medvedev and Oveido 2013).

Third, IEG's case studies confirmed the observations that improvement in outcome indicators of regulatory indicators is not sufficient to guarantee impact on investments, employment, and growth. Rwanda has been a champion of Doing Business reforms since 2005, has been nominated as top performer, and has sustained the momentum of investment climate reforms over time thanks to strong political commitment. Yet expectations of FDI inflows have not materialized (Figure 3.5). Even though some increase in FDI was recorded after the initial reforms, the actual value has been far short of expectations.[20]

In contrast, Cambodia has embarked on fewer regulatory reforms, has a more modest level of regulations in the country, and has rampant corruption. Yet FDI has been flowing in the country over the last few years, growth rate has been exceeding 7 percent per year, and poverty has dropped dramatically. Recent research on FDI has identified the size of the market and its growth prospects, distance to important markets, relative labor endowments, and openness to trade as important drivers of FDI. And Cambodia has almost all of them: low labor cost; stable political environment; favorable tax regime for FDI (20 percent corporate tax and free repatriation of dividends), integrated regionally and globally (World Trade Organization accession in 2004); few barriers to entry and exit for most business activities; smaller presence of state-owned enterprises; access to significant markets (for example, All but Arms Agreement on free access to the European Union market); and praise by the International Labour Organization for raising labor working standards in the garment industry.

Regulatory reforms are not a sufficient condition to attract FDI. Other factors play an important role for foreign investors, such as cost of electricity, logistics costs, labor cost, and market access. In Cambodia, the All but Arms agreement that provides duty and quota free access to the European Union market has been estimated as providing the equivalent of 11–16 percent *ad valorem* reduction on cost for goods in the destination markets. No regulatory reform can hope to accomplish such a momentous impact on production costs, absent huge initial regulatory distortions (Box 3.2).

FIGURE 3.5 Foreign Direct Investment, Net Inflows (percent of GDP)

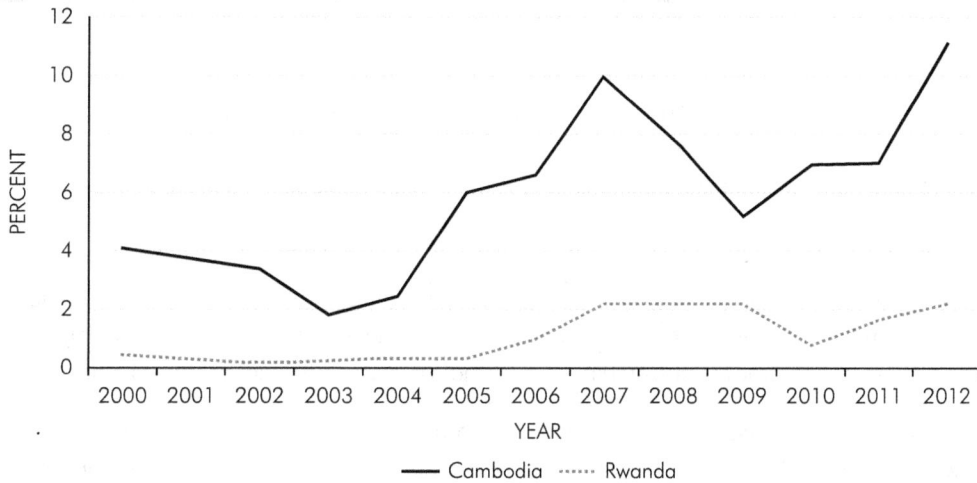

SOURCE: World Development Indicators, World Bank.
NOTE: GDP = gross domestic product.

Finally, a proper assessment of the impact of investment climate interventions must take into account that regulatory reforms should improve outcomes for society as a whole, not just for businesses. Regulations are typically seen as a burden, cost, or constraint for businesses (Kitching 2006; Chittenden, Kauser, and Poutziouris 2002; Djankov 2009; Crain and Crain 2010); consequently, their assessments focus on the real or alleged impact on businesses alone. Yet, as discussed in detail in the next chapter, regulations affect a much wider set of stakeholders, such as consumers, employees, and investors. Furthermore, they produce highly variable outcomes that go beyond firms and include unequal treatment of employees and consumers, unequal distribution of wealth and resources, and unequal access to goods and services. Accordingly, properly estimating the true impact of regulatory reforms on society requires a consideration of its impact on a range of key social stakeholders, practices, and institutions beyond the narrow aspect of business activity. This will better align regulatory reform interventions to the strategic World Bank Group objective of shared prosperity.

In sum, IEG found evidence that, within the limits of available data, the World Bank Group support to regulatory reforms in client countries has improved their business environments, as measured by the simplification of procedures and reduction of time and costs to businesses. This notwithstanding, the impact of regulatory reforms on firm creation, jobs, and investment is not clear.

Rwanda

In Rwanda much improvement has been achieved in the investment climate—especially along the dimensions of Doing Business reforms. But Rwanda is not an easy place to do business. In enterprise surveys and interviews IEG conducted with private enterprises operating in Kigali, IEG heard complaints about access to finance, availability, and cost of land, electricity, transport, and skills as well as uncertainties related to tax administration, investor aftercare, and competition with politically connected firms. The country remains risky, especially in view of presidential elections in 2017. Still too much depends on a charismatic leadership, and formal processes are not quite institutionalized.

The government-private sector relationship is somewhat unbalanced. The private sector is weak, and the government is setting the pace in everything. The government of Rwanda is an "impatient government"—it wants to do business and get things done quickly. It thus has little patience to wait for the private sector and it takes on initiatives itself to seed business, creating government-related companies. This makes some private investors nervous and complicates public-private dialogue on prioritizing reforms.

At the same time, there are clear signals that the government does not promote economic and business interests at the expense of social and environmental values. Environmental and social rules are strict and well enforced. IEG heard of a case where, in trying to simplify the Doing Business "dealing with construction permits" indicator, the government did not accept simplifications that could jeopardize building safety and quality. IEG also heard cases where companies have been relocated because they were encroaching on wetlands. No plastic bags are allowed in Rwanda, and street vendors are restricted to designated areas.

The country is one of the fastest growing in Africa, and expectations are high. Relative to the reform effort, however, the response in terms of private investment and FDI has been below expectations. The government is somewhat disappointed that reforms are not producing better results, but there are no signs that it is thinking of slowing down reforms. There is finally a realization that Doing Business reforms are not enough and so it is broadening the scope of reforms and methodically trying to address other binding constraints to private businesses.

Although Doing Business reforms are generally viewed as being not the most pressing or important, the consensus is that they have been useful and worthwhile. They have generated a strong and positive response—in terms of registrations and tax revenues—and have reduced costs for business. These reforms do not appear to have crowded out other reform efforts. They have generated a level of confidence among policy makers that the government can get things done and thus tackle more difficult reforms. Rwanda is a country that needs a change in image, and Doing Business reforms have helped in that respect.

Cambodia

Like Rwanda, Cambodia had a tragic past and has had to rebuild its social and economic institutions and physical infrastructure. However, unlike Rwanda, the country did not see the Doing Business indicators as a tool to improve the image of the country internationally, and not much progress on investment climate reforms has been made. The country's Doing Business ranking is worse than all other countries in the region, except Lao PDR (159).

Some government representatives spoke about progress that had been made (business registration, customs clearance, and so forth), but implementation takes time and is often slowed by individuals who impede reforms so they can protect their personal interests. Corruption at all levels of the economy remains rampant and imposes costs, delays, and uncertainty on existing investors and keeps many potential investors away, especially investors from the United States and Europe. The level of corruption in Cambodia has been well documented. In 2013, Transparency International ranked Cambodia as the second most corrupt country in East Asia, led only by North Korea. In 2011, IEG published a working paper noting that corruption was consistently the main constraint for most firms (Girishankar and others 2011).

Other impediments to PSD identified by respondents were cost of electricity and lack of skilled workforce.

Despite the challenges of doing business in Cambodia, FDI and exports continue to grow. Cambodia attracts mostly regional investors who wish to diversify their production base, reduce production costs, or take advantage of duty-free access to European and North American markets. As a consequence, Cambodia has experienced strong economic growth and high FDI inflows. GDP growth exceeded 10 percent leading up to the global financial crisis in 2008–09 and has exceeded 7 percent since 2010. This strong growth has contributed to a sharp decrease in poverty. In 2011 about one-fifth of the population lived below the national poverty line, compared to 50.1 percent in 2007.

Cambodia's achievements, according to people IEG met, are less attributable to regulatory reforms than they are to other factors, including Cambodia's location in East Asia, the country's accession to the World Trade Organization in 2004, and extension of the European Union's Everything but Arms to Cambodia, which gave the country tariff-free access to the European Union and cut local content requirements from 50 percent to 30 percent. One survey respondent estimated the impact of the free access to the European Union market as equivalent to a reduction of import duties of 11–16 percent *ad valorem*. No regulatory reforms can be expected to have the same impact.

SOURCE: IEG case studies.

Notes

[1] For the World Bank the rest of portfolio is defined as all non-investment climate projects in the networks that have investment climate projects, such as PREM, FPD, Human Development Network, and SDN. For IFC, the rest of portfolio is defined as all the non-investment climate advisory service.

[2] World Bank lending projects and IFC advisory projects are assessed by comparing the results against the stated objectives. However, investment climate projects implemented by the two institutions have significant differences. In fact, many Bank projects aim at institutional reforms, whereas IFC projects usually aim at simplifying regulations and procedures. Furthermore, project implementation length in both institutions varies considerably (averaging three years for IFC versus six years for the World Bank), which could influence the likelihood of achieving results by project completion. Finally, the M&E frameworks and reporting rules of each institution are different. Consequently, a direct comparison of the ratings of the two institutions must be done with caution.

[3] Correlations with other gender indices were considered but presented limitations (the Country Policy and Institutional Assessment score is available for a limited number of countries; the Women, Business, and the Law indicators that more directly refer to entrepreneurship have very little variation across countries).

[4] A multivariate analysis of the correlation between individual reforms and the WEF Global Gender Gap economic participation score reveal a very poor correlation overall, with a couple of exceptions—interventions focused on tax policy, mediation, mining, and property rights are strongly associated with a lower WEF Global Gender Gap economic participation score.

[5] The World Bank Group started to produce *Women, Business and the Law* reports in 2012. The reports focus on setting out legal differentiations on the basis of gender in 143 economies around the world, covering 6 areas—accessing institutions, using property, getting a job, providing incentives to work, building credit, and going to court.

[6] An interesting question is whether positive outcomes for women can be achieved even without explicit targeting or whether, to maximize impacts, the project design needs to rest on a clear understanding of gender issues, identification of gender-specific bottlenecks, and specific gender-targeted actions.

[7] An impact evaluation conducted to evaluate the impact of the project found that women working in male-dominated sectors (like metal fabrication and foundry) earn substantially more than those working in traditional industries and also work fewer hours per week. At the same time, large informational gaps exist among women operating in traditional industries about the returns available in male-dominated sectors. The impact study conducted an analysis on the mechanisms to become a crossover to a male-dominated industry and advocated that informational campaigns combined with mentorship interventions can facilitate the growth of female entrepreneurship in nontraditional industries.

[8] The Ghana Land Administration Project; the Honduras Land Administration Project; the Lao People's Democratic Republic Second Land Titling projects; and the Uganda Private Sector Competitiveness II.

[9] All case study countries classified by the Bank Group as FCS for one or more year between FY07 and FY14: Guinea, Lao PDR, Liberia, Mali, Nepal, South Sudan, Sudan, and the Republic of Yemen.

[10] See chapter 5 for a more detailed discussion.

[11] Other data sets were also used, such as the Entrepreneurship Data, the Organisation for Economic Co-operation and Development regulatory index for FDI and its market competitiveness index, and the Enterprise Surveys.

[12] It must be noted that the analysis of impact does not discriminate impact of Bank Group interventions from impact of other donor's interventions. Although other donors might support investment climate reforms in countries where the Bank Group is engaged, the Bank Group is recognized by many as a key player in the investment climate reform area.

[13] Positive here indicates a change in the right direction (either positive or negative depending on the specific indicator). Note that few indicators are used for multiple tests.

[14] In a small number of instances (7), the indicators are significant but in the wrong direction.

[15] Variables used for propensity score matching include level of income, region, constant price GDP (as proxy for size of the economy), and gross fixed capital formation (as proxy for size of private sector).

[16] Contrary to propensity score match, difference in difference allows for unobserved characteristics to influence program participation, although they are assumed to be time invariant. IEG estimates difference in differences in a parametric model using indicator values at the beginning and end of period and including as control variables the level of income, the region, the constant price GDP (as proxy for size of the economy), and gross fixed capital formation (as proxy for size of private sector).

[17] Additional tests were performed to estimate the impact of these interventions, including the adoption of different classification of interventions and the use of one additional indicator from UNCTAD (the "Inward FDI Performance Index"). These additional tests were either inconclusive or confirmed the reported results.

[18] Apart from methodological issues presented in earlier assessments (IEG 2009), a more recent IEG review (IEG 2013) highlighted that, notwithstanding some improvements, the Doing Business indicators still present methodological problems. The first of them relates to its reliance on a limited number of contributors—in Doing Business 2013 (World Bank 2012), IEG found 60 instances in which the indicators relied solely on the input of one contributor, and another 22 (across 18 countries) in which the indicators did not draw on any contributors at all, yet still provided data. Second, the Doing Business shows a high turnover of contributors (although details have not been disclosed). Since participating in Doing Business is voluntary, not all firms choose to participate every year. Roughly one-third of the Doing Business 2010 firm cohort participated consistently across the four years ending in 2013, which implies a 66 percent turnover rate. Third, the contributors' qualifications are not clear. The Doing Business report does not specify in detail the process used to verify that contributors have the required expertise. Fourth, the Doing Business process does not provide any information on the variability of contributor estimates. Doing Business estimates and reports the median when several local partners provide different values (World Bank 2011a). However, the reports provide no indication on the number of instances in which experts differ on their assessment of indicators nor on the magnitude of these differences. Finally, the value of panel data is limited because of partial adjustments to changes in methodology. Although, in response to earlier criticisms, the Doing Business team has back-calculated the data to adjust for changes in the methodology and any revisions in data arising from corrections, when income per capita data are revised by the original data sources, Doing Business does not update the cost measures for previous years; thus, variables are noncomparable across time.

[19] The Enterprise Survey values are estimated for SMEs and domestic firms and are median values (as per assumptions followed by the Doing Business report).

[20] Enhancing Private Sector Competitiveness in Rwanda. Increasing Private Investment in Rwanda: Options for Reform with Greater Impact. World Bank. Finance and Private Sector Development, Africa Region. Draft, May 2014.

References

Abidoye, B., P. F. Orazem, and M. Vodopivec. 2009. "Firing Costs and Firm Size: A Study of Sri Lanka's Severance Pay System." World Bank SPD Discussion Paper 0916, Washington, DC.

Aghion, P., and Marinescu. 2008. "Cyclical Budgetary Policy and Economic Growth: What Do We Learn from OECD Panel Data?" *NBER Macroeconomics Annual 2007* 22: 251–78. Chicago: University of Chicago Press.

Ahsan, A., and C. Pages 2009. "Are All Labor Regulations Equal? Evidence from Indian Manufacturing." *Journal of Comparative Economics* 37: 62–75.

Alcázar, L., R. Andrade, and M. Jaramillo. 2011. "Panel/Tracer Study on the Impact of Business Facilitation Processes on Enterprises and Identification of Priorities for Future Business Enabling Environment Projects in Lima, Peru." Report 6, Mimeo, Grupo para Analysis de Desarollo, Lima, Peru.

Altenburg, T., and C. van Drachenfels. 2006. "The 'New Minimalist Approach' to Private-Sector Development: A Critical Assessment." *Development Policy Review* 24: 387–411.

Amin, M. 2009. "Are Labor Regulations Driving Computer Usage in India's Retail Stores?" *Economics Letters* 102: 45–8.

Arnold, J., and C. Schwellnus. 2008. "Do Corporate Taxes Reduce Productivity and Investment at the Firm Level? Cross-Country Evidence from the Amadeus Dataset." CEPII Research Center Working Papers 2008–19, Paris, France.

Bobonis, G. J., and H. J. Shatz. 2007. "Agglomeration, Adjustment, and State Policies in the Location of Foreign Direct Investment in the United States." *Review of Economics and Statistics* 89 (1): 30–43.

Branstetter, L., F. Lima, L. J. Taylor, and A. Venâco. 2010. "Do Entry Regulations Deter Enterpreneurship and Job Creation? Evidence From Recent Refroms in Portugal." National Bureau of Economic Research Working Paper 16473, Cambridge, MA.

Bruhn, M. 2008. "License to Sell: The Effect of Business Registration Reform on Entrepreneurial Activity in Mexico." Policy Research Working Paper 4538, World Bank, Washington, DC.

———. 2013. "A Tale of Two Species: Revisting the Effect of Registration Reform on Informal Business Owners in Mexico." *Journal of Development Economics* 103: 275–83.

Bruhn, M., and D. McKenzie. 2013. "Entry Regulation and Formalization of Microenterprises in Developing Countries." World Bank Policy Research Working Paper 6507, Washington, DC.

Cárdenas, M., and S. Rozo. 2009. "Informalidad empresarial en Colombia: problemas y soluciones." *Revista Desarrollo y Sociedad*, Universidad de Los Andes-Cede, Colombia.

Chari, A. V. 2011. "Identifying the Aggregate Productivity Effects of Entry and Size Restrictions: An Empirical Analysis of License Reform in India." *American Economic Review: Economic Policy* 3(2): 66–96.

Charlton, A., and N. Davis. 2006. "Does Investment Promotion Work?" Mimeo, London School of Economics.

Chittenden, F., S. Kauser, and P. Poutziouris. 2002. "Regulatory Burdens of Small Business: A Literature Review." UK Small Business Service, online at: http://www.berr.gov.uk/files/file38324.pdf.

Clarke, G. R. G. 2014. "Firm Characteristics, Bribes, and the Burden of Regulation in Developing Countries." *Journal of Academy of Business and Economics*.

Crain, N., and M. Crain. 2010. "The Impact of Regulatory Costs on Small Firms, US Small Business Administration." Available at: http://www.sba.gov/sites/default/files/The%20Impact%20of%20Regulatory%20Costs%20on%20Small%20Firms%20(Full).pdf.

Dall'Olio, A., M. Iootty, N. Kanehira, and F. Saliola. 2013. "Productivity Growth in Europe." World Bank Policy Research Working Paper 6425, Washington, DC.

De Giorgi, G., and A. Rahman. 2013. "SME Registration Evidence from a Randomized Controlled Trial in Bangladesh." World Bank Policy Research Working Paper Series 6382, Washington, DC.

Djankov, S. 2009. "The Regulation of Entry: A Survey." *World Bank Research Observer* 24 (2): 183–203.

Djankov, S., T. Ganser, C. McLeish, R. Ramalho, and A. Shleifer. 2010. "The Effect of Corporate Taxes on Investment and Entrepreneurship." *American Economic Journal: Macroeconomics* 2: 51–64.

Djankov, S., C. McLeish, and R. Ramalho. 2006. "Regulation and Growth." *Economics Letters* 92: 395–401.

Dong, X. Y., and L. C. Xu. 2008. "The Impact of China's Milllennium Labor Restructuring Program on Firm Performance and Employee Earnings." *Economics of Transition* 16: 223–45.

——. 2009. "Labor Restructuring in China: Toward a Functioning Labor Market." *Journal of Comparative Economics* 37: 47–61.

Economisti Associati. 2011. *Investment Climate in Africa Program: Four Country Impact Assessment, Liberia Country Report.* Bologna: Economisti Associati.

Eifert, B. 2009. "Do Regulatory Reforms Stimulate Investment and Growth? Evidence from the Doing Business Data, 2003–07." Center for Global Development Working Paper 159, Washington, DC.

Gelb, A., V. Ramachandran, M. K. Shah, and G. Turner. 2006. "What Matters to African Firms? The Relevance of Perceptions Data." World Bank, Washington, DC.

Girishankar, Navin, David DeGroot, Raj Desai, Susan Stout, and Clay Wescott. 2011. "Cambodia: World Bank Country-Level Engagement on Governance and Anticorruption." IEG Working Paper 2011/6, World Bank, Washington, DC.

Hallward-Driemeier, M. 2013. *Enterprising Women: Expanding Economic Opportunities in Africa.* Washington, DC: World Bank.

Hallward-Driemeier, M., and L. Pritchett. 2011. "How Business is Done and the 'Doing Business' Indicators: The Investment Climate When Firms Have Climate Control." World Bank, Policy Research Working Paper 5563 Washington, DC. Online at: http://elibrary.worldbank.org/doi/pdf/10.1596/1813-9450-5563.

Hanusch, M. 2012. "The Doing Business Indicators, Economic Growth and Regulatory Reform." World Bank Policy Research Working Paper 6176, Washington, DC.

Harding, Torfinn, and Beata Javorcik. 2011. "Roll Out the Red Carpet and They Will Come: Investment Promotion and FDI Inflows." *The Economic Journal* 121 (December): 1445–76.

Head, K., J. Ries, and D. Swenson. 1999. "Attracting Foreign Manufactoring: Investment Promotion and Agglomeration." *Regional Science and Urban Economics* 29 (2): 197–218.

IEG (Independent Evaluation Group). 2009. "ICRR—Third Lao PDR Poverty Reduction Support Operation." World Bank, Washington, DC.

——. 2011. *Peru: Country Program Evaluation for the World Bank Group, 2003–09.* Washington, DC: World Bank.

——. 2013. *An In-Depth Follow up on the Management Action Record for the Doing Business Evaluation.* Washington, DC: World Bank.

Kaplan, D. S., E. Piedra, and E. Seira. 2011. "Entry Regulation and Business Start-Ups: Evidence from Mexico." *Journal of Public Economics* 95: 1501–15.

Kitching, J. 2006. "A Burden on Business? Reviewing the Evidence Base on Regulation and Small Business Performance." *Environment and Planning C: Government and Policy* 24 (6): 799–814.

Klapper, L. F., R. Amit, and M. F. Guillen. 2010. "Entrepreneurship and Firm Formation Across Countries." In *International Differences in Entrepreneurship*, eds. J. Lerner, A. Schoar, 129–58. Chicago: University of Chicago Press.

Klapper L. F., and I. Love. 2014. *The Impact of Business Environment Reforms in New Firm Registration.* Washington, DC: World Bank.

Lawless, M. 2013. "Do Complicated Tax Systems Prevent Foreign Direct Investment?" *Economica* 80: 1–22.

Lee, Y., and R. H. Gordon. 2005. "Tax Structure and Economic Growth." *Journal of Public Economics* 89: 1027–43.

McKenzie, D., and Y. S. Sakho. 2010. "Does It Pay Firms to Register for Taxes? The Impact of Formality on Firm Productivity." *Journal of Development Economics* 91: 15–24.

Medvedev, D., and A. Oviedo. 2013. "Informality and Profitability: Evidence from a New Firm Survey in Ecuador." World Bank Policy Research Working Paper 6431, Washington, DC.

Morisset, J. P. 2003. "Does a Country Need a Promotion Agency to Attract Foreign Direct Investments? A Small Analytical Model Applied to 58 Countries." World Bank Policy Research Working Paper 3028, Washington, DC.

Pierre, G., and S. Scarpetta. 2006. "Employment Protection: Do Firms' Perceptions Match with Legislation?" *Economics Letters* 90: 328–34.

Sentance, A. 2013. "An Economic Analysis. Taxation, Economic Growth and Investment." In *Paying Taxes 2013. The Global Picture*, eds. A Lopez Claros, A. Packman, 23–28. Washington, DC: PwC and World Bank.

Simavi S., C. Manuel, and M. Blackden. 2010. "Gender Dimensions of Investment Climate Reform: A Guide for Policy Makers and Practitioners." World Bank, Washington, DC.

World Bank. 2008. *Development and Climate Change: A Strategic Framework for the World Bank Group* (Vol. 1 of 2). Washington, DC: World Bank.

———. 2009. *Global Investment Promotion Benchmarking 2009: Summary Report.* Washington, DC: World Bank.

———. 2011a. *Doing Business 2012: Doing Business in a More Transparent World.* Washington, DC: World Bank.

———. 2011b. *Global Study on Gender in SEZs.* Washington, DC: World Bank.

———. 2012. *Doing Business 2013: Smarter Regulations for Small and Medium-Size Enterprises.* Washington, DC: World Bank.

———. 2014. *Women, Business and the Law 2014: Removing Restrictions to Enhance Gender Equality.* Washington, DC: World Bank.

4

Evaluating the Social Value of Regulatory Reforms

HIGHLIGHTS

• Estimating the social benefits of regulatory reform requires consideration of its impact on a range of important social stakeholders, practices, and institutions—not only on businesses.

• Formal impact assessments are conducted in only a minority of World Bank Group projects with investment climate intervention—about 15 percent of them—and formal assessments do not always refer to all regulatory reforms implemented as part of an intervention.

• Regulation should be thought of in terms of both economic and social costs and economic and social benefits. In practice, though, discussion focuses only on business costs.

Promoting social value lies at the heart of the World Bank Group mission of ending poverty and promoting shared prosperity. The twin goals of poverty elimination and shared prosperity that guide the new Bank Group Strategy demand that regulatory reform be understood in the context of broader social values and goals, to augment the narrower perspective of business compliance cost reduction. This chapter conducts a review of Bank Group methods used to evaluate the social value (or benefits) of the regulatory reforms it supports with the aim of providing a better understanding of the range of impacts of reform, thereby developing the capacity to implement better reforms in future.

Governments typically implement regulatory reform to correct perceived market failures and improve market efficiency (Veljanovski 2010). Through regulation, however, policy makers often seek to promote market activity, but also to safeguard employee and consumer interests and protect the environment. Improving the social benefits of regulatory reform requires consideration of its impact on a range of important social stakeholders, practices, and institutions—not only businesses. Hence, regulation should be thought of in terms of both economic and social costs and economic and social benefits. In practice, though, discussion usually focuses only on business costs.

Regulatory Reform and Its Effects: Theoretical Foundations

Regulation is often treated in academic and policy discourses as a burden, cost, or constraint on business activity (Kitching 2006). This is principally because assessments of regulatory reform focus on the real or perceived impact on *businesses* rather than the full range of stakeholders affected by regulation—consumers, employees, investors, and others. Regulation is customarily defined as generating negative impacts on firms, particularly SMEs (Chittenden, Kauser, and Poutziousis 2002; Djankov 2009; Crain and Crain 2010). Large national and cross-national surveys of business compliance typically claim that regulation hampers success (BIS 2013), increases costs (de Jong and Kloeze 2013), and produces adverse effects on macro-level indicators such as business entry rates, productivity, labor mobility, and growth (for example, Jalilian, Kirkpatrick, and Parker 2007; Djankov and others 2010; Caballero and others 2013). Although SMEs consider themselves to be well informed about regulation, they are more likely to report positive effects of regulation (Anyadike-Danes and others 2008).

Such cross-sectional surveys can be criticized on a number of grounds (Kitching, Hart, and Wilson 2013). First, few studies attempt to specify the mechanisms through which regulation produces effects (Frontier Economics 2012) or how effects are generated over time. Many studies simply correlate variables and assume causal connections on the basis of correlation. Second, surveys tend to work with rather crude proxy measures of the quality of national regulatory regimes, compressing the complex influence of regulatory reform into a straightforward quantitative indicator. Third, cross-national surveys take the country rather than the firm as the unit of analysis, focusing on macro- rather than microlevel effects. Studies therefore are unable to specify the microlevel adaptations to, and dynamic effects of, regulatory reform. This generates the unintended implication that all firms in a particular country are affected by regulatory reform in similar ways when reform redistributes the risks, burdens, and benefits of regulatory change *between* businesses and *between* businesses and other stakeholders.

Regulation is not, however, solely a burden on businesses. It performs a necessary function in enabling markets to function; it can be market constituting rather than market distorting (Polanyi 1957; Fligstein 1996; Elder-Vass 2009). Without a comprehensive framework of regulation—for example, effective property rights, contract dispute measures, and laws forbidding anticompetitive practices—market economies would function poorly. Regulation permits and enables firms to trade, facilitating a variety of potential social benefits, including wealth creation, employment, product innovation, increased consumer choice, and reduced prices. But regulation enabling market activity also produces outcomes that can reduce social value, including pollution, congestion, inequitable treatment of employees and consumers, unequal distribution of wealth, and unequal access to goods and services.

Therefore, although regulatory reform often generates public goods, not all members of a population are guaranteed to benefit equally, and some may not benefit. Reform impacts stakeholder groups unevenly; some groups may suffer serious disadvantages as a consequence of reform. Reform enables, motivates, and constrains stakeholder groups to adapt to a changed regulatory landscape in different ways, with variable consequences. Both increases and reductions in social value are possible consequences of regulatory reform, impacting stakeholders in various ways. Assessment of the impact of regulatory reform should attempt to capture these diverse tendencies.

Analytical Framework: Assessing the Social Value of Regulatory Reform

The concept of social value resonates with the longstanding notion of economic welfare (Pigou 1920) and with contemporary ideas of human development, capabilities, quality of life, well-being, happiness/life satisfaction, and sustainability (Sen 1979; Bleys 2012). Conventional measures of economic growth such as GDP and the beliefs, discourses, and policy stances that support such measures have been criticized for ignoring some of the human and environmental consequences of development (Van den Bergh 2009). Economic growth is not an end in itself but rather a means to the end of improved human welfare; broadly understood, it is a point increasingly recognized by governments and supranational organizations.[1]

Definitions of social value are likely to be contested within and across societies; social value means different things to different people. How societies define social value is likely to be influenced by a wide range of factors, including the policies of national, subnational, and supranational governments; the wealth of the population and its distribution; availability of public services and access to infrastructure; the role and influence of civil society organizations (political parties, business associations, trade unions, and pressure groups); and demographic factors such as age, ethnicity, language, religion, and location. For example, some might perceive regulatory reform intended to provide a minimum income standard through a national minimum wage as enhancing social value by raising employment incomes and reducing poverty. In contrast, others might believe a national minimum wage reduces social value because of anticipated adverse impacts on economic efficiency, business profitability, and employment. So in proposing a set of empirical indicators of social value, it is important to recognize the contested character of the concept and the indicators that attempt to operationalize it.

Regulatory reform is a dynamic force shaping the activities of business and nonbusiness stakeholders, enabling and motivating action as well as constraining it (Anyadike-Danes and others 2008; Kitching, Hart, and Wilson 2013; Kitching, Kašperová, and Collis 2013). Consequently, the appropriate analytical framework comprises a theory of change connecting regulatory reform, the actions of businesses, and the wide variety of stakeholders with whom they interact (consumers, suppliers, employees, investors, and others) to the wide range of social value effects (Figure 4.1). By influencing business and stakeholder activities, regulatory reform generates (or fails to generate) diverse forms of social value. Some studies highlight, for instance, the potential for regulation to contribute to improved environmental protection (for example, Leiter, Parolini, and Winner 2011; Testa, Iraldo, and Frey 2011; Wilson, Williams, and Kemp 2012), whereas others question it (Kneller and Manderson 2012) or suggest that stricter enforcement might make things worse (Cheng and Lai 2012).

Measuring the benefits and costs of regulatory reform is a difficult task. National governments and supranational bodies such as the European Commission have adopted impact assessment procedures to estimate likely costs and benefits as an aid to regulatory decision making, including consideration of whether to regulate at all (for example, Radaelli and de Francesco 2010; Staroňová 2010; Dunlop and others 2012). Wood and Leighton (2010) identify a number of methods and tools that have been developed to quantify or monetize such costs and benefits; others offer detailed prescriptions of how to measure the related concept of social return on investment (SROI Network 2012).[2]

FIGURE 4.1 How Regulatory Reform Generates Social Value Impacts

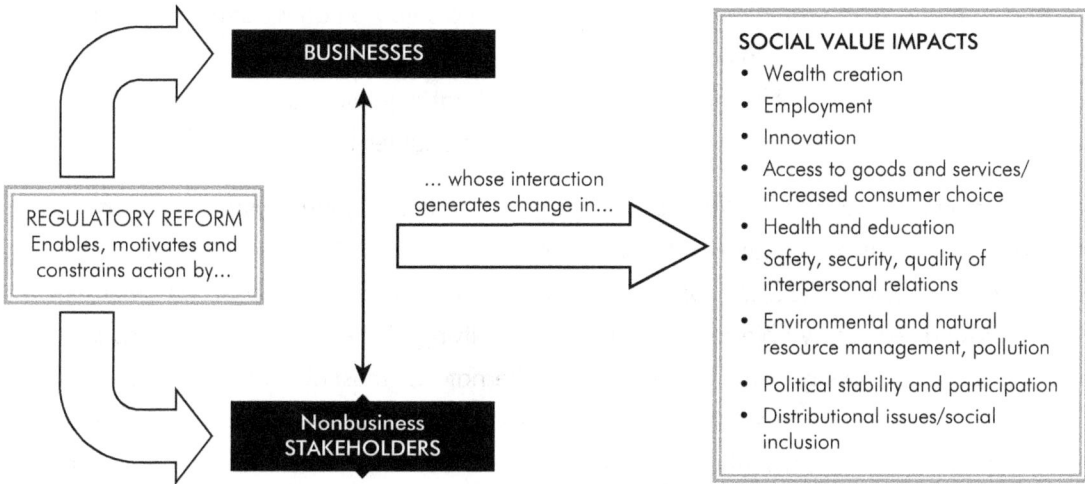

SOURCE: IEG.

The social return on investment approach seeks to quantify and put a monetary value on social value outcomes (Wood and Leighton 2010; SROI Network 2012). Social return on investment methodologies vary, but all take into account the range of stakeholders involved in the impact value chain, specify relevant indicators and quantitative or financial measures for the indicators, and outline the types of data required. And they make adjustments for deadweight and displacement.

Where regulatory reforms are complex and far reaching, capturing social value outcomes might be difficult, because identifying relevant stakeholders, mapping impact chains that link reforms to indicators, finding appropriate data sources, and quantifying (and monetizing) social value may be very challenging, particularly where outcomes differ for stakeholder groups or occur over long time periods.

The standard cost model (SCM) provides a methodology to estimate the administrative costs and burdens of regulation (SCM Network n.d.). The model distinguishes direct financial, compliance, and long-term structural costs. Compliance costs are further subdivided into substantive and administrative compliance costs: the former refer to those needed to comply with a regulatory requirement, the latter to those needed to document or disclose compliance. The SCM measures administrative costs from central government regulation for the normally efficient business. The SCM has been a key instrument in the European Union Programme for Reducing Administrative Burdens (see Rambøll Management 2007)[3] and national governments have used variants of the model to conduct impact assessments to assess the likely economic, social, and environmental effects of regulatory proposals

(European Commission 2009; Radaelli and de Francesco 2010). Hence the scope of the SCM as a measure of regulatory obligations in focusing solely on administrative costs is rather narrow. But it is arguably even narrower as a measure of social value, because it ignores any benefits of regulation. Use of the SCM can only treat regulation as a burden, cost, or constraint on businesses—but never as something that enables benefits.

Regulatory impact assessment (RIA) is a process of systematically identifying and assessing the expected effects of regulatory reforms, using a consistent analytical method, such as benefit/cost analysis (OECD 2008). RIA is a comparative process: it is based on determining the underlying regulatory objectives sought and identifying all the policy interventions that are capable of achieving them. These "feasible alternatives" must all be assessed, using the same method, to inform decision makers about the effectiveness and efficiency of different options and enable the most effective and efficient options to be systematically chosen. RIA should be integrated with a public consultation process, as this provides better information to underpin the analysis and gives affected parties the opportunity to identify and correct faulty assumptions and reasoning.

Application of the Framework: Analysis of Cross-Country Evidence

To identify evidence of the extent and depth of social assessment in investment climate projects across the World Bank Group, IEG follows the framework shown in Table 4.1.

All 819 projects in the investment climate portfolio were reviewed by keyword search and subsequent closer examination. This review identified 108 projects (87 for IFC and 21 for the World Bank) with some formal impact assessment of social value.[4]

Several key findings emerge from this analysis (Table 4.2). First, formal assessments are conducted in only a minority of World Bank Group projects—about 15 percent of the total. There is, however, a significant difference between the two institutions, with IFC including some formal assessment in 25 percent of its projects and the World Bank only in 5 percent. Second, formal assessments do not always refer to all regulatory reforms implemented as part of an intervention. There were large differences between IFC and World Bank projects: approximately two in ten of IFC reports refer to all regulatory reforms (17 percent), whereas almost none of World Bank reports do so. Third, there are a large number of projects for which there are no data; this is especially true for the World Bank, where nine in ten projects provided no information (16 percent for IFC).

Fourth, some estimate of social value is reportedly made in only 16 percent of IFC projects and 1 percent of World Bank projects. In virtually all IFC projects for which data

TABLE 4.1 Indicators of the Social Value of Regulatory Reform

Procedural Indicators

Does the World Bank undertake any of the following when assessing the value of regulatory reform?

Are formal impact assessments undertaken?

Do assessments refer to all regulatory proposals—or only a subset (all interventions or a subset)?

If formal impact assessments undertaken: Do assessments incorporate estimates of social value?

If estimates of social value incorporated: Are they presented in quantitative or discursive form?

If estimates are quantified: Is it a single point or a high/low range?

Does the social valuation refer to a single category or multiple categories? Which category? (see below)

If yes: Are specific recipients of social value of regulation identified? For example, stakeholder assessment of regulatory reform proposals, recording number and diversity of stakeholders (business versus nonbusiness [consumers, employees]; small firms versus large firms); other

If yes: Is regulatory quality measured (for example, volume of regulation, reduced complexity, rate of change, reduced administrative burden/compliance costs, clearer guidance on inspection and enforcement mechanisms, other)?

Impact Indicators

Is regulatory reform argued/demonstrated to generate changes in any of the following indicators?

"Economic" indicators: macroeconomic stability; GDP; private sector cost reduction; investment; employment; productivity; innovation; prices; capacity for market entry and competition; consumer choice

"Social" indicators: health, happiness, and well-being; behavioral changes; access to education and training; employee protection; personal safety/freedom from crime, or perceptions of crime; community regeneration; access to goods and services and infrastructure; political stability and participation; quality of interpersonal interaction and social capital; environmental quality and footprint; sustainability

For all those benefits, do they also look at distributional issues (economic and social outcomes/ social inclusion) economic equality for socially excluded individuals (for example, job training, education, products that directly address economic inequalities for the socially disadvantaged), and communities (for example, low-income housing, access for underserved communities to water, Internet, utilities, and so forth)?

SOURCE: IEG.
NOTE: GDP = gross domestic product.

TABLE 4.2 Analysis of Cross-Country Evidence: Summary

	No. of IFC Sample (%)	No. of World Bank Sample (%)
Number of World Bank Group interventions in portfolio	343 (100)	476 (100)
Are formal impact assessments undertaken?	87 (25)	21 (5)
Assessments refer to all regulatory proposals	59 (17)	2 (0.4)
Assessments refer only to a subset	14 (4)	0
No data reported	14 (4)	19 (4)
Do assessments incorporate estimates of social value?	54 (16)	6 (1)
Assessments presented in quantitative form	50 (15)	1 (0.2)
Assessments presented in qualitative/discursive form	0	5 (1)
Assessments presented in both	4 (1)	0
No data reported	33 (10)	15 (3)
If quantitative:		
Assessments presented as single-point estimates	48 (88.9)	1 (100)
Assessments presented as ranges	6 (11.1)	0
Does the social valuation refer to a single category or multiple categories?	36 (14)	6 (1)
Single category effects	23 (7)	2 (0.4)
Multiple category effects	13 (4)	4 (1)
No data	51 (15)	15 (3)
Are specific recipients of social value of regulatory reform identified?	46 (13)	6 (1)
Is regulatory quality measured?	35 (10)	6 (1)
For all those benefits do they also look at distributional issues?	7 (2)	0

SOURCE: IEG.

NOTE: Percentages do not sum to 100 due to rounding; percentages of single-point or range estimates refer to all 55 evaluations reporting quantitative estimates of social value (either alone or in combination with qualitative/discursive formats).

are available, the estimates are quantitative; 80 percent of World Bank assessments are presented in qualitative/discursive form. Nearly all quantitative assessments are provided as single-point estimates of particular indices rather than as a value range (90 percent of IFC evaluations and the single World Bank evaluations). Single-point estimates might provide useful indications of likely social value in terms of particular indicators, but they risk conveying a spurious precision and lack sensitivity to the changing circumstances that support higher- or lower-value outcomes.

Fifth, as social value is a multidimensional concept, intended to refer to different kinds of social benefit for a variety of stakeholder groups, IEG looked at whether the assessments are based on a single category or on multiple categories. Only 4 in 10 IFC evaluations and 3 in 10 World Bank evaluations provided any data on this issue. Of those that provided data, two-thirds of IFC evaluations and half of the World Bank evaluations considered only a single type of reform effect. This suggests a narrow rather than a multistranded conception of social value and leaves a large gap in the understanding of how regulatory reform might contribute to social value. The qualitative analysis shows that the vast majority of projects focus on the impact of reform on investment (reported in 28 of the 36 for IFC, and 1 of the 6 for World Bank).

Other indicators of economic value were also reported: employment, prices, productivity, infrastructure, business creation, exports, and access to education and training. In addition, a number of social indicators were also mentioned—environmental protection and sustainability, political stability and participation, tackling corruption, and, interestingly, the quality of interpersonal interaction and social capital. Although it is difficult to know precisely what is meant by each of these terms in the context of brief descriptions in projects documents, their inclusion does suggest that the World Bank Group emphasizes the *economic* effects of regulatory reform and assumes that changes in the economy will necessarily bring about desirable changes in social value. Economic changes *might* be associated with improvements in one or more aspects of social value, but they do not guarantee them and might also lead to reductions in social value where regulatory reform leads to a redistribution of benefits among different social groups.

Sixth, in only 13 percent of IFC projects and 1 percent of World Bank projects were specific recipients of the social value of regulatory reform identified. In 45 of the 46 IFC evaluations and 3 of the 6 World Bank evaluations were businesses specified as the major beneficiaries of regulatory reform; SMEs were mentioned specifically in five IFC projects. Other beneficiaries identified included taxpayers, consumers, investors, and employees. Businesses were the primary beneficiaries identified. Again, the logic appears to be that where businesses benefit from reform, it is assumed that this necessarily feeds into increases in social value, implicitly defined in terms of benefits for nonbusiness stakeholders.

Seventh, distributional issues were examined in only seven evaluations—corresponding to 2 percent of the IFC portfolio and none of the World Bank projects, the latter of which usually related to the formalization of informal businesses. This suggests that important distributional issues are neglected in World Bank Group projects; these are essential to understanding social value outcomes and the extent to which shared prosperity is achieved. Again, this could be an unintended consequence of the underlying assumption that regulatory reform is assumed to generate changes in economic behavior that, in turn, necessarily produce social benefits.

Conversely, there is no automatic relationship between the two; economic and social changes are connected in complex ways. Bank Group projects provide very limited evidence of the links between regulatory reform and economic and social impacts. It is not clear whether regulatory reform produces benefits that extend to entire populations or are confined to particular social groups—businesses, investors, men, or urban populations, for example. To explore whether, and how, the social benefits of regulatory reform reach social groups lacking economic assets—with restricted access to goods, services, and infrastructure, often located in rural or remote areas, and suffering from exclusion and discrimination—more sophisticated forms of evaluation need to be undertaken.

In summary, IEG's analysis offers some interesting lessons as to how regulatory interventions and their evaluations might be improved to provide more meaningful evidence of the benefits and costs of regulatory reform. First, attention should be drawn to the limited and narrow scope of assessments. In line with a declining Bank-wide trend in conducting cost-benefit analysis during project design (IEG 2010), a very small proportion of investment climate projects conducts any formal assessment of social value of regulatory reforms. Furthermore, businesses are not the only stakeholders affected by regulatory reform, and reducing costs and increasing investment are not the only objectives of such reforms. Other stakeholder groups and regulatory reform effects should be incorporated within evaluations.

Second, serious consideration should be given to distributional issues. Regulatory reform need not necessarily benefit all members of the population equally. Indeed, some groups may be worse off after reform because some stakeholders are enabled to act in ways that, intentionally or inadvertently, disadvantage or exclude such groups. Last, evaluations are not conducted according to a common template, so there would be gains from standardizing the questions asked and data obtained. This would at least enable cross-project comparisons that might stimulate new thinking about how to implement initiatives as well as how to evaluate them.

Application of the Framework: Qualitative Analysis of World Bank Group Project Reports

Out of the portfolio of 819 projects, IEG reviewed a sample of 19 projects in Africa, Asia, Europe, and Central America; these were selected from among those that conducted a social evaluation of regulatory reform. The 19 projects comprised 13 IFC projects (Appendix Table D.1), drawn from the 87 identified as involving some form of impact assessment, and all 6 World Bank projects (Appendix Table D.2) identified as doing so. The IFC reports include seven that set out the methods and assumptions underpinning their assessments of regulatory reform (starred in Appendix Table D.1). To examine the social value of reform, IEG examined the methods used to draw conclusions and looked for evidence of procedural and impact indicators set out in Table.

Both IFC and World Bank clients are typically national or subnational governments; in one case, clients included financial intermediaries. Projects vary in financial scale. World Bank projects tend to be larger, varying from $9 to 84 million. IFC planned project expenditures ranged from $100,000 to $5 million.[5] These IFC projects identify their intended beneficiaries. Large companies were cited as intended beneficiaries in 16 projects; SMEs in 16 projects; national government in 14; subnational governments in 8; other intermediaries in 7; the public in 3; and financial intermediaries in 2. This profile of intended beneficiaries is reflected in the very business-centered analyses presented, presupposing that where business benefits, then social value is necessarily generated.

World Bank projects refer to nonbusiness stakeholders more often. Intended beneficiaries included public service users or consumers, government departments, and tax payers as well as business (or SMEs specifically). Although the primary focus of IFC advisory work is on businesses, assessments of social value outcomes should also seek to capture impacts on nonbusiness stakeholder groups.

To examine the effects of World Bank Group interventions, IEG distinguished three types of indicator: project output, procedural outcome, and impact indicators.[6] Project output indicators refer to whether intended activities were delivered. Procedural outcome indicators refer to changes in regulatory processes and institutions. Impact indicators refer to the social value benefits of regulatory reform. Impact indicators are the most important for a proper assessment of the social value outcomes of regulatory reform (Table 4.3).

The analysis leads to six key points. First, and fundamentally, none of the projects explicitly defined social value in relation to regulatory reform initiatives, although some used close synonyms, such as social development outcomes (in Thailand). The absence of social value criteria and indicators means IEG had to rely on external criteria such as those sketched in

TABLE 4.3 Indicators Used for Evaluation

Category	Description	Examples
Project output indicators	Refer to whether intended activities were delivered	Number of stakeholders involved
		Entries receiving advisory services
		Number of training courses/workshops/events/seminars organized
		Number of participants attending training courses and so forth (including specific groups such as women)
		Number of service recipients providing feedback on or reporting satisfaction with participation in a workshop/event/seminar
		Reports, surveys, manuals produced, or assessments completed
		Whether training provided for key project service delivery providers
		Creation or improvement of service monitoring, evaluation, enforcement, and communication mechanisms
		Media appearances
Procedural outcome indicators	Refer to changes in regulatory processes and institutions	Number of procedures, policies, and practices removed or amended (or proposed for removal or amendment), such as registering new business
		Number of businesses completing a new or amended procedure
		Time or costs estimated to be saved as a result of changes in regulatory processes
		Number of people reporting accurate knowledge/attitudes/practices
		Creation of public or public-private bodies to monitor regulatory reform

Category	Description	Examples
Impact indicators	Refer to social value benefits of regulatory reform. These are potentially very wide-ranging and might include any of the benefits listed in Table 4.1	Aggregate private sector savings
		Increased business investment
		Enhanced access to the energy infrastructure
		Improvement in population health

SOURCE: IEG.

Table 4.1, drawing out the implications on the basis of projects' stated objectives, intended beneficiaries, activities, and outcomes. Furthermore, the specification in IFC projects of broad categories such as "other intermediaries" and "public benefits" might disguise variable outcomes for different groups. "Other intermediaries" are defined as business associations, chambers of commerce, nongovernment organizations, and other business service providers. This is a broad group that might include trade unions, professional bodies, and consumer groups (it is not clear whether these are included).

Second, the assessments focus heavily on project output and outcome indicators. These are useful to determine whether reforms have been implemented as intended and to detail changes in regulatory processes and institutions, but they provide limited insight into substantive impacts.

Third, some projects present impact indicators of social value, but only in a very general sense. These include increased investment in the national economy, stakeholder collaboration, social assessments, job creation, improving environmental, and health and safety standards— or maintaining existing standards at reduced cost. IFC projects typically discuss the aggregate private sector compliance cost savings involved in discovering and interpreting regulatory requirements, and in submitting applications. One project in Kenya showed how the SCM methodology was applied using administrative-level wage costs, although this arguably might underestimate costs where business owners are personally responsible for ensuring compliance.

It is unclear precisely how estimates of increased levels of investment (or other indicators) have been made. More important, it is debatable how far procedural outcome indicators reflect changes in social value. The assumption underpinning regulatory reform—that reform *necessarily* generates positive substantive impacts (however defined)—could be challenged. The relationship between regulatory reform and substantive impact is much more complex than the time and monetary savings alleged to arise from the removal and simplification of regulations.

One project in Sudan sought to improve the investment climate and increase business competitiveness through aggregate cost savings for businesses of 10 percent, with knock-on effects on growth and employment. The means to achieve these objectives was implementing reductions in four Doing Business indicators (paying taxes, property registration, registering businesses, and dealing with construction permits).[7] Although the Project Completion Report claims that targets were exceeded, the IEG Evaluation Note (IEG 2011) provides a more critical commentary, stating that the claimed reductions in the cost and time of doing business and wider impacts on private sector investment cannot be substantiated because of a failure to implement reforms, lack of data, the limited timeframe for evaluation, and problems of attribution.[8]

But even where more clear-cut criteria of social value are adopted, there is evidence of the prioritization of economic over social value. One project in Kenya (World Bank 2012) identifies reduced time and cost of inspections together with no decrease (and possibly even an improvement) in health and safety. Such an approach arguably prioritizes cost reductions over the social benefits of improved health and safety.

The six World Bank projects take into account a wider range of issues that are relevant to making assessments of social value. Several projects specify that the environmental, social, and cultural impacts of intervention were considered. A Central African States project discusses the benefits of greater regional integration for the population as a whole. Documents for a Thailand project discuss possible impacts on ethnic minorities and indigenous peoples in particular regions, particularly with regard to resettlement; loss of business, income, or assets; processes of stakeholder participation (including nongovernmental organizations and civic organizations); capacity-building measures to enable the national government to undertake social assessments, promote public participation, and improve service performance; processes for monitoring projects' social development performance; and policies safeguarding environmental, social, and cultural goods. Each provides a useful potential indicator of social value, although it is often difficult to isolate the specific effects of regulatory reform from the broader program of financial and technical support. Regulatory reform is often only a minor component of the interventions.

Fourth, regulatory reform may generate contradictory effects at the individual firm level (Kitching, Hart, and Wilson 2013; Kitching, Kašperová, and Collis 2013) and unpredictable effects at the macro level. Regulation affects businesses directly, by mandating or prohibiting action by them, for example, requiring registration and licensing to trade lawfully. But regulation also impacts businesses indirectly by mandating, prohibiting, or enabling action by actual and prospective stakeholders with whom businesses deal. Licensing procedures, for instance, might restrict start-up and reduce social value in terms of the benefits generated by market competition—product and process innovation, lower prices, and increased consumer choice. But they might also prohibit poorly capitalized and badly managed firms from engaging in activities that undermine market confidence and the social value that arises from market activity.

For example, a minimum statutory capital requirement might deter poorly capitalized firms whose market entry might generate problems for existing participants without compensating benefits. More sensitive analyses of the macro-level impact of particular licensing requirements, and their removal, is required. In Ukraine, a law requiring mandatory certification of selected food products was repealed. Given the absence of detailed information on its effectiveness, it is difficult to determine the impact on social value. Deregulation is not *necessarily* a remedy for market failure, particularly where it enables market actors to behave in ways that undermine market confidence and/or harm consumers.

Fifth, the use of impact indicators raises the very difficult challenge of establishing *additionality*—of attributing a causal connection between regulatory reform and its purported social value consequences. Firms undertake their economic activities in open systems, where the actions of many agents—domestic and international—influence their activities and performance.[9] Regulation is one influence among many on business behavior and the substantive social benefits alleged to flow from it (increased business numbers, reduced private sector costs, higher investment and employment); it may or may not be a significant influence on particular events or outcomes.

Attributing causality to regulatory reform is particularly problematic where regulatory reform is just one component of a wider reform program. Even if the impact claims presented in PCRs are accepted, it is unclear whether such gains and savings are *additional* to what would have occurred in the absence of the intervention. Some caution in assuming that reform *caused* the changes is recommended. Regulatory reform makes particular actions possible; agents must interpret and act on the basis of regulatory change for reforms to generate effects.

Finally, the Doing Business data analysis is underpinned principally by the assumption that regulation necessarily burdens firms, adding to costs and constraining action. There is some recognition that regulation might benefit businesses by enabling stakeholders with whom businesses deal to act in particular ways—for instance, investor protection laws might encourage the supply of equity—but similar arguments might be applied to regulation imposed directly on firms themselves. More rigorous and time-consuming procedures for starting a business, for instance, might also contribute to higher levels of social value by deterring market entry by unscrupulous business owners unwilling or unable to comply with other regulatory standards, thus leading to price undercutting and competitive threats to law-abiding businesses, with adverse consequences for existing businesses, consumer choice, and those whom the regulations are intended to safeguard.[10]

Regulation arguably generates contradictory effects at the level of the firm. How such effects aggregate up to the country level is a complex process. There are likely to be important intracountry distributional impacts on firms, with some managing to secure more benefits than others and others suffering more burdens. Intracountry variations, for example, in the time firms take to comply with particular regulatory requirements are obscured by the provision of average estimates (Hallward-Driemeier and Pritchett 2011). Such differences are glossed over in country-level analyses and rankings (Kitching, Hart, and Wilson 2013). Furthermore, the assumption that business owners are aware of and comply with relevant regulations is particularly important for social valuation. In fact, social value in its various forms might be increased, or reduced, by noncompliance.

In summary, although the 19 interventions provide slightly more detail regarding the social value of regulatory reform, they offer few insights beyond the procedural indicators set out in Table 4.3. PCRs do not define social value explicitly, so IEG has to draw inferences from the data presented. There are some indications of a broader notion of social value with World Bank projects making reference to environmental, health, and safety, and other types of impact and to nonbusiness stakeholders—but these are generally discussed briefly or do not appear to be fully integrated into the assessment of impact.

Procedural indicators such as compliance cost savings do not tell very much about social benefits. Business stakeholders are treated as paramount; nonbusiness stakeholders are barely visible in many IFC PCRs. Moreover, compliance cost savings data are presented as though they are necessarily benefits for all businesses, yet such benefits are likely to be distributed unevenly, because some are better able to exploit regulatory change than others, and this might even generate adverse impacts for some businesses.

Notes

[1] See the U.K.government measuring national well-being website: http://www.ons.gov.uk/ons/guide-method/user-guidance /well-being/index.html and the OECD Better Life Initiative website: http://www.oecd.org/statistics/betterlifeinitiativemeasuring well-beingandprogress.htm.

[2] Although many of these methods have been developed with the specific aim of assessing the social value of social enterprise activities, several might be applied to regulatory reform initiatives.

[3] http://ec.europa.eu/smart-regulation/refit/admin_burden/index_en.htm.

[4] Nine keyword search terms were used: RIA, research impact assessment, impact assessment, cost benefit analysis, cost benefit, compliance cost saving, private sector saving, social value, and standard cost model. Interestingly, the term "social value" was identified in only one publication.

[5] Actual expenditure may vary from planned expenditure.

[6] These three indicator categories are similar to the classification used in IFC reports.

[7] The program also involved major changes to the administration of the tax system, customs reform, trade logistics, and other measures, many of which had a regulatory dimension, despite not being described in such terms.

[8] Since the project was completed in 2010, Sudan has become two countries. South Sudan became independent in 2011 but has been subject to persistent internal conflict since then.

[9] Mali, for example, suffered a military coup during an IFC intervention, leading to the drastic curtailment of the private sector investment that the intervention sought to stimulate. Both Kenya and Ukraine experienced delays in project implementation following government elections with secondary effects on regulatory reform.

[10] Any such effects are *in addition to* those deterring law-abiding prospective business owners. Which effects predominate in particular country contexts has to be determined by empirical research.

References

Anyadike-Danes, M., R. Athayde, R. Blackburn, M. Hart, J. Kitching, D. Smallbone, and N. Wilson. 2008. "The Impact of Regulation on small Business Performance: Report for the Enterprise Directorate of BERR." Department of Business, Enterprise and Regulatory Reform Project Report, London, UK.

BIS (Department for Business Innovation and Skills). 2013. *Small Business Survey 2012: SME Employers*. Available at: https://www.gov.uk/government/uploads/system/uploads/attachment_data/file/193555 /bis-13-p74-small-business-survey-2012-sme-employers.pdf.

Bleys, B. 2012. "Beyond GDP: Classifying Alternative Measures of Progress." *Social Indicators Research* 109 (3): 355–76.

Caballero, R., K. Cowan, E. Engel, and A. Micco. 2013. "Effective Labor Regulation and Microeconomic Flexibility." *Journal of Development Economics* 101 (1): 92–104.

Cheng C. C., and Y. B. Lai. 2012. "Does a Stricter Enforcement Policy Protect the Environment? A Political Economy Perspective." *Resource and Energy Economics* 34 (4): 431–41.

Chittenden, F., S. Kauser, and P. Poutziouris. 2002. "Regulatory Burdens of Small Business: A Literature Review." UK Small Business Service, online at: http://www.berr.gov.uk/files/file38324.pdf.

Crain, N., and M. Crain. 2010. "The Impact of Regulatory Costs on Small Firms, US Small Business Administration." Available at: http://www.sba.gov/sites/default/files/The%20Impact%20of%20Regulatory%20Costs%20on%20Small%20 Firms%20(Full).pdf.

de Jong, G., and R. Kloeze. 2013. "Institutions and the Regulation of Business—An International Firm-Level Study of Compliance Costs." *American Journal of Industrial and Business Management* 3 (6A): 1–11.

Djankov, S. 2009. "The Regulation of Entry: A Survey." *World Bank Research Observer* 24 (2): 183–203.

Djankov, S. T. Ganser, C. McLeish, R. Ramalho, and A. Shleifer. 2010. "The Effect of Corporate Taxes on Investment and Entrepreneurship." *American Economic Journal: Macroeconomics* 2: 51–64.

Dunlop, C., M. Maggetti, C. Radaelli, and D. Russel. 2012. "The Many Uses of Regulatory Impact Assessment: A Meta-Analysis of EU and UK Cases." *Regulation and Governance* 6 (1): 23–45.

Elder-Vass, D. 2009. "Towards a Social Ontology of Market Systems." Centre for Research in Economic Sociology and Innovation Working Paper 2009–06 Colchester, UK. Available at: http://repository.essex.ac.uk/2298/1/CWP-2009-06 -Soc-Ontol-Mkt-Systems-Final.pdf.

European Commission. 2009. *Action Programme for Reducing Administrative Burdens in the EU. Delivering on Promises.* Bruxelles: European Commission.

Fligstein, N. 1996. "Markets as Politics: A Political-Cultural Approach to Market Institutions." *American Sociological Review* 61 (4): 656–73.

Frontier Economics. 2012. *The Impact of Regulation on Growth.* London: Frontier Economics. Available at: https://www.gov .uk/government/uploads/system/uploads/attachment_data/file/32107/12-821-impact-of-regulation-on-growth.pdf.

Hallward-Driemeier, M., and L. Pritchett. 2011. "How Business is Done and the 'Doing Business' Indicators: The Investment Climate When Firms Have Climate Control." World Bank Policy Research Working Paper 5563 Washington, DC. Online at: http://elibrary.worldbank.org/doi/pdf/10.1596/1813-9450-5563.

IEG (Independent Evaluation Group). 2010. *Cost-Benefit Analysis in World Bank Projects.* Washington, DC: World Bank.

———. 2011. *Evaluative Note, Sudan Administrative Barriers Reform Program.* Washington, DC: World Bank.

Jalilian, H., C. Kirkpatrick, and D. Parker. 2007. "The Impact of Regulation on Economic Growth in Developing Countries: A Cross-Country Analysis." *World Development* 35 (1): 87–103.

Kitching, J. 2006. "A Burden on Business? Reviewing the Evidence Base on Regulation and Small Business Performance." *Environment and Planning C: Government and Policy* 24 (6): 799–814.

Kitching, J., M. Hart, and N. Wilson. 2013. "Burden or Benefit? Regulation as a Dynamic Influence on Small Business Performance." *International Small Business Journal.* doi: 10.1177/0266242613493454.

Kitching, J., E. Kašperová, and J. Collis. 2013. "The Contradictory Consequences of Regulation: The Influence of Filing Abbreviated Accounts on UK Small Company Performance." *International Small Business Journal.*

Kneller, R., and E. Manderson. 2012. "Environmental Regulations and Innovation Activity in UK Manufacturing Industries." *Resource and Energy Economics* 34 (2): 211–35.

Leiter, A. A. Parolini, and H. Winner. 2011. "Environmental Regulation and Investment: Evidence from European Industry Data." *Ecological Economics* 70 (4): 759–70.

OECD (Organisation for Economic Co-Operation and Development). 2008. *Introductory Handbook for Undertaking Regulatory Impact Analysis (RIA).* Paris: OECD.

Pigou, A. 1920. *The Economics of Welfare.* London: Macmillan.

Polanyi, K. 1957. *The Great Transformation.* Boston: Beacon Press.

Radaelli, C., and F. de Francesco. 2010. "Regulatory Impact Assessment." In *The Oxford Handbook of Regulation,* eds. R. Baldwin, M. Cave, and M. Lodge. Oxford: Oxford University Press.

Rambøll Management. 2007. *Study on Administrative Costs of the EU Company Law Acquis.* Copenhagen: Rambøll Management. Available http://ec.europa.eu/internal_market/company/docs/simplification /final_report_company_law_administrative_costs_en.pdf.

SCM Network. *International Standard Cost Model: Measuring and Reducing Administrative Burdens for Business*. Available at http://www.oecd.org/regreform/regulatory-policy/34227698.pdf.

Sen, A. 1979. "Equality of What? The Tanner Lecture on Human Values." Stanford University. Available at: http://www.tc.umn.edu/~ston0235/3302/readings/sen.pdf.

SROI Network. 2012. *A Guide to Social Return on Investment*. Available at: http://www.thesroinetwork.org/publications/cat_view/29-the-sroi-guide/223-the-guide-in-english-2012-edition.

Staroňová, K. 2010. "Regulatory Impact Assessment: Formal Institutionalization and Practice." *Journal of Public Policy* 30 (1): 117–36.

Testa, F., F. Iraldo, and M. Frey. 2011. "The Effect of Environmental Regulation on Firms' Competitive Performance: The Case of the Building and Construction Sector in Some EU Regions." *Journal of Environmental Management* 92 (9): 2136–44.

Van den Bergh, J. 2009. "The GDP Paradox." *Journal of Economic Psychology* 30 (2): 117–35.

Veljanovski, C. 2010. "Economic Approaches to Regulation." In *The Oxford Handbook of Regulation*, eds. R. Baldwin, M. Cave, and M. Lodge. Oxford: Oxford University Press.

Wilson, C., I. Williams, and S. Kemp. 2012. "An Evaluation of the Impact and Effectiveness of Environmental Legislation in Small and Medium-Sized Enterprises: Experiences from the UK." *Business Strategy and the Environment* 21 (3): 141–56.

Wood, C., and D. Leighton. 2010. *Measuring Social Value: The Gap Between Policy and Practice*. London: DEMOS. Available at: http://www.demos.co.uk/files/Measuring_social_value_-_web.pdf?1278410043.

World Bank. 2012. "Project Completion Report for Kenya: Improving Regulatory Performance and Capacities." Project ID 551987. World Bank, Washington, DC.

5 Factors Affecting Performance

HIGHLIGHTS

- Aspects of project design under the control of the World Bank Group—such as simpler project design, good supervision, and good risk assessment—can reduce or eliminate the negative effects of factors not under its control, such as inadequate borrower performance and the onset of a crisis.

- Two aspects of project implementation—simplicity of design and good risk assessment—can reduce or eliminate the negative impact of most implementation problems.

- Inadequate technical design cannot be compensated by any good aspects of project design and hence is the factor most likely leading to unsatisfactory performance.

- Political instability remains one of the main problems affecting the effectiveness of investment climate reforms.

- Collaboration within the World Bank Group is mostly driven by informal factors. Systems and formal organization are seen as mostly discouraging collaboration. Factors related to roles and strategy can foster collaboration if properly handled.

- Successful collaboration rests on complementarity of roles, complementarity of perspectives, and complementarity of instruments. The new T&C Global Practice has the opportunity to take advantage of two business models provided that governance and accountability systems, funding, pricing, human resources policies, and operational systems are properly integrated.

In this chapter IEG presents evidence on factors that help explain the success or failure of investment climate interventions. As discussed earlier, although both IFC and the World Bank support investment climate reforms, they have adopted two distinct business models. The World Bank includes investment climate components in larger lending or budget support operations; IFC supports investment climate reforms only through smaller, technical assistance operations.

In its analysis IEG first tries to identify if and when each institution is better able to handle implementation problems in investment climate projects, and which implementation problems more significantly affect the development objectives in investment climate operations. Then IEG looks at the lessons that can be learned from investment climate interventions on FCS and in industry-specific projects. Finally, IEG analyzes the factors that foster collaboration between the World Bank and IFC units working on investment climate.

For each project in the investment climate portfolio, IEG identified implementation problems, distinguishing problems related to the World Bank Group's role from those related to the borrower/client's role. In its analysis IEG included only closed projects with a rating for individual investment climate components, that is, 197 projects: 150 for the World Bank and 47 for IFC.

IEG's analysis identified 330 implementation problems, classified as shown in Table 5.1. In IFC the majority of problems relate to factors beyond its control—implementation delays, crisis, and stakeholder involvement; these account for 70 percent of all problems. In contrast, the corresponding share in the World Bank is 40 percent, showing that the Bank is better able to handle these issues.

It is interesting to note that M&E is the most important problem for the World Bank and the least for IFC; for both institutions, however, implementation delays and the onset of a crisis are major implementation problems as well. This is in part because of the critical importance that political stability plays on the success of investment climate projects. Because most of the investment climate work relies on the enactment of laws, regulations, and coordination among different ministries and agencies, a committed and strong government is key to success.

IEG's 25 country case studies have clearly shown that political (in)stability, strong or limited political commitment, absence or presence of a reform champion, and stakeholder analysis are key factors that explain performance of regulatory reforms across countries.

With respect to political (in)stability, a solid understanding of political economy is essential for the success of the regulatory reform process. Kenya illustrates the importance of political (in)stability. The country initiated many investment climate reforms over the last decade with some degree of success. In 2007 it was recognized as one of the top 10 reformers in the world by the Doing Business report. More recently, however, the reform process has slowed down. This was primarily a result of the postelection violence in 2007–08. Following the

TABLE 5.1 Implementation Problems in Investment Climate Projects

Project Problem	IFC Achievement of DO			World Bank Achievement of DO		
	No	Yes	Total	No	Yes	Total
Task team leader change	3	2	5	—	1	1
Skills mix	—	1	1	1	2	3
Risk assessment	—	—	—	10	4	14
Technical design	1	7	8	14	2	16
Supervision	2	1	3	9	1	10
Unrealistic target	1	4	5	2	4	6
M&E	—	1	1	20	35	55
Too many components	2	—	2	13	2	15
Stakeholder involvement	6	9	15	10	4	14
Borrower performance	4	—	4	12	8	20
Crisis/natural disaster	17	7	24	16	28	44
Implementation delays	18	14	32	21	11	32
Total	**54**	**46**	**100**	**128**	**102**	**230**

SOURCE: IEG portfolio review.
NOTE: DO = Development Outcome; M&E = monitoring and evaluation; — = not available.

unrest, a coalition government was established. During this period, the government did not make decisions and regulatory reforms lost momentum. The government focused on reconciliation rather than challenges of regulatory reforms.

More recently, with the new government, there seems to be renewed interest in regulatory reforms. For example, KenInvest (Kenya Investment Authority) indicated that there is a lot of pressure from the president to complete the one-stop shop for investors. Recently the president himself opened the first Huduma center (one-stop shop for citizens), and reform targets, including regulatory reforms, are included in the government staff's performance contract.

Rwanda exemplifies the presence of strong commitment. The government of Rwanda has made significant progress in the business regulation area at the highest level. It paid a lot of attention to Doing Business-type reforms and established a dedicated team to coordinate such reforms. Reform efforts have been timed so they enter into the annual Doing Business ranking. As a result of this high level of commitment and dedication, Rwanda is a now top reformer in Doing Business. For the government of Rwanda, Doing Business is an important tool to improve the country's image in general and among investors in particular. Reforms are not only on paper, but are also effectively implemented. The government has broadened reforms to focus on SEZs, trade logistics and regional integration, support to key sectors such as tourism and agribusiness, and more long-term efforts focused on power generation and transport.

An example of lack of government commitment can be found in the experience with SEZ reforms in general. IFC assisted the Cambodia SEZ Board in reforming the legal, regulatory, and institutional framework for SEZs. Cambodia was mainly interested in getting a draft law but was not prepared to begin the interministerial consultation process during the project. It would have been useful, in the project design if IFC had a Memorandum of Understanding that detailed client commitment to the project, with a clear timeframe, so the planned activities could have been implemented effectively.

Similarly in Nepal, the SEZ law component was deemed a failure; IFC took a risk by embarking on what it believed was a useful tool to get investment and job creation kick-started, yet the tense and immature political situation ultimately undermined efforts to fully achieve SEZ objectives. In particular, there was strong resistance to SEZs because of a lack of understanding of a potentially new SEZ regime and politically motivated resistance to SEZs, which threatened entrenched interests that were supportive of the existing Industrial Zones regime.

Bangladesh illustrates the combination of the importance of both political stability and commitment. In Bangladesh, the 2007–08 military-backed government created a stable political environment for advancing public financial management and procurement reform. The caretaker government worked to root out corruption from all levels of government; the government also pushed forward with regulatory and other reforms. It granted legal independence to the judiciary, the election commission, and the Anti-Corruption Commission and established the Bangladesh Better Business Forum and the

Regulatory Reform Commission to promote state responsiveness through dialogue with the private sector.

The World Bank and IFC both had access to the caretaker government. This close relationship allowed them to keep the momentum of regulatory reform programs. The U.K. Department for International Development and the IFC-managed Bangladesh Investment Climate Fund supported the latter two initiatives, which encouraged public scrutiny and debate for draft laws and identified key investment climate reforms, which the transitional government began to implement.

However, once the elected government took office in 2009, the Better Business Forum did not meet; it was formally dissolved in 2010, although the need for public-private dialogue continues to be acutely felt. The Regulatory Reform Commission was set up in 2007 to prepare recommendations to modernize government rules and regulations. Some regulations were adopted. The new government rejected the Commission initiative on political rather than substantive grounds, because it had been undertaken by the caretaker government, despite a general recognition of the useful role that the agency had played. The reform agenda was left to individual ministries to follow up, and although there was incremental progress, most of the bolder measures that had been proposed were off the table.

Linked to political instability, the presence or absence of a reform champion is another critical factor of success. In Kenya, there was no government champion to push the regulatory reform process with the change in the government. The weakness of the RIA project was a lack of local participation and buy-in from the government. Similarly, at high levels (ministry/prime minister) there was no champion to support the business regulatory bill.

In Bangladesh, the program was restructured after a change in government because it lacked a champion at the highest levels. Nevertheless, working with line ministries, despite being time consuming and resource intensive, has improved the sustainability of the program. Overall, the impact is measured through the SCM, which includes only benefits for firms and assumes that all firms benefit from the reforms. BICF shows some of the benefits of a sustained program on investment climate reforms over a scatter-shot approach of individual projects, despite some initial missteps. Prior to 2009, during the caretaker government, IFC had access to the Chief Advisor's office as a broad commitment to investment climate reform and pushed forward with initiatives that were later reversed by the elected government of 2009. The programmatic approach allowed BICF to step back and re-engage with the line ministries at all levels to push a program forward.

Unsuccessful efforts in regulatory reforms often focus on improving the technical quality of legislation but ignore the importance of the process to move a bill through the parliamentary process. Although the World Bank and IFC cannot and should not be engaged in these processes, successful regulatory reform requires understanding this part of the policy-making process and engaging relevant stakeholders. The experience in Kenya shows that stakeholder analysis should be a critical part of project design and implementation. This is particularly important in investment climate projects, because they are implemented in countries with a high level of political instability (and hence, a high risk of short-lived commitment) (Figure 5.1).

Virtually all regulatory reforms include several parties with different interests. Therefore, it is critical to perform a systematic stakeholder analysis at the stage of project design. Interviews with IFC staff suggest that project teams do this type of analysis informally. However, operational teams need to be more aware of the political economy of reform and develop strategies for mitigating potential risks posed by vested interests opposing reforms.

Because the distribution of problems is different across institutions, as shown in Table 5.1, IEG attempted to understand how each institution is equipped to handle different implementation problems. IEG conducted this analysis with a set of Probit regressions, where the dependent variable is the achievement of the intervention's Development Outcome[1] plus an interaction term between project problems and a dummy for the World Bank. Control variables include dummies for region, income level, and being a major investment climate project. The results presented in Figure 5.2 show that the IFC business model is better at handling problems related to the World Bank Group's role—technical design, M&E, and supervision, as well as

FIGURE 5.1 Political Stability Index in Countries With and Without Investment Climate Interventions

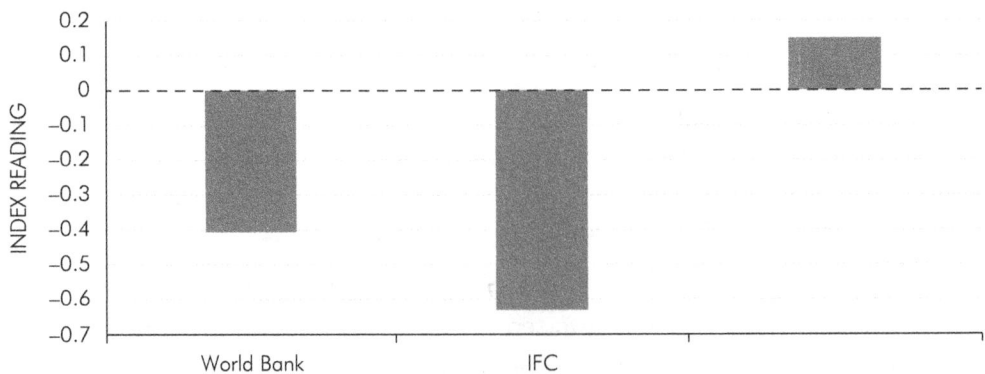

SOURCE: IEG calculation using Worldwide Governance Indicators.
NOTE: Control group includes countries with no World Bank Group investment climate support.

FIGURE 5.2 Probabilities of Achieving the Development Outcome of Each Intervention, by Implementation Problem and Business Model

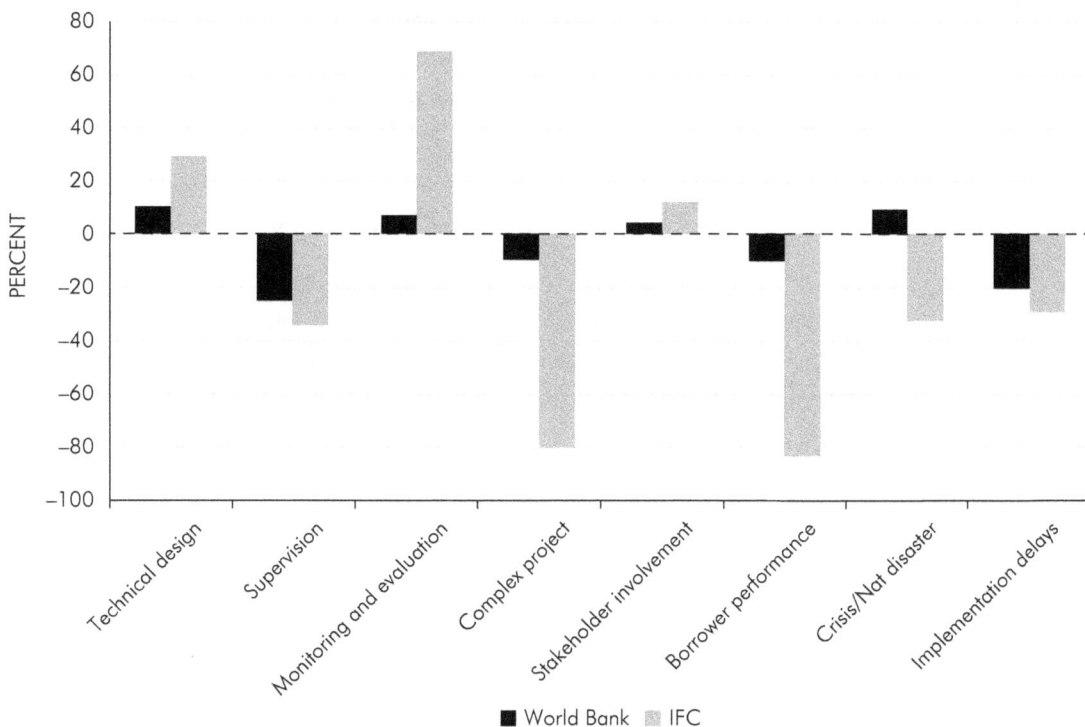

SOURCE: IEG portfolio review.

stakeholder involvement. The World Bank is better equipped to deal with problems related to external factors, such as borrower performance, crisis, and implementation delays, as well as problems related to poor supervision.

One finding from this analysis is that all investment climate projects are affected, one way or the other, by implementation problems. Setbacks occur not only in projects that do not achieve their development objectives, but also in projects that successfully achieve their goals. Approximately 45 percent of problems identified in IEG's review occur in projects that achieve their developmental objectives. This raises a legitimate question: among all the issues identified, are some more binding than others? For instance, IEG observed that a good proportion of projects with poor stakeholder involvement still succeeded (see Box 5.1). Similarly, implementation delays appear almost as often in successful projects as in unsuccessful ones.

To answer this question, IEG adopted two strategies. First it ran a series of multivariate regressions to control for a number of concurrent factors. Then it estimated a series of

BOX 5.1 Findings From the Field—Stakeholder Analysis Matters

In Kenya, IFC supported drafting of the Business Regulatory Act as the foundation to legalize the Business Regulatory Reform Unit, a move to a single business registration system and a one-stop shop. The bill was seen as best practice by IFC staff.

However, the bill has been stalled in the Parliament for some time. In the meantime, the government recently passed a statutory instrument act that includes some components of business regulation bill and made some parts of the business regulatory act irrelevant.

Knowledge of this parallel work was limited among IFC staff. It is interesting to note that during the preparation no formal stakeholder analysis was done, although the bill affected many different groups with conflicting interests.

SOURCE: IEG review.

regressions with interaction terms to establish the combined effect of problems occurring simultaneously. In all regressions, IEG controlled for a number of fixed factors that have been shown to be significant in similar work:[2] length of project implementation (as proxy of complexity), value of project lending, sector, region, GDP growth of country, level of economic development as proxy for institutional development, and a dummy for network and project being restructured. Overall, the only variable that is consistently significant is GDP growth, with a positive effect on the probability of achieving the development objectives.

In a first set of regressions IEG examined the project problems related to the World Bank Group role and those related to borrower behavior separately. The results show that three factors under the Bank Group's control are particularly important: complexity of design, which reduces the probability of success by around 50 percent; inadequate risk assessment, which reduces the probability of success by almost 50 percent; and inadequate M&E, which has the potential to reduce the success rate by a quarter (Table 5.2, regression 1). On the borrower/client side, after controlling for other factors, borrower performance and crisis are significant correlates of success, indicating that lack of borrower engagement reduces the probability of success by 50 percent and the occurrence of a crisis by 25 percent (Table 5.2, regression 2). These results maintained their significance even when IEG ran a Probit model with all projects problems, both Bank and borrower/client (Table 5.2, regression 3).

TABLE 5.2 Probit Regression for World Bank Group Projects on Investment Climate

Variables	(1) iegoutcome	(2) iegoutcome	(3) iegoutcome
Task team leader change	0.0226 (0.129)		0.104 (0.921)
Skills mix	0.0128 (0.109)		0.0467 (0.486)
Risk assessment	−0.442** (−2.000)		−0.444* (−1.860)
Technical design	−0.143 (−1.115)		−0.0278 (−0.244)
Supervision	−0.213 (−1.247)		−0.271 (−1.453)
Unrealistic target	−0.187 (−1.061)		−0.0977 (−0.615)
Monitoring and evaluation	−0.228*** (−2.590)		−0.257*** (−2.896)
Many components	−0.527*** (−3.067)		−0.514*** (−2.500)
Stakeholder involvement		−0.0774 (−0.764)	−0.00196 (−0.0204)
Borrower performance		−0.499*** (−3.853)	−0.457*** (−2.825)
Crisis/Natural disaster		−0.237*** (−3.064)	−0.192** (−2.424)

continued on page 126

VARIABLES	(1) iegoutcome	(2) iegoutcome	(3) iegoutcome
Implementation delays		−0.110 (−1.567)	−0.0309 (−0.458)
Control variables	Yes	Yes	Yes
Observations	241	241	241

SOURCE: IEG calculations.
NOTE: z − statistics in parentheses; *** = p<0.01, **p<0.05, *p<0.1.

Can the developmental objectives be achieved when good supervision and complex design are present in the same project? As seen previously, many implementation problems are present in both successful and unsuccessful projects. IEG observed that borrower performance and the occurrence of a crisis are factors with the most (negative) impact on the achievement of the project's objectives. Does this result hold even when inadequate borrower performance happens with, say, good supervision? To detangle these combined effects, IEG estimated a number of Probit models with interaction terms. This helped identify which, if any, positive aspects of investment climate projects design reduce or eliminate the negative impact of implementation problems on achieving the development objectives.

Figure 5.3 presents the probabilities of achieving the development outcome when a series of project problems is paired with positive aspects of project implementation. The results show that a good risk assessment can help reduce the negative outcome associated with poor borrower performance and the event of a crisis. Furthermore, the negative impact of a crisis can be reduced with a simpler design and good supervision. Similarly, the chances of achieving the development outcome are higher if a poor M&E is associated with a simpler design, if a complex design is associated with a good risk assessment, and if a poor risk assessment is paired with a simpler design. These results are consistent with previous IEG work on quality of Advisory Service projects and development effectiveness ratings, showing a positive association between high work quality in project design and success in Development Outcome (IEG 2014b).

In summary, the findings of this analysis reveal three interesting patterns. First, there are aspects under the control of the World Bank Group that can reduce or eliminate the

FIGURE 5.3 Probability of Achieving the Development Outcome when Project Problems Occur with Good Design Features

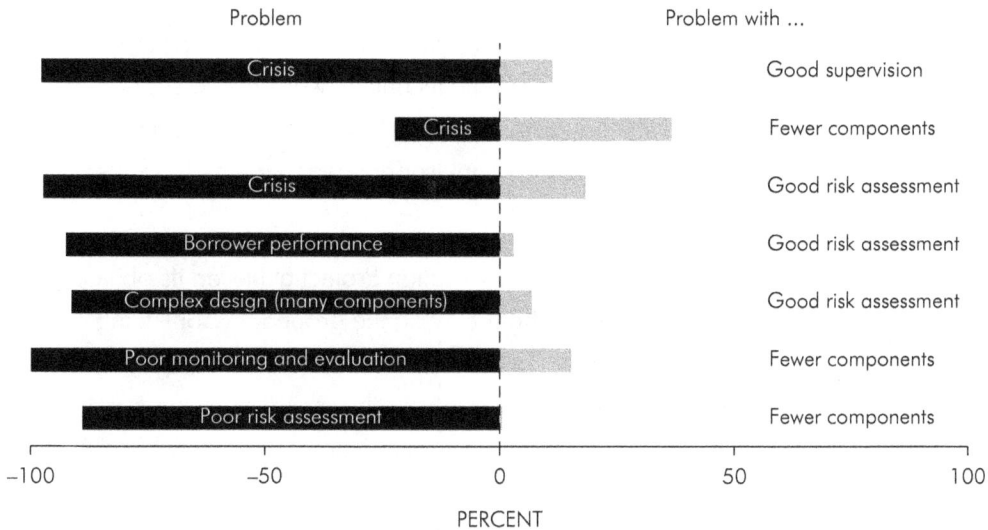

SOURCE: IEG portfolio analysis.

negative effect of factors not under its control. More specifically, inadequate borrower performance can be alleviated by having a simpler project design, and a crisis can be dealt with better if the project does not have a complex design, has a good supervision, and has a good risk assessment. Second, two aspects of the project implementation—simplicity of design and good risk assessment—can reduce or eliminate most implementation problems. Finally, there is one implementation problem for which no other aspect of the design can alleviate its negative impact: inadequate technical design.

Fragile and Conflict-Affected Situations

In FCS, evidence from success and failures in case studies provides the following lessons.

In many FCS, overambitious projects—in terms of scope or timing—led to less than satisfactory results. In the Republic of Yemen, the Bank's Port Cities Development Project ambitiously aimed to strengthen local institutions from the bottom up. However, national and local reforms are difficult to combine over a short period of time in an FCS environment, and hence the right sequencing starting with the national level is required to achieve results. The Bank's Private Sector Growth and Social Protection Project also had overambitious objectives and did not perform well. The promotion of growth in non-oil sectors in the Republic of Yemen—as the project envisioned—would necessitate that a series of actions be taken over time. In the context of a single tranche operation, only initial measures in this area could be envisioned, leaving open the question of how these reforms would be sustained on completion of the operation.

In contrast, in Lao PDR the Bank took into account the unsatisfactory outcomes of earlier budget support operations and provided adequate technical assistance to support its program. In light of the country's limited technical capacity, program objectives were not overambitious, as the programmatic nature of Bank support was expected to foster continuity of reform (IEG 2009).

The Republic of Yemen's Business Start-Up Simplification Project achieved its objectives thanks to its flexible design and ability to adjust to the reality on the ground, discontinuing activities that had minimal added value at the time. For example, the project did not pursue business simplification in the city of Aden as planned because of other activities by the parallel Bank project. The project also did not work with the General Investment Authority because of another IFC project working with the Authority.

Thus, selectivity and flexibility in project design is essential in contexts characterized by political instability and weak capacity. Consistent with IEG's FCS evaluation, these projects also highlight the need for phasing and sequencing of investment climate support based on a timely diagnostic of the most urgent needs and constraints (Box 5.2).

In FCS, institutional capacity building and implementation assistance have been instrumental in determining the success of interventions. In Sudan and South Sudan, the Bank Group's investment climate interventions immediately followed the signing of the 2005 Comprehensive Peace Agreement. The timing of the interventions was considered appropriate; in South Sudan, for example, the Bank Group saw the need for a quick and effective strategy that would demonstrate that the country was stabilizing and that investors were welcome (IFC 2011). Yet the difference in the design and implementation strategy between Sudan and South Sudan led to vastly different results.

In Sudan, IFC's project design was flexible to allow organic growth as traction was achieved (IFC 2010). However, the program lacked enough focus on implementation assistance and was ill suited to the country's postconflict condition. In light of the weak institutional capacity, less emphasis on areas of reform and more attention to implementation assistance might have been a better strategy.

A similar approach was applied successfully in South Sudan. IFC's investment climate project, rated successful by IEG, focused on the creation and strengthening of critical institutions and the establishment of a basic legal framework rather than the streamlining of existing procedures. IFC's approach in South Sudan was also incremental—partly

BOX 5.2 Timing of Impact of Investment Climate Reforms

Part of the literature and practice of investment climate reforms in FCS refers to the timing of regulatory reforms. The argument is that, regulatory reforms being "low hanging fruits" that are easy and fast to implement, they produce results quickly and help motivate additional reforms as well as the peace-building process.

IEG tested this hypothesis by estimating a regression discontinuity model for each of the interventions most commonly implemented in FCS for which intermediate outcome indicators exist, that is, regulations and trade.[a] Using the outcome indicators presented in Chapter 3, IEG tested whether two years after project approval—that is, most likely when such reforms have been implemented—the outcome indicators show a significant improvement.

The results for regulations show a significant impact only for the number of procedures and time to complete registration. In contrast, no outcome indicator for trade shows any significant improvement just two years after approval. This implies that trade reforms take more time (than the average two years) to produce measurable results.

FIGURE Regression Discontinuity of Reforms in Regulations Before and Two Years after Project Approval

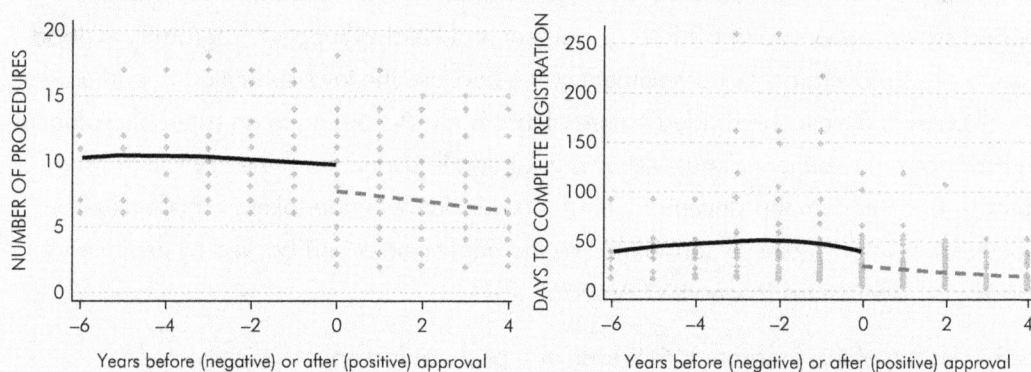

SOURCE: IEG calculations.
a. The test is applied to all countries, not just to FCS, for reason of sample size.

driven by lack of secured funding. Unlike in Sudan, IFC's role in South Sudan made major contributions in some areas (IEG 2013a). For example, the project supported the re-established business registry and helped enact the Investment Promotion Act, among other regulatory reforms. Project activities not only included support to drafting the laws but also involved intensive hands-on support through every step of the enactment and implementation process.

Post-conflict Liberia also faced capacity deficits. However, the country stands out as an example where several positive factors contributed to largely successful investment climate reforms. Project design was kept simple, and was thus appropriate to circumstances in a postconflict country (IEG 2011c). Although the 2011 elections and local capacity limitations were an implementation constraint, technical support by the World Bank Group helped overcome some of these weaknesses. For example, the Reengagement and Reform Support Program II was accompanied by substantial, intensive technical assistance for capacity improvement by the World Bank and other donors in the areas covered by the operation. Similarly, in Lao PDR, the Bank was cognizant of severe local capacity limitations and subsequently increased technical assistance during the progression of its budget support operations.

The Bank Group's success in fragile situations such as South Sudan and Liberia highlight that even in a postconflict country with limited implementation capacity, reform programs can be successful if, in addition to conservative targets, the program is supported by a critical mass of technical assistance and institutional strengthening to make up for local capacity shortcomings (IEG 2011b).

Government ownership is also a vital success factor in FCS. In Liberia the government exhibited strong ownership of the Reengagement and Reform Support Program II. A good measure of the government's commitment came because the laws submitted to parliament were all passed, despite the divided nature of that body. According to an external evaluation, the relevance of investment climate reforms in Liberia is evident from the participatory approach and the demand-driven nature of many initiatives undertaken, with detailed requests for assistance directly formulated by the beneficiaries and backed by preliminary analyses and discussions (Economisti Associati 2011).

One key lesson of this program is that even in a post-conflict country with limited implementation capacity, a reform program can be successful if there is genuine and strong government commitment. In the Republic of Yemen, government commitment was a vital condition for the success of IFC's Mining Policy Reform and Investment Climate Tax Projects. Both projects experienced continued government ownership manifested through extensive engagement in follow-up activities (IFC 2008).

Ensuring government commitment might require having a champion of reforms. IFC did not have a constant client within the government of Nepal, which could consistently champion the cause of investment climate reforms (IEG 2012). Although the investment climate reform project was successful in setting up a public-private dialogue that was instrumental in building trust between the government and the private sector, both this dialogue and the SEZ components were dependent on having a stable counterpart in government and a political consensus. However, three government reshuffles in three years led to changes in local counterparts (IEG 2012). IFC nevertheless built a constituency for reforms through a sustained communication campaign and took these topics to the forefront of discussions on PSD and investment climate reforms. It also adopted other means, such as building solid partnerships and relationships with relevant line ministries, and leveraging and utilizing relationships with senior and mid-level bureaucrats. In the process, some political economy concerns may have been overlooked, such as political sensitivities associated with land allocation in the SEZ project.

Both government and stakeholder engagement, therefore, are keys to ensure the success of interventions. Facilitating government ownership of reforms involves a careful assessment of the political feasibility of the proposed interventions, as well as identification of measures to reduce diminishing client interest in reforms. Tools to accomplish this include a consistent communication strategy to highlight the relevance and necessity of the reform process, having "champions" within the government to create stakeholder engagement, and developing strategic alliances with other World Bank Group projects to accommodate different client interests in reforms.

The fragile political economy has a fundamental bearing on the success of investment climate interventions. In Nepal, investment climate reforms immediately followed the end of the conflict in 2006. An investment climate minidiagnostic noted that analyzing and recommending priority reform areas in the investment climate are a key to embarking on a postconflict reform program. With increasing stability, a good investment climate becomes essential in realizing latent investment. Nepal's fluctuating political economy, however, was a tremendous constraint. Successive elections, the abolishment of the monarchy, and constitutional changes led to perpetual political uncertainty. Regardless, IFC has been supporting the country, for example, by implementing the second phase of the Nepal Investment Climate Reform Program to enhance the transparency and accountability of service delivery at the Office of the Company Registrar.

In the Republic of Yemen, civil unrest disrupted the progress of several Bank Group projects. The Bank's Private Sector Growth and Social Protection Project, for example, was affected by civil unrest in 2011. Although the unrest caused significant disruption in the country, it was not unforeseeable and the related risk was not adequately addressed in the program's design—which was too ambitious for such a fragile situation. To counter political uncertainties, the project was designed as a single tranche operation with the option to offer a programmatic series to the new administration. However, this mitigation measure was ineffective in the face of civil unrest. Given the systemic risk of political uncertainty, Bank engagement through analytical work rather than lending might have been more appropriate, or prior actions that could be accomplished quickly but were of an irreversible nature might have been preferable.

In Guinea the World Bank Group suspended all engagement following the 2008 military coup, and IFC's mining sector technical assistance was forced to close before the government could adopt any reform. The project was found to have an inadequate evaluation of political risks. The Guinea CASCR Review also noted that the Bank Group did not appear to have a real strategy for dealing with FCS (IEG 2013b). Following Bank Group re-engagement in 2011, IFC immediately re-engaged with a regulatory reform agenda.

In conclusion, the Bank Group's mixed implementation record demonstrates the complexity of achieving regulatory reform in FCS. Examples reviewed by IEG illustrate the importance of properly assessing the political economy of the country; properly tailoring the scope, complementarity, and timing of any reform program; and properly gauging and supporting the institutional and technical capacity to bring investment climate reforms to completion and thus support long-lasting and sustained PSD and growth.

Industry-Specific Intervention

IFC's agribusiness and tourism investment climate projects are more likely to be flagged for technical design issues and less likely to be flagged for having implementation delays than World Bank investment climate projects, although implementation delays are the leading problem identified for IFC investment climate interventions. World Bank projects are more likely to be flagged for having too many components and less likely to be flagged for implementation delays. For World Bank projects, M&E is the most common problem.

A review of project evaluations suggests that three factors are associated with success or failure: counterpart commitment, local capacity and human resource quality, and project complexity. For the first two factors, greater commitment and better capacity (or explicit attention to capacity building) appear to aid effectiveness. For complexity, a larger number of "moving parts" (components and subcomponents) appears negatively related to success (see Box 5.3).

World Bank Group Collaboration and Results

Collaboration and how it occurs are not recorded formally in the World Bank Group. This explains why the extent of collaboration reported by the two institutions is substantially different. Of the 819 projects reviewed by IEG, 44 percent (147) of IFC projects are flagged as having collaboration with the World Bank, but only 6 percent of

BOX 5.3 Inclusive Growth through a Diversified Agricultural Sector

In India, the Orissa Socio-Economic Development Loan/Credit II sought to promote inclusive growth by diversifying the agriculture sector through strengthened property rights, improved income-earning opportunities for forest dwellers, privately led agro-industrial growth, withdrawal of the state from commercial activities to create space for the private sector, and improvements in the reliability and accessibility of electric power.

IEG found the project to be well designed and found that Bank staff had developed excellent working relationships with the client. In spite of low capacity on the counterpart side and serious data deficiencies on results, the project appears to have produced an expansion in irrigated land under water user group management and an improved investment climate (including reduced barriers to entry), which may have contributed to accelerated growth led by private industrial investments "with effective environmental due diligence."

SOURCE: IEG.

TABLE 5.3 Bank-IFC Collaboration in Investment Climate Projects

	IFC—Number of Projects (%)	Bank—Number of Projects (%)
Without collaboration	185 (56)	447 (94)
With collaboration	147 (44)	29 (6)
Total	**332 (100)**	**476 (100)**

SOURCE: IEG portfolio review.

World Bank projects report collaboration with IFC, a rate seven times lower than IFC's (see Table 5.3).[3]

The main reason coordination within the World Bank Group is important is that it can enhance the effectiveness of Bank Group support to clients. Unfortunately, presenting evidence of such links in practice is difficult because the effectiveness discussion in project

FIGURE 5.4 Success Rate by Degree of Collaboration

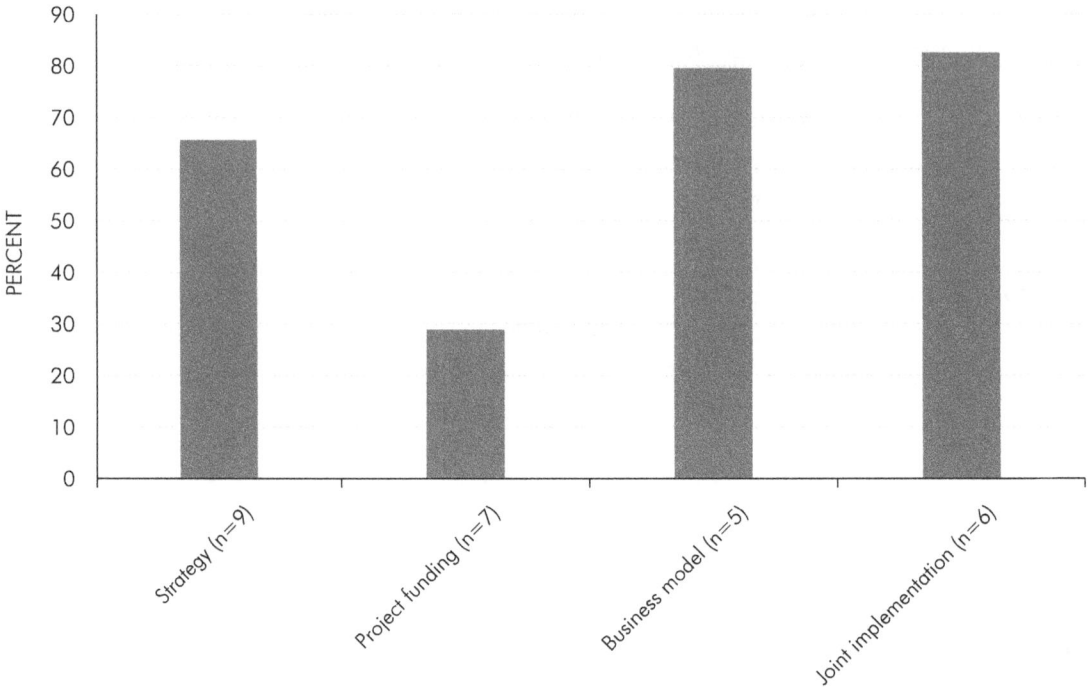

FIGURE 5.4 Success Rate by Degree of Collaboration

SOURCE: IEG portfolio review.

documents is not generally linked to the presence or absence of collaboration. Nevertheless, in the investment climate portfolio 33 projects with IEG ratings were characterized as having some form of coordination. On the basis of PCRs and Evaluation Notes, IEG classified such collaboration in four categories that denote an increasing level of collaboration: strategy/ broad collaboration, project funding business model, complementarity of institutions (that is, IFC Advisory Services complements a World Bank Development Policy Loan [DPL]), and joint design or implementation. IEG estimated the share of projects in each category that has a successful outcome. As shown in Figure 5.4, the higher the degree of collaboration, the higher the share of achievement of the Development Outcome. It must be recognized, however, that these findings are based on a small number of observations.

Given this limitation, IEG reviewed projects with examples of collaboration to draw anecdotal evidence. A number of investment climate projects led IEG to conclude that successful collaboration rests on complementarity: of roles, of perspectives, and of instruments.

COMPLEMENTARITY OF ROLES

When the roles of each institution are clear and do not overlap, results can be successful. In Cambodia's Alternative Dispute Resolution Project IFC played an active role in providing global knowledge of international best practices to both the government and the private sector by bringing in a lead legal counsel from the World Bank Group. He provided extensive comments on the draft National Arbitration Center of Cambodia subdecree, led one consultation session with the private sector and government, and met frequently with high-level officials in the government to advise them on the major issues related to the establishment of the Center.

In Serbia, IFC, the World Bank Europe and Central Asia Financial and Private Sector Development, and the World Bank Institute collaborated on the Regulatory Impact Analysis Project. In 2010 a Regulatory Reform Conference was organized jointly by the government of Serbia, the World Bank, the World Bank Institute, IFC, and the Balkan Center for Regulatory Reform. All parties had different *modus operandi*, but there was a clear division of tasks, accompanied by continuous communication between task team leaders, especially before endorsing with the client any action and requirement; this guaranteed full cooperation of all the agencies and successful delivery of the project.

COMPLEMENTARITY OF PERSPECTIVES

A second requirement for fruitful collaboration is complementarity of outlook. IFC's Philippines Investment Promotion Policies Project was inherently complex and controversial. Multiple World Bank Group players were involved, including IBRD, CIC/ FIAS, MIGA, and IFC. IFC Private Enterprise Partnership's field presence and existing relationships with key stakeholders placed it naturally in the position to manage client relationship in day-to-day operations. It provided funding to support FIAS work. Bank staff led work on fiscal incentives, with FIAS support. IFC managed work on institutional assessment with critical support from MIGA. IFC also led interventions at the subnational level. Yet many members of the project team were working toward different outcomes. Team members did not always share the same perspective. Although this was not main factor behind the failure of the project, it certainly detracted from performance.

In Madagascar an IFC project on supporting Doing Business reforms was designed jointly with the World Bank PSD program. This joint approach allowed the Bank Group to face the client with just one interface and add depth and breadth to the scope of reforms that were already ongoing when this project was launched. The project helped build the first-ever comprehensive inventory of business licenses in Madagascar. Additionally, it pioneered the roll-out of "guillotine"-style licensing reform and the application of the standard cost model methodology to estimate the cost to Malagasy companies of complying with the licensing regime.

Finally, collaboration will not succeed unless complementarity of instruments exists. The different business models of the World Bank and IFC provide opportunities to exploit the complementarity of instruments and approaches. Tunisia had more than one PREM-led DPL, with collaboration from FPD. However, IFC supported the government of Tunisia in a good proportion of reforms that triggered the disbursement of the budget support loan. Regulations, FDI policy, tourism, debt management, and bankruptcy were all areas of reform. As IFC's support opened the doors to the implementation of the DPLs, the DPLs in turn offered a policy umbrella to guide IFC's reform interventions.

Bosnia-Herzegovina is another example where IFC's reform work encouraged the government and the Bank to consider a DPL. IFC had conducted a substantial amount of investment climate advisory work in the country and was in close dialogue with the government there. In light of the progress in implementing many of the IFC investment climate recommendations, a DPL focusing on the business environment was developed to provide additional support for reforms. The investment climate team became an integral part of the DPL Bank team. Although formally the task team leader was Bank staff (as the system does not accommodate a coleader), an IFC staff member did act as co-task team leader. Bank budget covered the costs of both Bank and IFC staff working directly on the DPL, and IFC funded its own technical assistance activities. The Bosnian government saw one World Bank Group team.

In contrast, when complementarity of roles between the two institutions is not recognized and the World Bank and IFC are seen as providing similar services to the clients, collaboration is not achieved and "turf" competition is generated. There have been instances where staff and management have questioned the legitimacy of IFC working with governments, even for advisory services. Some see it as intruding into a well-established Bank space. Some see the technical assistance business as a zero-sum game. A few see the Advisory Services in IFC as not being relevant, as it is of narrow scope compared to the Bank's work.

For example, in a country in South Asia, staff in the Bank reacted strongly to a request IFC received from the Ministry of Commerce for technical assistance work. They questioned whether IFC Advisory Services should be involved in tax and trade regulation. Questions were even raised about IFC working in licensing and regulatory reform and regarding whether IFC should be expanding its investment climate program in the country. Both IFC and the Bank had separate competent teams to conduct the work requested by the Ministry of Commerce. A compromise was finally reached by agreeing that IFC would focus on one subnational region in the country.

Similarly, when collaboration is driven by other factors, such as funding, positive results cannot be expected. About three years ago, the government of a Central Asian country sent a request for technical assistance for land reform to donors and to units in the World Bank Group, including FPD and CIC. A CIC mission went to the country to better define the technical assistance and signed an agreement with the government to focus on the land registry and construction permits. As CIC did not have the staff to meet the government timetable, it entered into an agreement with FPD to manage the technical assistance. The reports and recommendations were made available to FPD, IFC/investment climate, SDN, and others, for review and to be used as inputs in their respective work program in the country. The government accepted the recommendations and requested assistance to implement them.

As of now, funding has not materialized through either the government (Bank loan) or other sources. According to SDN, because of resource constraints, funds are available only for a scoping mission, but not to implement the recommendations. So SDN is preparing to repeat the scoping mission it undertook more than three years ago. Recommendations addressing the land registry and construction permits have been accepted by the government and were praised by Bank staff—but have yet to be implemented.

Finally, it is important to recognize that collaboration is not a sufficient condition for success in achieving development outcomes. Other critical factors, such as political stability or the level of commitment from the government, play a crucial role in achieving the development objectives of a project. There are cases where the collaboration was successful but the results were not (or vice versa). For example, in the Madagascar licensing simplification project, a political crisis brought the project to a halt just before the first set of reform recommendations was delivered to the client. In the Democratic Republic of the Congo, although the government counterparts were verbally supportive of an IFC/FIAS project on tax and Doing Business reforms, there was very little follow-up or local ownership.

Regardless of the coordination efforts within the World Bank Group, a clear commitment from the government is critical to having a successful project. Finally, in Bihar state (India), the World Bank and IFC conducted joint scoping activities and collaborated on some of the same initiatives related to investment climate reforms. However, the scope and goals of this project were not fully consistent with conditions on the ground. In spite of the government of Bihar's general reform-mindedness, the government did not have a strong level of commitment to the project. It seems that the project's scope was more ambitious than the government was willing or able to embrace and that on-the-ground elements such as political will and departmental capacity should have been considered during the first project.

Strong government buy-in should have been established prior to initiating implementation. Yet the business taxation recommendations were fully incorporated into the Bihar budget because it received strong support and a public endorsement from the Deputy Chief Minister (who was also the Finance Minister).

In Mali, government commitment outside of Doing Business indicator reforms was limited (IEG 2011a). After the completion of the first phase of investment climate reform, IFC sensitized the government to the fact that Doing Business reforms are only the start, and not the final stopping point, for reforms. Yet IFC initiated a second phase of investment climate reforms with minimal government commitment outside of Doing Business reforms. The program assisted in drafting laws and regulations, including the laws to set up and regulate industrial zone authorities; it also provided advisory services to various government entities over the course of the program (IEG 2014a).

WORLD BANK GROUP STAFF VIEWS ON BUSINESS MODELS

As shown in Chapter 1, IFC and the World Bank use two different business models in supporting investment climate interventions. The institutions have some differences and similarities in their activities, execution, and funding (Box 5.4). To find the views of World Bank Group staff on the value of each business model, IEG conducted a survey of staff involved in investment climate work[4] (Appendix E). The survey addressed issues related to the collaboration between and within the Bank Group units. It asked staff whether these two business models would foster collaboration, discourage collaboration, or both (for example, at times foster and at times discourage collaboration). Interestingly, only a very small share of staff (6 percent) perceived the difference between the IFC model and the World Bank model as a positive factor fostering collaboration. A significant share, 30 percent, saw them as discouraging collaboration.

Almost 50 percent of staff see the difference in the two models as either an opportunity to foster collaboration or an obstacle that hampers collaboration. They do not dismiss the value of each business model; rather, they show a much more nuanced perception, saying that the differences can both foster and discourage collaboration. Hence, if properly understood and implemented, these differences in business models might represent an opportunity for collaboration, and impact, in investment climate work.

Some interesting differences could be noted across units and categories of staff. Staff who typically manage projects (grades GF and GG) and staff that are closer to the client (staff in country offices) have a much more positive attitude toward the two business models than senior staff and staff in headquarters (82 percent and 66 percent, respectively).

In recent years, some joint Bank-IFC collaboration took place around DPLs, exploiting the complementarities presented in the Bank's and IFC's business models. To obtain budget support, clients have to meet a set of conditions, which generally include a set of reforms. For those investment climate-related reforms, the Bank seems to be increasingly calling on IFC investment climate staff to support reforms in client countries. The fit seems to work well, as the interventions of IFC investment climate tend to be focused, limited in scope, and delivered in a very short period of time. In most of IFC's interventions in DPLs, IFC adopts its own business model, credits the projects to its portfolio, and avails itself of its own funding. This was the case in Tunisia and Bosnia-Herzegovina, where IFC support opened the door to World Bank budget support.

With the events of the Arab Spring, there has been an increase in demand for investment climate advisory work in the Middle East and North Africa, resulting in growth of the project portfolio of both IFC and FPD. Also, new topics are gaining attention, such as job creation and women in business.

With a growing portfolio, there is less concern about competition between IFC and the Bank and more concern about the need for collaboration. The Bank's macro approach to investment climate reform is complemented by IFC's narrow, practical, short-term interventions, such as in regulatory reform and simplification, the development of an investment policy, or improving the investment climate for a sector, for example, agribusiness or tourism.

The presence of a collaborative mindset among the management team in IFC/investment climate and FPD in the region, as well as with CIC at headquarters gave the impetus to act on that complementarity. Proximity (Cairo) or co-location (Rabat) of field staff has helped significantly. Finally, to make the working relationship even closer, CIC embedded a staff member in FPD in the Middle East and North Africa Region at headquarters. Whether in the Arab Republic of Egypt, Lebanon, Morocco, South Sudan, Tunisia, or the Republic of Yemen, the units are involved jointly in a number of areas, including regulatory reform and simplification, trade logistics, tax, debt management, sector development (such as tourism), and bankruptcy.

SOURCE: IEG interviews with World Bank Group staff and managers.

Further, the more distant staff are from IFC mapped staff, the more the perception of value of the two business models drops (Figure 5.5). This could be explained by the fact that the more staff are familiar with the IFC model—as in the case of FPD investment climate staff—the more they appreciate its value and hence see it as an opportunity for collaboration.

FIGURE 5.5 Perception of Value of Two Business Models by World Bank Group Staff Involved in Investment Climate Work (percent)

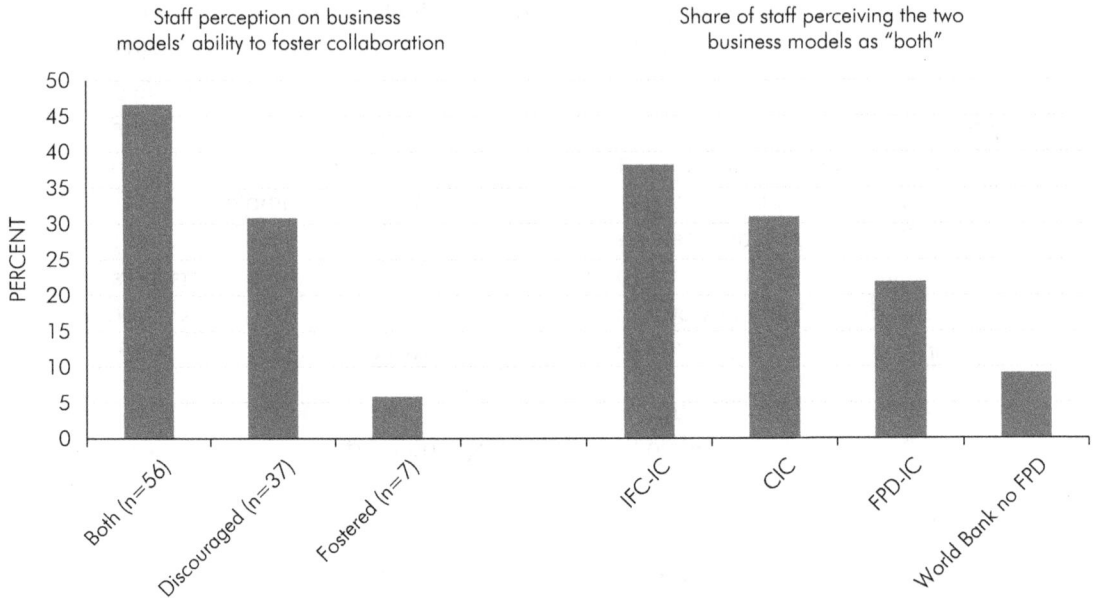

Staff perception on business models' ability to foster collaboration

Share of staff perceiving the two business models as "both"

SOURCE: IEG staff survey.
NOTE: CIC = Investment Climate Practice; FPD = Finance and Private Sector Development; IC = Investment Climate business line.

NATURE OF COLLABORATION

Collaboration can take different forms and degrees of intensity, from merely exchanging information all the way to joint implementation of projects. In the World Bank Group the nature of collaboration can include sharing information about the project with Bank/IFC colleagues, peer reviewing and/or providing comments on the project documents, going on missions for the project, designing the projects (that is, concept, Project Appraisal Document, Project Data Sheet—Technical Assistance and Advisory Services, or implementing projects).

IEG's review of 25 country case study reveals that at the strategic level, collaboration among the institutions seems to be more common; it is less so at the operational level. Nepal was selected (starting with the FY11 Interim Strategy Note) as a pilot country to implement an enhanced joint strategy to leverage IDA and IFC resources and realize synergies. For the FY11 Interim Strategy Note, private sector consultations led by IFC in Kathmandu were coordinated with the Bank team and IFC advised on the joint donor consultation agenda. The Bank and IFC had joint offices, and staff and worked closely on issues such as e-payments, infrastructure, hydropower, and business enabling environment. On an intervention level, IFC and the World Bank were coordinated in implementing an investment climate strategy.

Similarly, both IFC and the World Bank have demonstrated harmony and integration in their work on regulatory reforms in Rwanda. One project was designed as a joint project; however, all other projects have been designed and implemented in close collaboration with existing projects to maximize the comparative advantage offered by both IFC and the World Bank. In Colombia, there was a strategic level coordination, but it is hard to say whether the collaboration among the World Bank Group members was based on respective comparative advantages.

In its survey, IEG also asked Bank Group staff the degree of collaboration they have experienced. The results are shown in Figure 5.6, with the degree of intensity increasing in a clockwise direction.[5] Survey results show, not surprisingly, that lighter collaboration is more frequent than deeper collaboration. Overall, half the time collaboration involves simple activities such as information sharing and peer reviewing. Only one-third of the time is collaboration deep enough to involve design and implementation of projects.

Headquarters staff are 20 percent more likely to be involved in any type of collaboration than field staff. This is understandable, as most of them play a formal or informal anchor role. They also are substantially more involved in deeper forms of collaboration, such as going on joint missions, joint design of programs and projects, and joint project implementation. In contrast, field staff report a higher rate of sharing information than headquarters staff, perhaps because of increased colocation of field offices. These results fit in with the respective roles and situations of headquarters and field staff.

FIGURE 5.6 Extent of Collaboration Within the World Bank Group

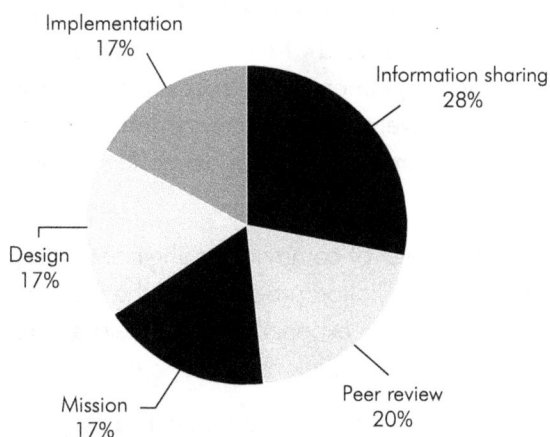

SOURCE: IEG staff survey.

BOX 5.5 Donors' Support to Investment Climate

The investment climate program received a significant amount of financial support from a number of donors. Overall, since FY07, 60 percent of the financial cost of investment climate operations managed by FIAS has been sponsored by donors. Only 2 percent of such cost has been contributed by the client countries and the remaining 38 percent has been sponsored by the World Bank. Main donors include Austria, the Netherlands, Norway, Switzerland, Sweden, the United States, and the United Kingdom (see figure below). Another seven bilateral donors and a number of multilateral donors (for example, the European Union, Trade Mark East Africa, and so forth) support the FIAS program of investment climate reforms.

FIGURE Trust Fund Contributions to the FIAS Program

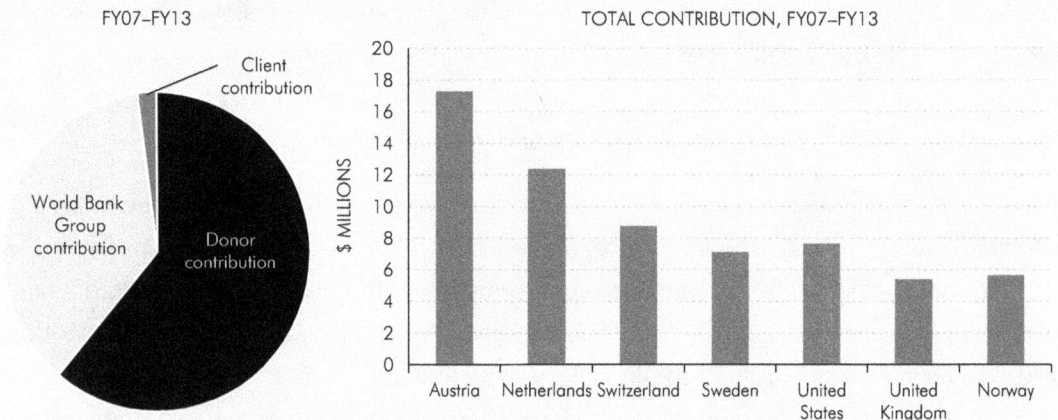

FY07–FY13

TOTAL CONTRIBUTION, FY07–FY13

IEG interviewed seven donors to gather their feedback on their relationship with FIAS on investment climate projects.

All interviewed donors expressed their satisfaction in working with FIAS. They all appreciated the quality of work and expertise in the field (a number of donors pointed out that IFC is the only place in the word where so many experts can be found working exclusively on the regulatory environment), their cost effectiveness in implementing reforms, their good access to government officials, and their good M&E system. One donor also appreciated the integrated approach across the whole World Bank Group (IFC, World Bank, and MIGA).

Donors also appreciate FIAS's level of commitment, their ability to participate in FIAS's strategy design, the constant consultation process, and the feedback they receive regularly. At times, though, they have experienced long delays in receiving feedback, especially when there is difference of opinions.

They decided to sponsor investment climate work because they share the strategic goal of helping PSD through the improvement of the regulatory environment. When their contribution decreased over time, they attributed that to either their own budgetary constraints or their own portfolio reorganization, not to lack of satisfaction with the collaboration with FIAS.

All donors appreciate the M&E system developed by FIAS and acknowledge that it has improved over time, moving from measuring of number of reforms to cost compliance savings, investment, and number of firms registered. In terms of impact, though, they recognize that this is hard to measure and that the methods used need to be improved. Similarly, they pointed out that the impact on the poor is not measured. More specifically, improvements should be made in measuring who is benefitting from the regulatory reforms. This is important for them, as they will be able to report to their Ministers and Parliamentarians answers on impact.

In terms of implementation, some donors pointed out that the World Bank Group should focus more on the political economy of reforms, as this is key to ownership and sustainability of investment climate reforms.

One other aspect that should be taken into account is pricing policy. Some donors pointed out that, at times, finalizing a financial (cash) contribution for advisory services can require a long, complex approval process including legislative action. Where these contributions are relatively nominal in size, there is a trade-off between the possibility of an extended delay (and missing a potential reform window) and the concrete demonstration of buy-in for the project. Consequently some flexibility in the application of the pricing policy should be considered as long as there are other strong signals of client commitment (such as in-kind contributions, demonstration of acting on quick-win recommendations, and so forth).

Another problem raised by some donors is the issue of branding, that is, receiving enough credit for the financial support provided. At times they are not satisfied with the acknowledgment they receive.

In terms of interventions, some donors pointed out that the set of areas offered is not comprehensive. For instance, environmental regulations are not properly addressed, in the health sector, demand is much higher than supply, and agriculture interventions are few and not focused. Finally, some products might be obsolete (for example, entry) and hence could be discontinued.

Other donors mentioned that occasionally the diagnostic work done to identify reforms is driven more by availability of IFC expertise than by the situation on the ground, and IFC should more often take into account the limited capacity of recipients (as to ensure sustainability of reforms).

One donor familiar with the reorganization process said that FIAS is a good example of cooperation and that the key to success is the having exceptional leadership.

SOURCE: IEG interviews with donors.

Interviews with different stakeholders in Bangladesh, Cambodia, Kenya, and Rwanda confirmed some unique qualities of the World Bank and IFC. Stakeholders highly appreciated IFC's access to international technical expertise, timeliness, and pragmatism, as well as flexibility. Access to government institutions and ability to provide substantive funding were the most common strengths identified of the World Bank. World Bank staff have a broader view on investment climate reforms, whereas IFC staff are much more focused on implementation.

In Bangladesh and Kenya, some stakeholders indicated that IFC's ability to handle political economy was not as strong as its technical capacity. One respondent pointed out, "Political economy is out of IFC's comfort zone." The World Bank is seen as slow to respond and implement projects. Some stakeholders indicated that the World Bank requires too much documentation. One stakeholder reported that after two years, "We are still exchanging documents with the World Bank."

SOURCE: IEG interviews.

Compared to other regions, staff in Sub-Saharan Africa and Latin America and the Caribbean report a higher degree of deep collaboration than other regions, including going on joint missions and collaborative design and implementation of programs and projects. In Africa, there has been a long history of collaboration between the Bank and IFC because of the well-funded and large IFC Investment Climate Business Line presence in the region. The Latin America and the Caribbean Region benefits from a "unitary" Bank/IFC management (Box 5.7).

Factors Affecting Collaboration between the World Bank and IFC

In identifying the factors that play a role in fostering collaboration, IEG compiled a list of 15 factors and included them in the staff survey. They are grouped in three categories: role of the unit and its strategy, systems or formal organization, and informal organization (Table 5.4). For each factor, the survey asked the respondent whether a factor strictly discourages or fosters collaboration, or both (that is, in some cases have fostered and in others have discouraged collaboration).

The survey results first point out the primary role of informal factors in fostering collaboration (Figure 5.7). Fifty-eight respondents identified informal factors as playing a key role in facilitating collaboration between the two institutions. However, systems and formal organization—such as different pricing policy, accountability matrix, M&E framework,

As part of the reorganization of FPD in FY11, joint management for investment climate was established in the Latin America and the Caribbean Region, with one person covering the positions of Director of FPD Investment Climate Global Practice and FPD for the region and co-Director of CIC. Since FY13, the IFC investment climate service line and FPD for the region have established a strong collaborative working relationship, with the idea of using the complementarity of IFC and World Bank strengths for a greater impact to clients. The IFC investment climate service line and FPD for the region have developed and will implement the first-of-a-kind tripartite (donors, IFC, and the Bank) multidonor program. The program responds to priorities expressed by client governments in more than 10 countries in the region and follows a joint IFC-World Bank results framework. The joint fundraising effort attempted to leverage external and internal partnerships, and to create a platform for setting common goals for the region.

For that, a jointly conceptualized proposal on a regional investment program for the region was designed between IFC region staff, CIC, FPD region staff, and PREM tax teams and was presented to the Canadian International Development Agency and the Swiss State Secretariat for Economic Affairs. The legal agreement, work plans, and M&E framework were also jointly prepared for the donors. The teams worked extensively to make sure that work streams were coordinated and complimentary. Such coordination helped improve discussions and communications not only with the clients, but also with donors.

In support of that joint management and program, the region has developed a set of joint—Bank and IFC—accountability matrices for the region. The matrices—necessary for that high level of collaboration—were not easy to design, develop, or use, as they had to be built on top of two not entirely compatible systems.

The Latin America and the Caribbean Region is an example where synergies between the Bank and IFC have enabled better client management, more joint project development, with more readily available global expertise and solutions to clients, though at a high administrative cost.

SOURCE: IEG.

donor reporting, and human resources policies and staff incentives—are on average seen as discouraging collaboration. Finally, factors related to roles and strategy can foster collaboration if properly handled.

Personal networks, previous experience, and physical proximity play a key role in fostering collaboration. This is the case across all regions and networks. At the same time, staff identify the personalities of staff and signals from managers/directors as having a mixed impact

TABLE 5.4 Factors Affecting Collaboration

Roles and Strategies	Systems and Formal Organization	Informal Organization
Program project overlap (that is, both working in the same space providing similar services to clients)	IFC Advisory Services accountability matrix (processes and staff accountability during project cycle)/World Bank organizational structure	Degree of familiarity with each other's operations (for example, project cycle, product lines, human resources systems, funding)
Same client (that is, both agencies working directly with government)	Formal incentive structure (for example, cross-support measured, recognition of collaboration by project operational systems)	Proximity to colleagues from the other institution (for example, both institutions located in the same building in the field)
Complementarity of instruments (for example, combining rapid technical assistance and long-term lending)	Pricing policy	Personal networks
Strategies/priorities of the two institutions	Project funding	Staff personalities
	Staff presence in the field	Previous experience working with World Bank/IFC
		Signals/directions from management

SOURCE: IEG.

on fostering collaboration, especially in the Latin America and the Caribbean and Europe and Central Asia Regions. IEG's Bangladesh field study confirms that World Bank Group coordination is mostly informal and based on needs. The World Bank and IFC are coming together on the Country Assistance Strategy, the Doing Business reports, investment climate surveys, and the occasion of visits by senior Bank Group management. No formal process brings the staff together regularly.

In Kenya local staff stated that their country office was an example of where investment climate coordination has worked well. Many indicated that collaboration starts at the personal level and has been improving over time. However, some suggested that jointness should be

FIGURE 5.7 Factors Affecting Collaboration between the Bank and IFC (average number of respondents identifying each)

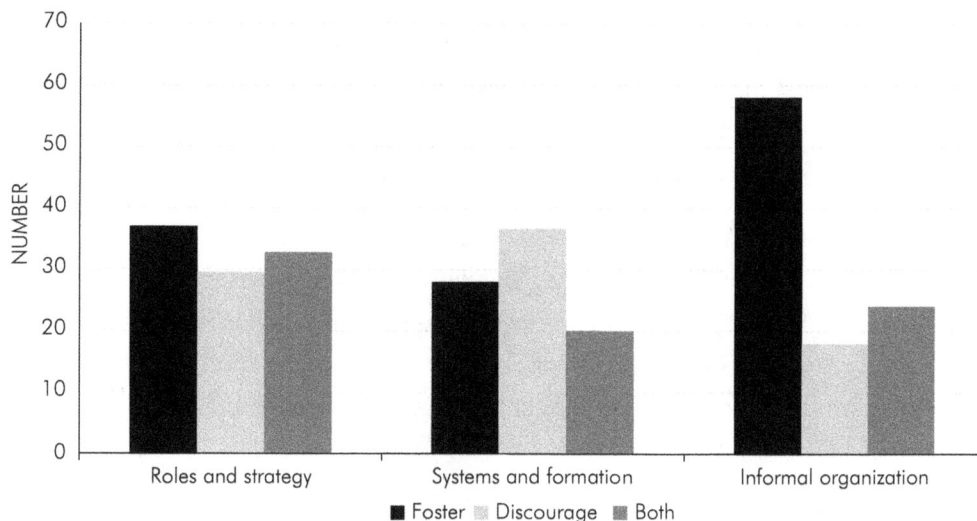

SOURCE: IEG staff survey.

an integrated solution and will not be achieved without adjusting managerial structures and staff incentives.

Among formal organizational factors, the different pricing policies and accountability matrices strictly discourage collaboration, with little opportunity to exert a positive role. This finding is valid across all networks. At the same time, presence in the field is the most important factor fostering collaboration across all networks, whereas project funding is perceived as the factor that most discourages collaboration.

Finally, the aspects of roles and strategy have shown mixed effects, at times fostering collaboration and at times discouraging it. Having the same client is seen more as fostering collaboration by IFC Investment Climate and CIC, but much less so by FPD Investment Climate (where it is seen at best as showing mixed results). Similar results are seen for complementarity of instruments. However, in the Africa and East Asia and Pacific Regions, strategies and priorities are perceived as much more aligned and as fostering collaboration.

WORLD BANK GROUP STAFF VIEWS ON THE NEW TRADE AND COMPETITIVENESS GLOBAL PRACTICE

Beginning in July 2014, all the investment climate units are going to operate under the T&C Global Practice. This practice will be the most integrated practice in the new World Bank Group structure. IEG interviews with Bank Group investment climate management and staff and surveys with staff provide some insights on how to optimize value to clients with the merger.

Most staff provided positive feedback, highlighting the complementarity and strengths of the Bank and IFC business models, such as, "We should learn from one another on the basis of facts and not rumors" and "IFC has a deep definition of products. [The] Bank has flexibility and wider knowledge. This should expand our engagement with clients."

However, some expressions of concern exist. In particular, one is the worry that the T&C Global Practice will be dominated by one institution and its business model. One staff member reported, "My worry is if investment climate advisory, as it is known in IFC, disappears, the perception within IFC might be that 'investment climate is going to Bank.'" Another staff member pointed out, "I expect that T&C will be Bank based, with a nice touch of IFC style."

The other fear is that the Global Practices will become silos. "In T&C, PREM Trade is macro; IFC-investment climate is micro. FPD-investment climate sits in the middle. How can we reconcile them?" asked one staff member. These expressions indicate the concern that the reorganization cannot be a simple juxtaposition of current systems and programs under one roof.

From an operational perspective, many staff hope that serious attempts will be made to remove impediments to collaboration that are found in the formal organization, for example, governance and accountability systems, funding, pricing, and human resource policies and systems. The need for such reforms has been raised repeatedly in interviews and confirmed by the surveys. "I hope the final design [of T&C] will not keep parallel tracks, but will integrate from the staff, responsibilities and systems, even if time is needed to integrate systems," said one staff member.

Some staff provided concrete suggestions to improve formal collaboration, such as implementing a multipractice budget system to mitigate the silo syndrome. "We need a multipractice budget code system on the Bank side," one staff member said, and the adoption of a dual sign-off system [region-anchor] in the World Bank. Today the systems do not require it, making "region-technical collaboration personal, ad hoc in the Bank," as another staff member noted.

Some staff highlighted the importance of the incentive system: "It is less important to put boundaries on perfect boxes than to provide incentives to collaborate and connect." Finally, as the composition of the portfolio has shown, a number of investment climate reforms will be undertaken in the future by sector Global Practices as well as Cross-Cutting Solution Areas.

Consequently staff and leadership should encourage cross-institutional collaboration in this area.

In sum, this chapter presents evidence that aspects of project design such as simpler project design, good supervision, and good risk assessment can reduce or eliminate the negative effects of most implementation problems. However, inadequate technical design cannot be compensated by any good aspects of project design and hence most likely leads to unsatisfactory performance. Furthermore, political instability is one of the main problems affecting the effectiveness of investment climate reforms.

Collaboration within the World Bank Group is mostly driven by informal factors. Systems and formal organization are seen as mostly discouraging collaboration and can pose significant challenges to the new global practice. Hence, although not easy to achieve, it is important to harmonize the back office functions of the global practice while maintaining the richness of the two delivery models.

Notes

[1] Successful projects are those with a rating of marginally satisfactory or better.

[2] This follows the approach of Denizer, Kaufman and Kraay (2013).

[3] IEG reviewed the investment climate project portfolios of both the Bank and IFC. The number presented here has been adjusted on the basis of that review. IEG has found a serious underreporting of collaboration by the Bank.

[4] See Appendix E for the questionnaire adopted. All task team leaders of investment climate projects in the IEG portfolio and all investment climate-mapped Bank Group staff received an invitation to participate. A total of 144 staff responded.

[5] There are five increasing levels of collaboration options: (i) sharing information; (ii) peer review of or commenting on project documents; (iii) going on mission for the project; (iv) taking part in the design of programs and projects; and (v) jointly implementing projects.

References

Denizer, C., D. Kaufmann, and A. Kraay. 2013. "Good Countries or Good Projects? Macro and Micro Correlates of World Bank Project Performance." *Journal of Development Economics* 105.

Economisti Associati. 2011. *Investment Climate in Africa Program: Four Country Impact Assessment, Liberia Country Report*. Bologna: Economisti Associati.

IEG (Independent Evaluation Group). 2009. "Lao PDR: Third Poverty Reduction Support Operation—Implementation Completion and Results Report Review." Report No. ICRR13162, World Bank, Washington, DC.

———. 2011a. *Evaluative Note: Investment Climate Reform in Mali*. Washington, DC: World Bank.

————. 2011b. *Evaluative Note: Sudan Administrative Barriers Reform Program*. Washington, DC: World Bank.

————. 2011c. "Implementation Completion Report Review—Liberia Reengagement and Reform Support Program 2." Report No. ICRR13612. Washington, DC: World Bank.

————. 2012. *Evaluative Note: Nepal Investment Climate Reform Program*. Washington, DC: World Bank.

————. 2013a. *Evaluative Note: Removing Barriers to Investment in Southern Sudan*. Washington, DC: World Bank.

————. 2013b. "Guinea Country Assistance Strategy Completion Report Review FY04-FY13." Report No. 81246, World Bank, Washington, DC.

————. 2014a. *Evaluative Note: Mali IC 2*. Washington, DC: World Bank.

————. 2014b. *Results and Performance of the World Bank Group 2013: An Independent Evaluation*. Washington, DC: World Bank.

IFC (International Finance Corporation). 2008. "Project Completion Report, Yemen IC Tax." World Bank, Washington, DC.

————. 2010. *PDS Approval, Sudan Administrative Barriers Reform Program*. Washington, DC: World Bank.

————. 2011. *Project Completion Report, Removing Barriers to Investment in Southern Sudan*. Washington, DC: World Bank.

6

Recommendations

HIGHLIGHTS

- The World Bank Group has supported a comprehensive menu of investment climate reforms. These reforms were generally supported in the right countries and generally addressed the right interventions. Diagnostic reports help design investment climate interventions, but their coverage is incomplete.

- Within the limits of available indicators, the World Bank Group was successful in improving the investment climate. However, success is mainly measured by number of laws enacted, streamlining of processes and time, or simplistic cost saving for private firms. Impact on investment, jobs, formation, and growth is not clear.

- Political instability remains one of the main factors hampering the effectiveness of investment climate reforms. Further, the social value of regulatory reform is not properly identified, measured, or reflected in design.

- The two institutions adopt two distinct business models with their own characteristics and complementarities. Coordination among the World Bank Group staff involved in investment climate reforms is higher than for the rest of the Bank Group but is mostly informal, relying mainly on personal contacts.

Investment climate reform as defined in this evaluation is the support of policy, legal, and institutional reforms intended to improve the functioning of markets and reduce transaction costs and risks associated with starting, operating, and closing a business in the World Bank Group's client countries. Improving the investment climate has been and remains a key objective of countries in their pursuit of economic growth through PSD.

This evaluation assessed the extent to which the World Bank Group has achieved the goal of helping its client countries improve the investment climate while taking into account the impact on different stakeholders in society. IEG looked at three main aspects of the Bank Group activities: relevance, effectiveness, and social value of regulatory reforms.

IEG's overall conclusion is that, within the limits of available measures of outcomes, the World Bank Group has been successful in improving the investment climate as available measures capture it. However, success is mainly measured by number of laws enacted, streamlining of processes and time, or compliance cost savings of private firms. Broader impact on investment, job formation, and growth is still not clear. Neither is the overall effect of these solutions when taking a holistic country-level view. Further, the social purpose of regulation and therefore the social impact of regulatory reform is not properly identified and measured.

The business models of the World Bank and IFC each have unique characteristics and advantages that must be nurtured. Coordination within the World Bank Group on the investment climate agenda is greater than for the rest of the Bank Group but is mostly informal, relying mostly on personal contacts.

Relevance

Relevance was assessed from three different perspectives: strategy, interventions, and diagnostic tools. At the corporate level, as well as in a number of sectors, improving the business climate is seen as a key to stimulating private sector investment. At the country level, nearly all World Bank Group country partnership and assistance strategies identify enhancing the business environment as a main objective to foster PSD. However, although Bank Group country strategies put a significant emphasis on improving the business environment, countries' own development strategies put much less emphasis on enhancing the investment climate. Only a few counties emphasized its role in their vision.

To establish whether the World Bank Group is offering a comprehensive set of regulatory reforms to its client countries, IEG constructed a comprehensive list of business regulations by reviewing the law library compiled by the Doing Business program in the eight countries that have the best regulatory environment. IEG classified the key regulatory areas covered. By matching the Bank Group intervention to this comprehensive compendium, IEG was able to establish that the Bank Group is indeed offering a comprehensive list of regulatory reforms to its clients. The mapping exercise provides evidence that, generally, World Bank Group interventions support relevant areas; that is, they cover the full set of regulations of a hypothetical country with a business-friendly regulatory environment. Using data from the Bank's Enterprise Survey, IEG was able to establish that the World Bank Group generally supports the reforms most needed by client countries and generally supports regulatory interventions in those countries that need them most.

Over the years a number of diagnostic tools have been used to design investment climate interventions. Recently new tools have been developed for specific areas of the regulatory environment. These tools cover in detail individual areas of the regulatory environment, but there is no comprehensive tool that allows an assessment of all regulatory aspects in client countries. Even for the analytical relevance of the most common diagnostic tools used to determine regulatory reforms—the Doing Business indicators and Enterprise Survey data—IEG presented evidence that they are incomplete; that is, they do not cover all areas of regulation as identified in the best practice list of regulations referred to earlier. Doing Business and the Enterprise Surveys cover only some areas—such as business registration, taxation, and trade—where most of the World Bank Group activities take place. Hence, although these diagnostic tools are often relied on to inform country strategies, they are used less frequently to design investment climate projects, even less so in IFC.

Recommendation—Expand the coverage of current diagnostic tools and integrate them to produce comparable indicators to capture the areas of the business environment not yet covered by existing tools.

Social Value

Regulatory reform should consider its impact on society as a whole, not just on businesses. The World Bank's focus on poverty elimination and shared prosperity implies that regulatory reform must be understood in the context of broader social values, including protection of the poor and vulnerable. Yet social value is not explicitly defined in any of the World Bank Group projects IEG has looked at. Without some definition of social value it is difficult to establish whether particular reforms have generated any particular benefits (or losses), or to identify the specific social groups that have benefitted or suffered as a result of reform. Furthermore, the absence of an explicit definition of social value encourages a reliance on customary approaches.

The Bank Group impact indicators include measures of aggregate cost savings for businesses or increases in private sector investment. Separate measures are needed to capture a wider range of sought-after benefits and potentially foregone benefits if existing regulations are changed. Some groups may benefit from regulatory reform, but other groups may become further marginalized or impoverished with regard to incomes; employment; access to goods, services, and infrastructure; or other indicators. An adequate set of social value indicators must attempt to capture this variety of experience. Social return frameworks suggest that projects should identify relevant stakeholders; an exclusive focus on businesses is too narrow. Nonbusiness stakeholders need to be incorporated within any evaluation of regulatory reform.

Recommendation—Develop a differentiated approach to identify the social effects of regulatory reforms on all groups expected to be affected beyond the business community. The approach should identify which groups are expected to be affected by the regulatory reform(s) within and beyond the business community, in order to ensure that reforms "do no harm" to people and the environment. The assessment should be differentiated depending on the expected impact of the regulatory reform(s) and may include qualitative or quantitative methods. The approach should be employed both ex ante (during the design of the project) as well as ex post (to assess the achieved impact of the reform). Such an approach should help better estimate the political economy risk associated with the reform, to identify potential groups that would sustain or oppose reforms and the extent of such support or opposition. The World Bank Group may also consider developing client capacity to conduct social value assessment to enable sustainability of investment climate reforms.

Coordination across the World Bank Group

The World Bank and IFC work in the same space and with the same clients through two distinct business models. The IFC business model is implemented through stand-alone advisory services. Projects are standardized, focused, and short term and include rapid interventions. They are mostly funded through internal budget and trust funds. The World Bank business model is implemented through lending and budget support and to a lesser extent through technical assistance. Projects are broader in scope and tend to be more long term. The client or the Bank executes the project.

Each model has unique features, and stakeholders appreciate their differences. Stakeholders interviewed across countries often appreciated IFC's international technical expertise, quick response and delivery, and close support. However, IFC's ability to handle the political economy was not as strong, nor was its ability to move beyond standardized products. The World Bank's main strength is the institutional access to government institutions, its comprehensive services, and its ability to provide substantive funding. Yet there was a common sense that the World Bank is slow to respond and to implement projects.

IEG's interviews with World Bank Group management and staff surveys indicated that there is collaboration among the institutions to varying degrees. Survey results show that simple activities such as information sharing are more frequent than formal engagements. Different systems and organizational structures are perceived as the main bottlenecks to collaboration. The interviews with investment climate management and staff indicate that staff have a positive perception of complementarity and strengths of the institutions with the new T&C Global Practice; however, some concerns exist regarding the dominance of one institution model over the other one.

Recommendation—Ensure that the Bank Group takes advantage of the complementarity and strengths of World Bank and IFC business models when designing the new T&C Global Practice. Exploit synergies by ensuring that World Bank and IFC staff improve their understanding of each other's work and business models. Maintain the richness of the two delivery models while addressing factors that discourage collaboration.

Appendix A
Methodology

The appendix includes the project portfolio selection and country case methodologies.

To identify potential projects, the IEG evaluation team adopted two approaches: (i) using Operations Policy and Country Services (OPCS) theme codes and (ii) using a keyword search.

OPCS Theme Code Approach

The OPCS theme code approach identified projects having "theme codes" relevant to Investment Climate. A list of these codes, made in consultation with the Finance and Private Sector Development (FPD) portfolio team, is as follows (from the OPCS website):

28 Tax Policy and Administration

31 Access to Law and Justice

34 Legal Institutions for a Market Economy

36 Personal and Property Rights

40 Regulation and Competition Policy

47 Regional Integration

49 Trade Facilitation and Market Access

66 Education for the Knowledge Economy

75 Rural Markets

77 Rural Policies and Institutions

The team identified projects that charged 20 percent or more volume of commitment to one or more of these ten theme codes. This approach identified 1,098 projects (647 closed, 451 active) out of the universe of 4,714 Bank projects approved since FY07. IEG reviewed Project Appraisal Documents for these projects to identify any components related to investment climate.[1]

Keyword Search Approach

World Bank projects do not have a flag for investment climate projects. Therefore, as a first step, the team created a comprehensive list of investment climate–relevant keywords to encompass the portion of the investment climate universe where the Bank had projects. Then, as a second step, the team identified potential projects by searching project approval and completion documents with the aforementioned keywords. In this second step, the team reviewed projects individually for their investment climate context, and interventions were characterized for the investment climate content.

The comprehensive list of investment climate–relevant keywords started with looking for "investment climate" in available World Bank analytical documents. This led to a set of 2,031 documents, which were sorted by date and filtered to capture World Bank activity over the last 12 years,[2] the most relevant period for the purpose of the research. This reduced the number of documents to 1,924. Documents outside the scope of this exercise were then dropped, bringing the number of documents to 733 reports comprising 108 Investment Climate Assessments, 433 working papers, 138 policy research working papers, and 54 Country Economic Memoranda.

Within each document, concepts associated with investment climate were listed and categorized. This conceptualization effort ultimately led to the engineering of a group of categories linked to the broad concept of investment climate. Initially, 91 categories were identified; this number was later aggregated into 29 broad categories (see Table A.1).

TABLE A.1 Categorization of Keywords Defining the Investment Climate Space in the World Bank Group

Category	Similar Terms		
A2F	access to finance	credit bureau	collateral regulations/ secured transactions
Competition	competition	competition policy	
Consumer	consumer protection	financial literacy	
Contract enforcement	alternative dispute resolution mediation	arbitration legal reform	contract law company law
Corruption	corruption	corporate governance	
Entry	business entry	barriers to entry	

Category	Similar Terms		
Exit	business exit insolvency	restructuring	bankcruptcy
FDI	foreign direct investment	FDI	FDI promotion
ICT	information communication technology	ICT	
Infrastructure	electricity telecom	water	transportation
Innovation	innovation	product standard	
Inspection	inspection	labor inspection	
Labor	skill quality	labor quality	
Land	access to land	land	
Market distortion	market distortion price control	taxes	subsidies
PPD	public private dialogue	consultative mechanism	business government consultation
PPP	public-private partnership	PPP	
Regulation	business regulation business registration regulatory simplification regulatory impact RIA (regulatory impact assessment) start-up procedure construction permit license	regulatory reform guillotine regulatory transparency red tape e-government online application labor regulation formalization	business regulatory environment regulatory streamlining one-stop shop e-registration electronic registration permit employment protection legislation
Remittances	remittance		
Security	security	crime	
Tax administration	labor taxation		
Trade	trade customs processing export processing zones	tariff logistics EPZ	trade facilitation regional integration

SOURCE: World Bank database.

TABLE A.2 World Bank Projects Identified and Selected for Portfolio Review

No. of Projects	OPCS Theme Codes Potential Projects Reviewed	Keyword Search Potential Projects Reviewed	Total
Closed	647	1,374	**327**
Active	451	1,196	**149**
Total	**1,098**	**2,570**	476

SOURCE: World Bank.
NOTE: OPCS = Operations Policy and Country Services.

These identified keywords were matched to project objectives and components text by running a search queries on all available Project Appraisal Documents[3] using AtlasTi software and also by scanning Independent Evaluation Group (IEG) Implementation Completion and Results Report Review databases. Adding these two queries resulted in a portfolio of 1,374 closed and 1,196 active projects.

The evaluation team reviewed the combined lists of closed and active projects derived from the approaches described above project by project, keeping in mind the scope of the evaluation. The final portfolio of World Bank projects with investment climate activities relevant to this evaluation stood at 327 closed and 149 active project (Table A.2).

Methodology for IFC Projects

For the International Finance Corporation (IFC), identification of the investment climate portfolio was straightforward because of the existence of an Investment Climate Business Line. The IEG team obtained a list of all IFC Advisory Services projects from MIS (management information system) and filtered for projects within the investment climate business line that were approved during or after FY07. Projects that were classified as non-client-facing were then filtered out. This resulted in a list of 343 projects in the IFC portfolio (Table A.3).

Methodology for Country Cases

The selection of 25 country case studies is based on the in-depth portfolio analysis and based on the following criteria: (i) stratified purposeful sampling by region, income and fragility; (ii) volume of operations; and (iii) types of instruments. The sample include 4 field based country cases among the 25 countries identified for the in-depth assessment (see Table A.4).

TABLE A.3 IFC Projects Identified and Selected for Portfolio Review

IFC Advisory Services	No. of Projects
Closed	175
Active	168
Total	**343**

TABLE A.4 Country Case Studies

Country	Country
Sub-Saharan Africa	**Europe and Central Asia**
Ghana	Armenia
Guinea	Azerbaijan
Kenya	Georgia
Liberia	Serbia
Mali	**Latin America and the Caribbean**
Rwanda	Brazil
Senegal	Colombia
South Sudan	Jamaica
Sudan	**Middle East and North Africa**
East Asia and Pacific	Jordan
Cambodia	Yemen, Rep.
Lao PDR	**South Asia**
Philippines	Bangladesh
Vietnam	India
	Nepal

Notes

[1] Project Appraisal Documents for World Bank projects.

[2] Although the evaluation period is FY07–13, documents that were searched for keywords extended past this period till the last IEG evaluation on investment climate (2006).

[3] There are more than 9,100 projects listed in World Bank operations since FY90 and 4,714 projects since FY07, and the official document repository stores nearly 41,000 Project Appraisal Documents. The IEG team ran AtlasTi queries on all available Project Appraisal Documents.

Appendix B
Portfolio Description of World Bank Group Support to Investment Climate Reforms

IEG's portfolio review identified 819 investment climate reform projects, of which 343 are IFC Advisory Services approved between FY07 and FY13 and 476 are World Bank lending.

For projects approved between FY07 and FY13, World Bank Group support to investment climate reforms has been an average of approximately $50 million for IFC and $475 million for the World Bank, excluding sector-specific interventions (sector-specific regulations increase World Bank lending commitments by $2.6 billion over this period).

Overall, although the number of approved projects declined between 2007 and 2013 from 144 to 81 projects, there was a year over year increase of 6 percent in 2011–12 and 21 percent in 2012–13. However, though project commitments averaged $1.1 billion for projects approved between FY07 and FY10, they dropped to an average of $664 million between FY11 and FY13 (an approximately 50 percent difference between 2007 and 2013). See Figure B.1.

The investment climate portfolio showed an almost equal distribution by number of projects and intervention amounts across income level and fragile and conflict situation (FCS) classifications.

Geographic Distribution of the Investment Climate Portfolio

Investment climate reform interventions were identified in 119 countries across all regions. Of these countries, two-thirds (74 countries) received support from both the World Bank and IFC, and the remaining 45 received support from just one of the two institutions.

Investment Climate World Bank Lending Figures

Overall, the number of investment climate projects as a proportion of all World Bank lending projects decreased from 18 percent in 2007 to 12 percent in 2013 at an average rate of 5 percent a year. The trend is more stable, however, when comparing investment climate-Finance and Private Sector Development network (FPD) projects against the rest of the FPD portfolio. This portfolio declined at an average 3 percent a year between 2007 and 2013, though excluding the drop between 2007 and 2008 reveals an increase of investment climate-FPD as a proportion of all FPD of 9 percent a year.

World Bank and IFC Portfolios by Investment Climate Amounts (approved FY07–13)

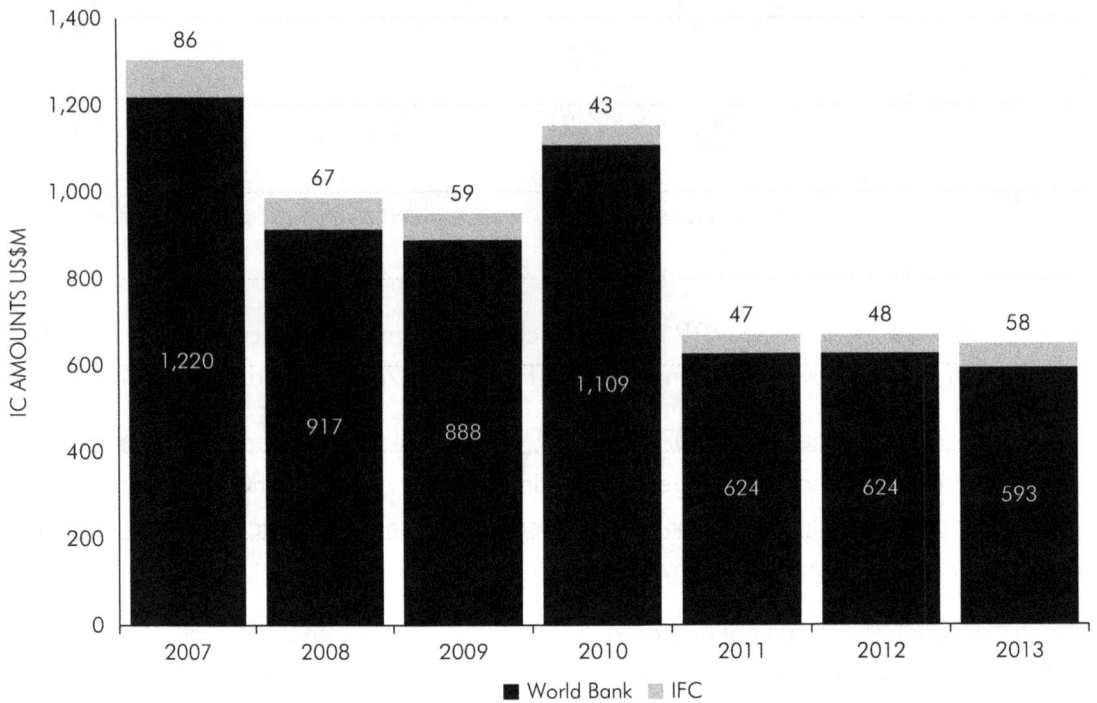

SOURCE: IEG portfolio review.
NOTE: To compare parallel portfolios, the bar graphs describe trends for projects approved FY07–13 and exclude the 176 World Bank lending projects closed FY07–13 but approved earlier.

FIGURE B.2.A Projects and Amounts, by Income Level (approved FY07–13)

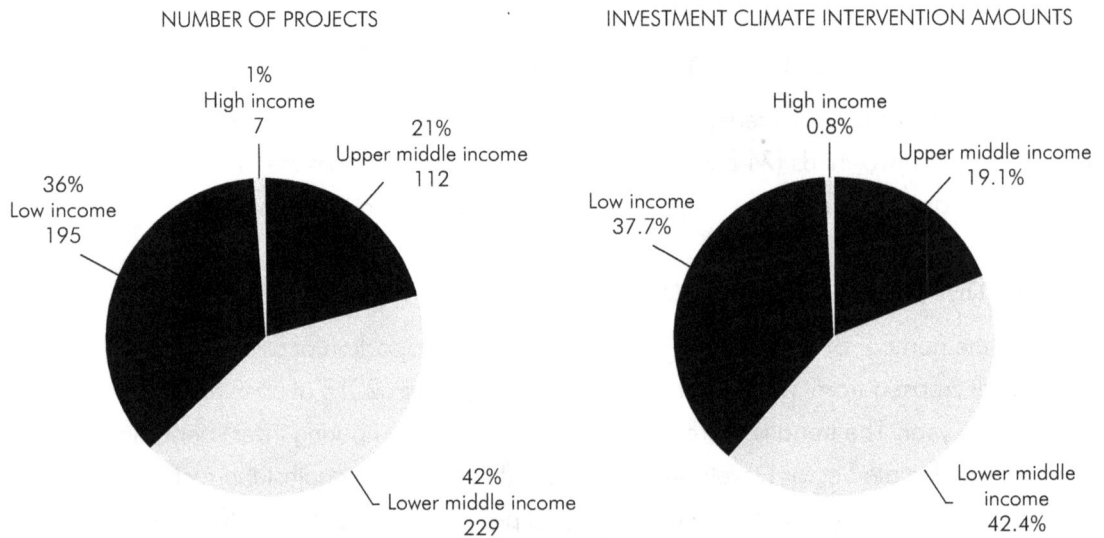

NUMBER OF PROJECTS

INVESTMENT CLIMATE INTERVENTION AMOUNTS

SOURCE: IEG portfolio review.
NOTE: Excludes regional projects.

FIGURE B.2.B World Bank Lending Projects and Amounts, by Income Level (approved FY07–13)

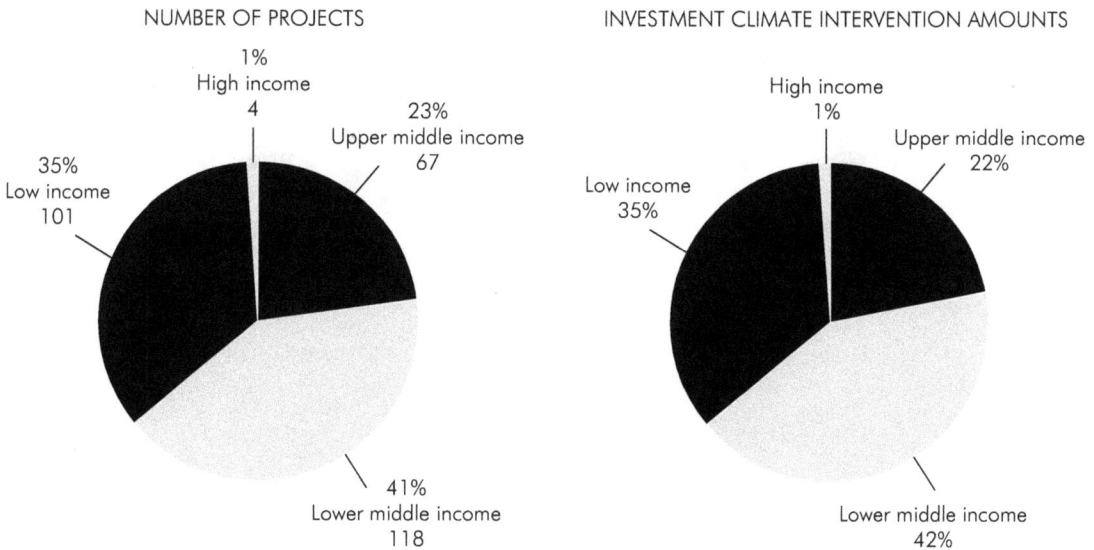

NUMBER OF PROJECTS

1%
High income
4

23%
Upper middle income
67

35%
Low income
101

41%
Lower middle income
118

INVESTMENT CLIMATE INTERVENTION AMOUNTS

High income
1%

Upper middle income
22%

Low income
35%

Lower middle income
42%

SOURCE: IEG portfolio review.
NOTE: Excludes regional projects.

FIGURE B.2.C IFC Advisory Projects and Amounts, by Income Level (approved FY07–13)

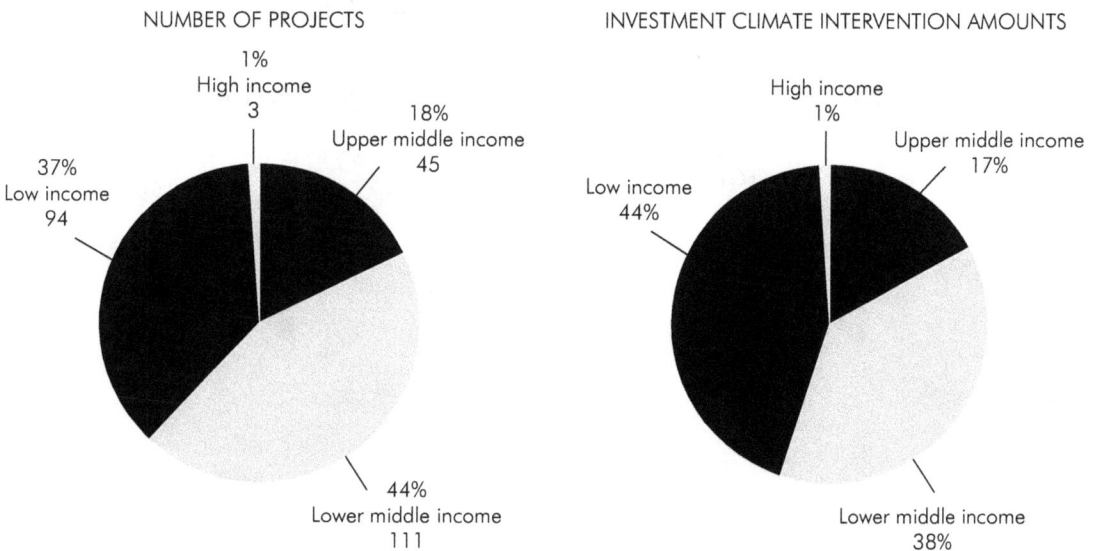

NUMBER OF PROJECTS

1%
High income
3

18%
Upper middle income
45

37%
Low income
94

44%
Lower middle income
111

INVESTMENT CLIMATE INTERVENTION AMOUNTS

High income
1%

Upper middle income
17%

Low income
44%

Lower middle income
38%

SOURCE: IEG portfolio review.
NOTE: Excludes regional projects.

FIGURE B.3.A Projects and Amounts, by Fragile and Conflict Situation Classification (approved FY07–13)

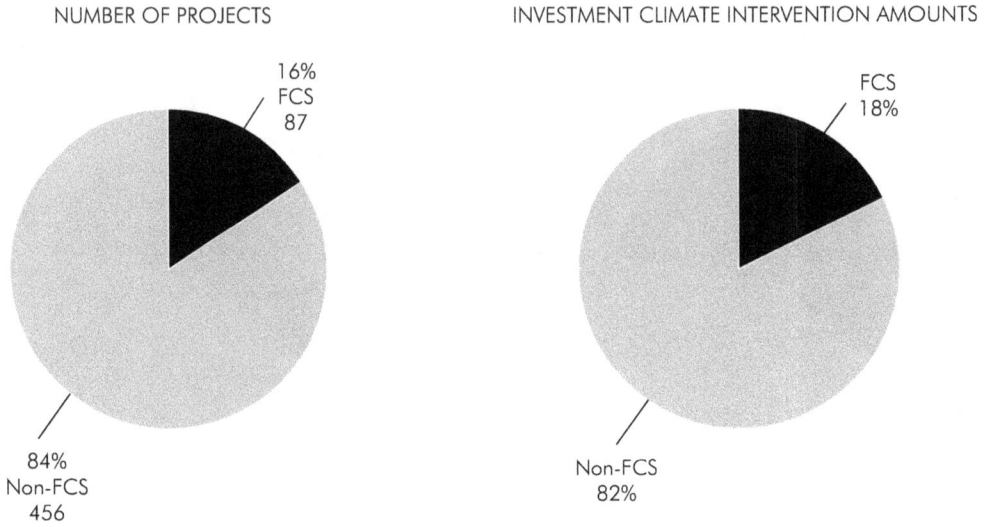

NUMBER OF PROJECTS

INVESTMENT CLIMATE INTERVENTION AMOUNTS

16%
FCS
87

84%
Non-FCS
456

FCS
18%

Non-FCS
82%

SOURCE: IEG portfolio review.
NOTE: Excludes regional projects.

FIGURE B.3.B World Bank Lending Projects and Amounts, by FCS Classification (approved FY07–13)

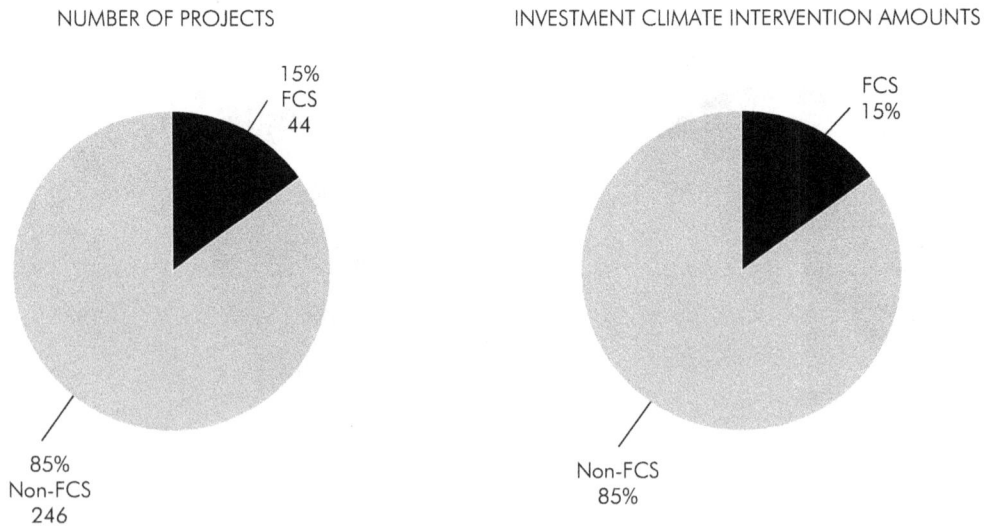

NUMBER OF PROJECTS

INVESTMENT CLIMATE INTERVENTION AMOUNTS

15%
FCS
44

85%
Non-FCS
246

FCS
15%

Non-FCS
85%

SOURCE: IEG portfolio review.
NOTE: Excludes regional projects.

FIGURE B.3.C IFC Advisory Projects and Amounts, by FCS Classification (approved FY07–13)

NUMBER OF PROJECTS

INVESTMENT CLIMATE INTERVENTION AMOUNTS

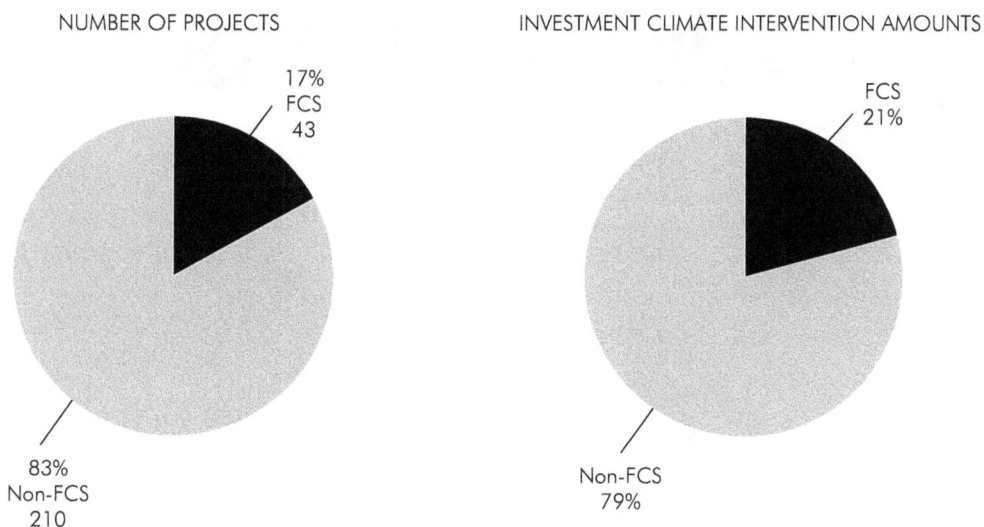

17%
FCS
43

83%
Non-FCS
210

FCS
21%

Non-FCS
79%

SOURCE: IEG portfolio review.
NOTE: Excludes regional projects.

TABLE B.1 Distribution of Investment Climate Interventions, by Network

Interventions	FPD	PREM	SDN
Alternative Dispute Resolution	4	5	1
Bankruptcy	2	4	0
Competition policy	7	11	5
Contract enforcement	10	11	2
Debt resolution/insolvency	5	18	1
Investment policy and promotion	24	47	34
Labor	5	22	0
Licensing	3	15	5
Property rights	13	35	50

continued on page 168

Distribution of Investment Climate Interventions, by Network

Interventions	FPD	PREM	SDN
Public-private dialogue	13	4	5
Registration	13	22	0
Regulation	22	54	17
Sector reform	27	97	130
Tax	12	48	4
Trade logistics	19	93	22
Total	**179**	**486**	**276**

SOURCE: IEG portfolio review.
NOTE: FPD = Finance and Private Sector Development; PREM = Poverty Reduction and Economic Management; SDN = Social Development.

FIGURE B.4 Geographic Distribution of Investment Climate Projects

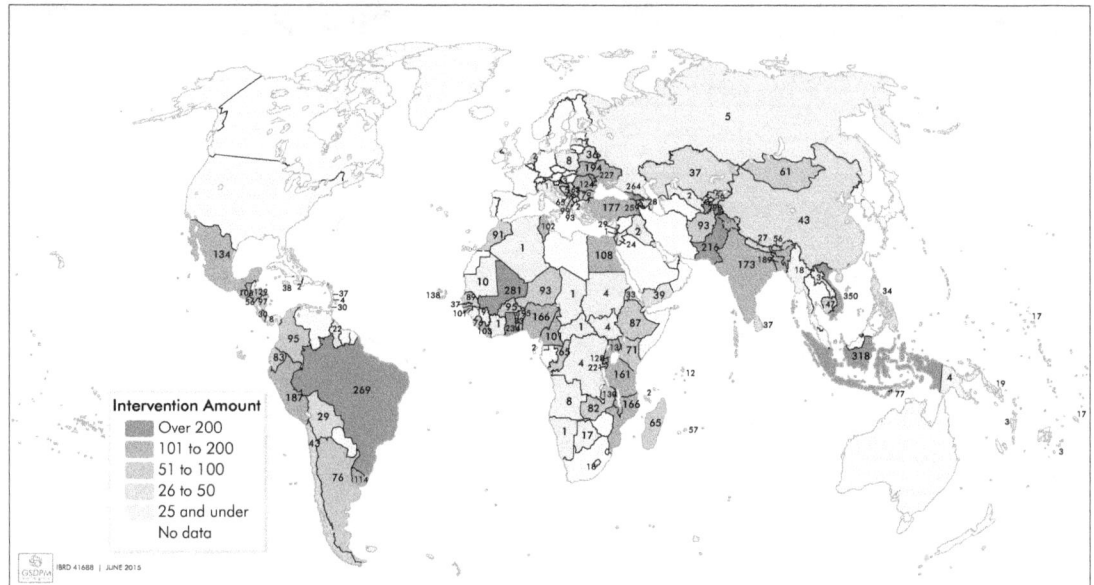

SOURCE: IEG portfolio review.

FIGURE B.5.A Total World Bank Investment Climate Projects (approval FY07–13)

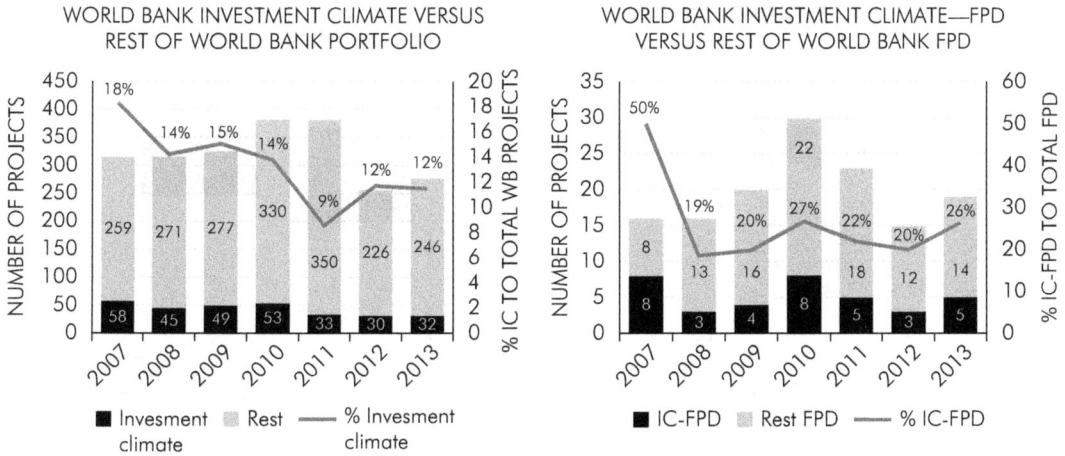

WORLD BANK INVESTMENT CLIMATE VERSUS REST OF WORLD BANK PORTFOLIO

WORLD BANK INVESTMENT CLIMATE—FPD VERSUS REST OF WORLD BANK FPD

SOURCE: IEG portfolio review.

NOTE: Number of projects (left axis) and share of investment climate projects among total Bank lending projects (right axis). FPD = Finance and Private Sector Development; IC = Investment Climate.

FIGURE B.5.B Total World Bank Investment Climate Projects, by Income Level (approved FY07–13)

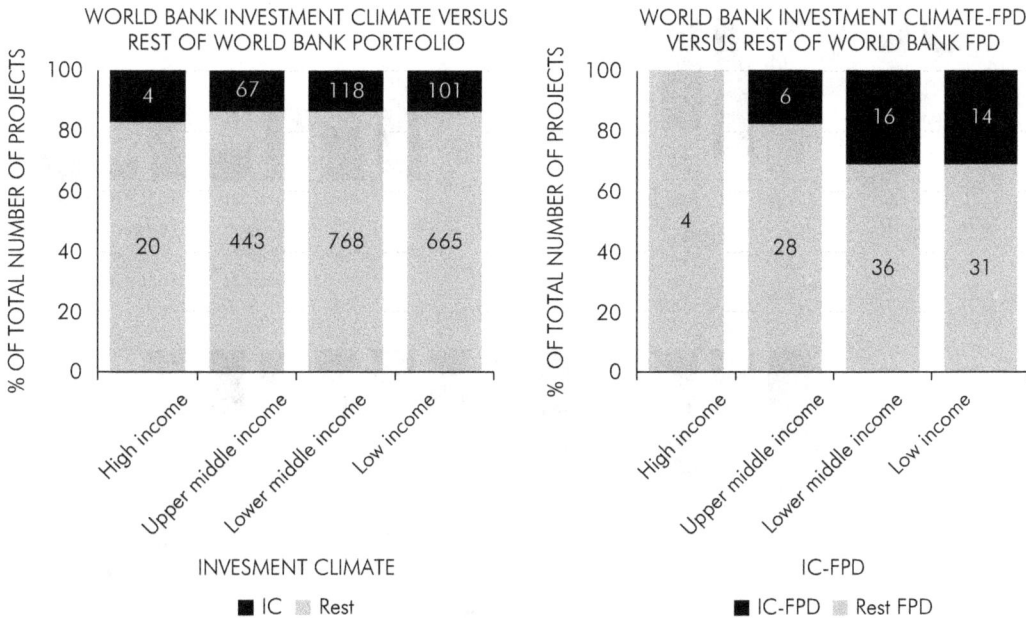

WORLD BANK INVESTMENT CLIMATE VERSUS REST OF WORLD BANK PORTFOLIO

WORLD BANK INVESTMENT CLIMATE-FPD VERSUS REST OF WORLD BANK FPD

SOURCE: IEG portfolio review.

NOTE: Excludes regional projects. FPD = Finance and Private Sector Development; IC = Investment Climate.

FIGURE B.5.C Total World Bank Investment Climate Projects, by Fragile and Conflict Situation Classification (approved FY07–13)

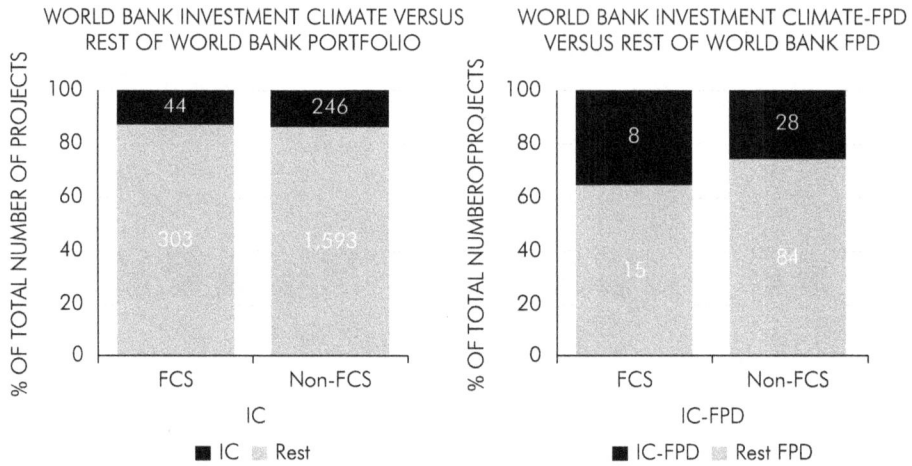

WORLD BANK INVESTMENT CLIMATE VERSUS REST OF WORLD BANK PORTFOLIO

WORLD BANK INVESTMENT CLIMATE-FPD VERSUS REST OF WORLD BANK FPD

■ IC ▨ Rest   ■ IC-FPD ▨ Rest FPD

SOURCE: IEG portfolio review.
NOTE: excludes regional projects. FCS = fragile and conflict-affected situation; FPD = Finance and Private Sector Development; IC = investment climate.

FIGURE B.6 Number of World Bank Investment Climate Projects Approved FY07–13 by Lending Instrument to Rest of World Bank Lending Portfolio (investment projects versus policy lending)

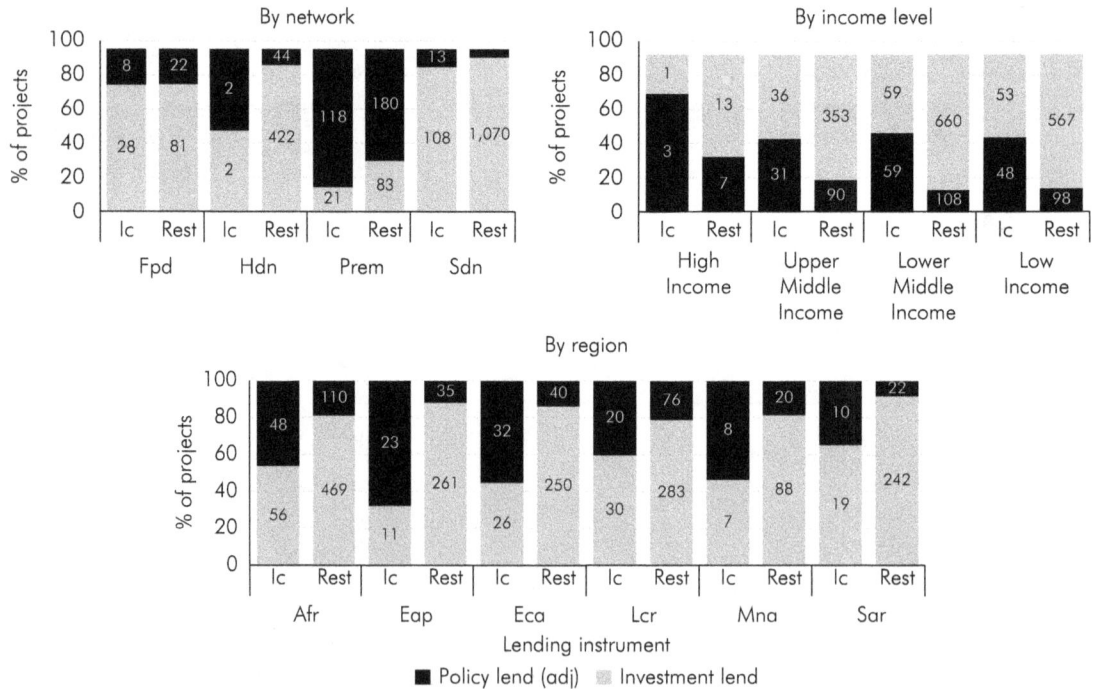

■ Policy lend (adj) ▨ Investment lend

SOURCE: IEG portfolio review.
NOTE: **Networks:** FPD = Finance and Private Sector Development; HDN = Human Development; PREM = Poverty Reduction and Economic Management; SDN = Sustainable Development. **Regions:** AFR = Africa; EAP = East Asia and Pacific; ECA = Europe and Central Asia; LCR = Latin America and the Caribbean; MNA = Middle East and North Africa; SAR = South Asia.

Investment Climate for Agribusiness and Tourism, by Number of Projects and Component Commitment Value, IFC Advisory Portfolios and World Bank Investment Portfolios (2007–13)

NUMBER OF PRODUCTS

IFC

WORLD BANK

23%
AgriTour
93

77%
Rest
315

24%
AgriTour
2,389

76%
Rest
7,446

COMPONENT COMMITMENT VALUE

IFC

WORLD BANK

16%
AgriTour
54

84%
Rest
289

18%
AgriTour
87

82%
Rest
389

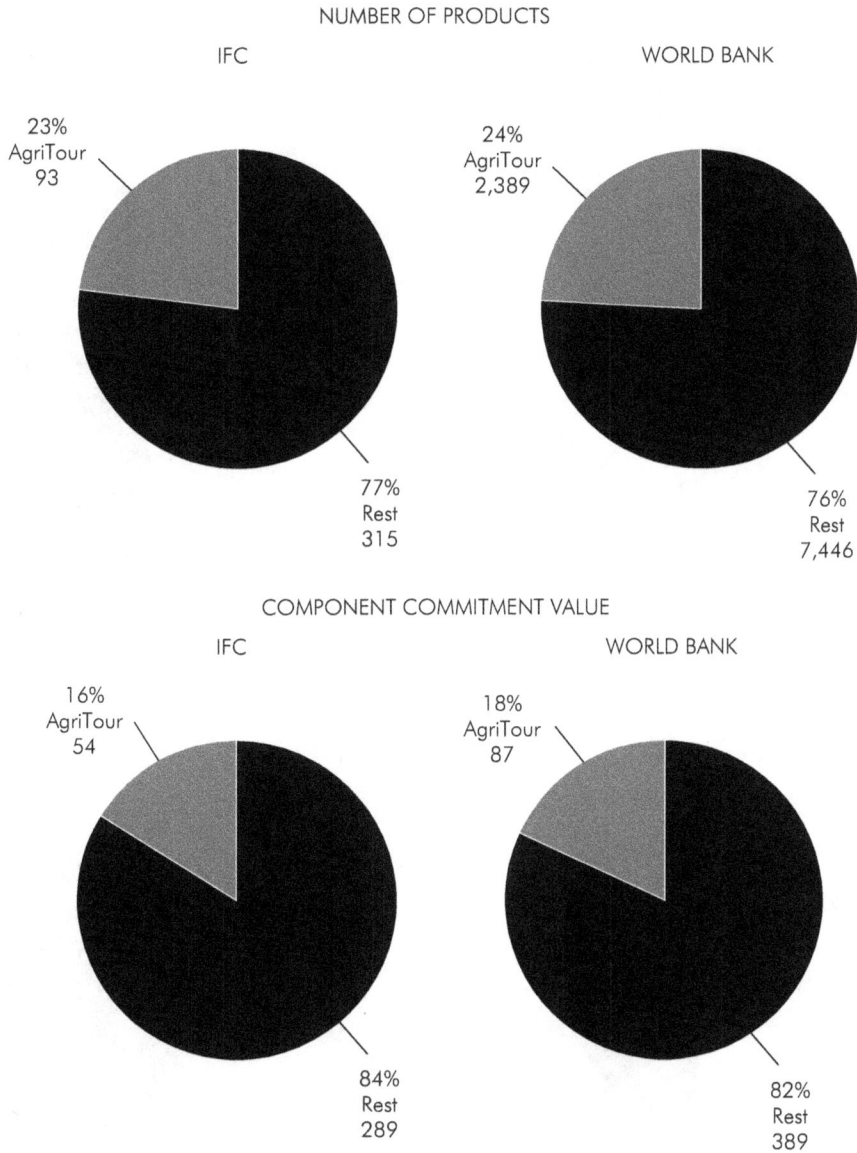

SOURCE: IEG portfolio review.

FIGURE B.8 Investment Climate for Agribusiness and Tourism, by Region, by Number of Projects, and Component Commitment Value, in IFC Advisory and World Bank Investment and Portfolios (2007–13)

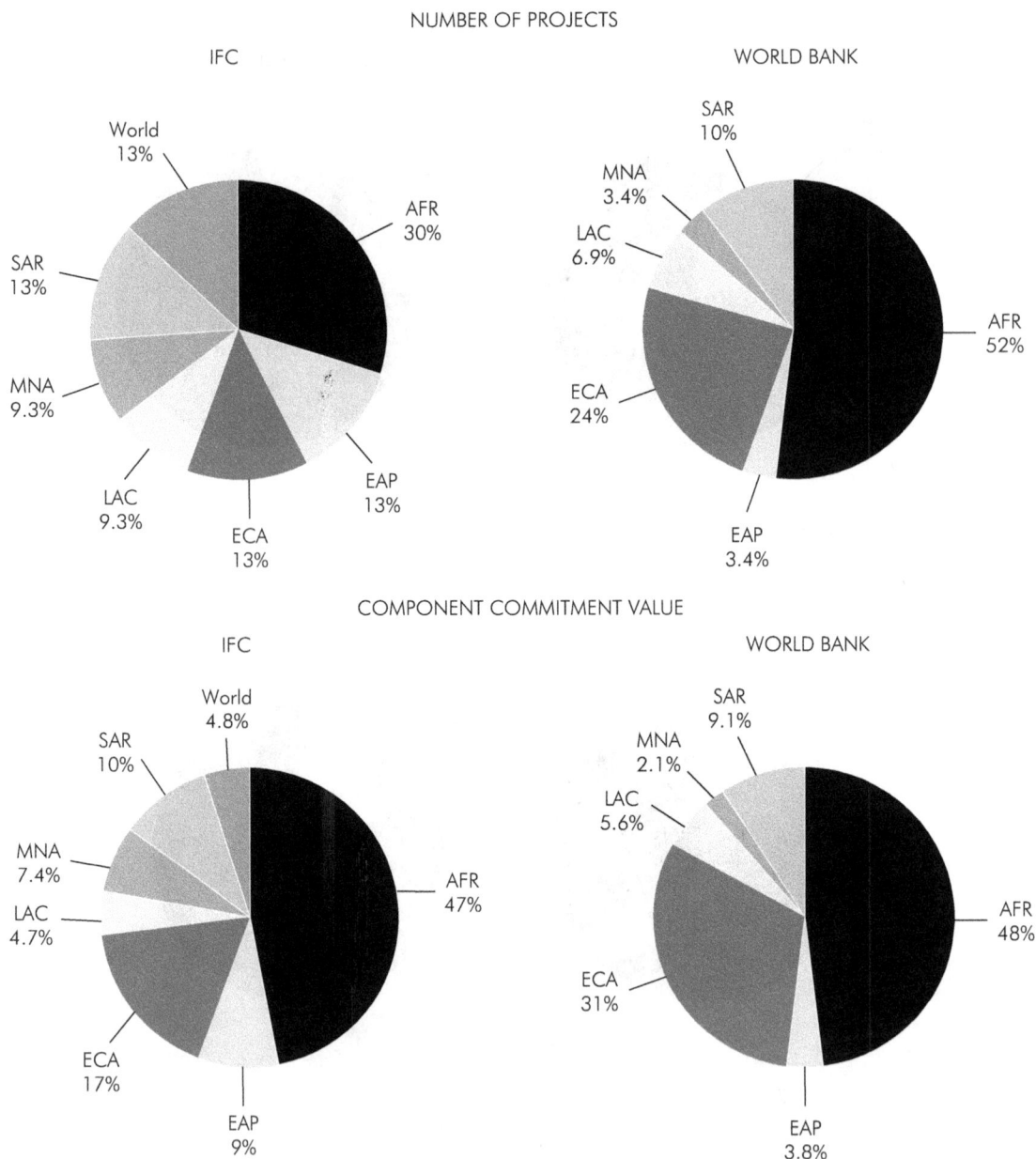

NUMBER OF PROJECTS

IFC

World 13%
AFR 30%
SAR 13%
MNA 9.3%
LAC 9.3%
ECA 13%
EAP 13%

WORLD BANK

SAR 10%
MNA 3.4%
LAC 6.9%
AFR 52%
ECA 24%
EAP 3.4%

COMPONENT COMMITMENT VALUE

IFC

World 4.8%
SAR 10%
MNA 7.4%
LAC 4.7%
AFR 47%
ECA 17%
EAP 9%

WORLD BANK

SAR 9.1%
MNA 2.1%
LAC 5.6%
AFR 48%
ECA 31%
EAP 3.8%

SOURCE: IEG portfolio review.
NOTE: AFR = Africa Region; EAP = East Asia and Pacific Region; ECA = Europe and Central Asia Region; LAC = Latin America and the Caribbean Region; MNA = Middle East and North Africa Region; SAR = South Asia Region.

FIGURE B.9 Investment Climate for Agribusiness and Tourism, by Country Income Level, by Number of Projects and Component Commitment Value, in World Bank Investment and IFC Advisory Portfolios (2007–13)

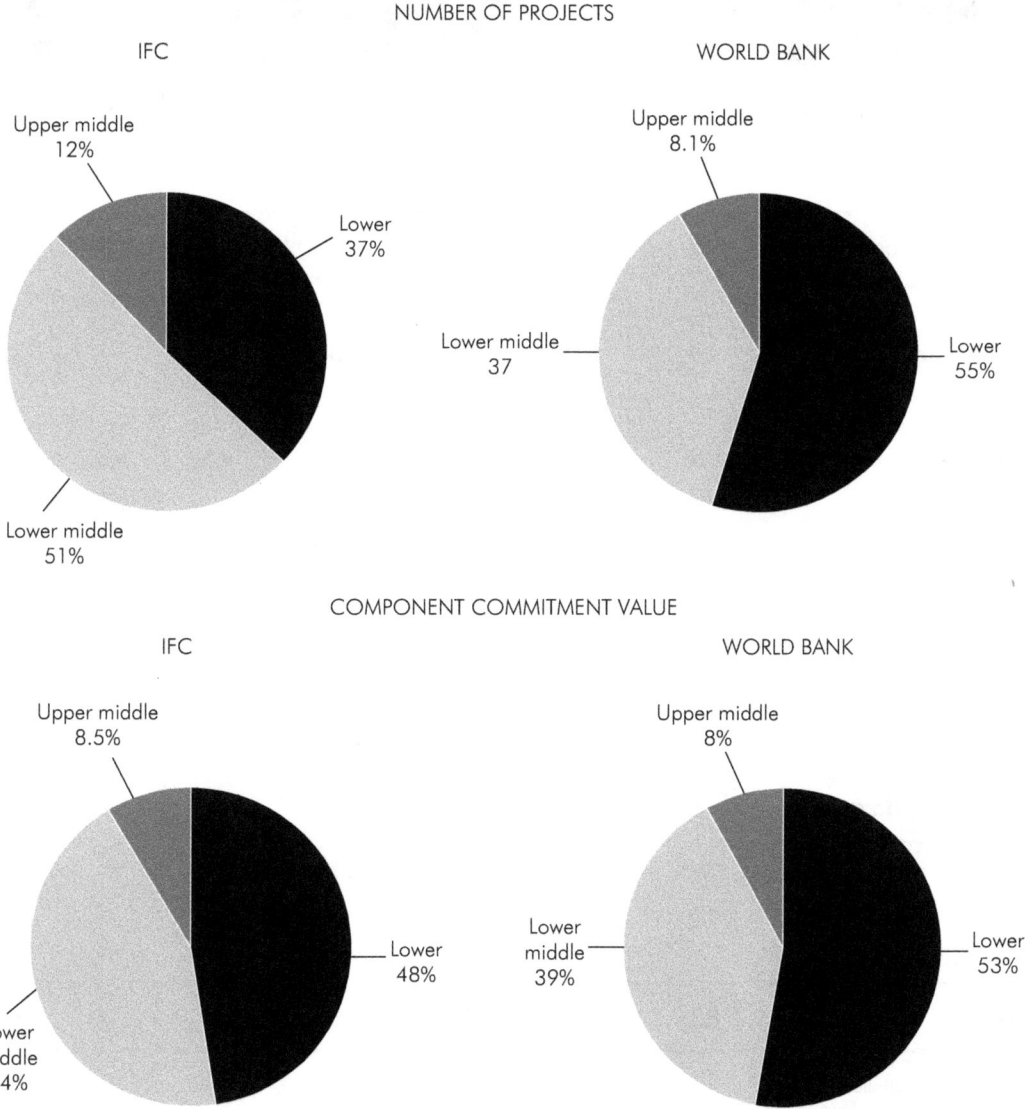

NUMBER OF PROJECTS

IFC

Upper middle
12%

Lower
37%

Lower middle
51%

WORLD BANK

Upper middle
8.1%

Lower middle
37

Lower
55%

COMPONENT COMMITMENT VALUE

IFC

Upper middle
8.5%

Lower
48%

Lower middle
44%

WORLD BANK

Upper middle
8%

Lower middle
39%

Lower
53%

SOURCE: IEG portfolio review.

TABLE B.2 Number of World Bank and IFC Activities in Agriculture and Tourism

Activities	World Bank			IFC			Total
	Agriculture	Tourism	Both	Agriculture	Tourism	Both	
Legal and institutional reforms and frameworks	28	3	n.a.	17	13	2	63
Sector diagnostics/ studies	5	n.a.	n.a.	11	9	3	28
Sector strategies and action plans	10	1	n.a.	6	4	1	22
Capacity building/ training	15	2	n.a.	4	n.a.	n.a.	21
Investment promotion	8	n.a.	n.a.	9	3	n.a.	20
Technology upgrading	8	2	n.a.	n.a.	2	n.a.	12
Physical infrastructure for investment	4	1	1	3	n.a.	n.a.	9
Product standardization and certification	5	n.a.	n.a.	3	n.a.	n.a.	8
Public-private development	n.a.	1	n.a.	2	2	1	6
Total	83	10	1	55	33	7	189

SOURCE: IEG portfolio review.
NOTE: n.a. = not applicable.

Appendix C
Statistical Tests for Regulatory Reform Indicators

IEG collected 39 regulatory environment indicators from different sources, such as the Doing Business, World Economic Forum, and Logistics Performance Index. For each indicator IEG estimated the average value in countries with and without Bank Group projects. For a regulatory intervention to be relevant, the expected average value of an indicator in countries with Bank Group–supported reforms would be worse than its value in countries without a Bank Group–supported project.

TABLE C.1 Statistical Test of Relevance in Countries With and Without World Bank Group Interventions

Regulatory Topic	Indicator***	Mean (Countries with no World Bank Group Intervention)	Mean (Countries with World Bank Group Intervention)	Difference	Significance
Registration	db_sbproc	7.96	9.37	−1.41	**
	db_sbipc	42.97	99.62	−56.64	**
Trade	lpi_score	2.91	2.51	0.40	**
	lpi_customs	2.70	2.27	0.42	**
	db_tabexpdoc	5.99	7.15	−1.16	**
	db_tabexptime	21.54	28.66	−7.12	**
	db_tabimpdoc	6.90	8.53	−1.62	**
	db_tabimptime	24.33	32.12	−7.79	**

continued on page 176

Statistical Test of Relevance in Countries With and Without World Bank Group Interventions

Regulatory topic	Indicator***	Mean (Countries with no World Bank Group intervention)	Mean (Countries with World Bank Group intervention)	Difference	Significance
	wef_6p09	4.68	4.28	0.40	**
	wef_6p10	5.32	6.99	−1.67	**
	wef_6p13	4.20	3.79	0.42	**
	dbdaysexport	6.25	7.27	−1.03	**
	dbdaysimport	7.77	9.36	−1.59	**
	dbexpdocprep	10.18	14.68	−4.50	**
	dbimpdocprep	11.37	16.86	−5.49	**
Tax	db_ptpmts	26.52	44.38	−17.85	**
	db_pttime	254.45	421.50	−167.05	**
	db_pttottax	42.18	69.11	−26.94	**
Regulation	Burden of government regulation (WEF)	3.42	2.97	0.45	**
	db_sbproc	7.83	9.87	−2.04	**
	db_sbipc	45.52	77.84	−32.32	**
	entr_newdensity	4.79	1.94	2.85	**
Investment Promotion	wef_6p11	4.77	4.92	−0.15	**
	wef_6p12	4.70	5.01	−0.30	**

Regulatory topic	Indicator***	Mean (Countries with no World Bank Group intervention)	Mean (Countries with World Bank Group intervention)	Difference	Significance
Bankruptcy	db_ritime	2.71	3.12	−0.41	**
	db_riout(recovery)	0.28	0.14	0.14	**
	db_rirec (recovery)	35.31	26.18	9.13	**
Property Rights	db_rpproc	5.98	6.62	−0.64	*
	db_rptime	62.86	86.75	−23.89	**
	wef_1p01	4.55	3.90	0.65	**

NOTE: *$p<0.01$; **$p<0.1$; ***$p<0.05$.

TABLE C.2 Indicator Names

Indicator	Source	Description
db_cpipc	Doing Business	Constr.Permit-Cost (% of income per capita)
db_cpproc	Doing Business	Constr.Permit-Procedures (number)
db_cptime	Doing Business	Constr. Permit – Time (days)
db_ptpmts	Doing Business	Paying Taxes – Payments (number per year)
db_pttime	Doing Business	Paying Taxes – Time (hours per year)
db_pttottax	Doing Business	Paying Taxes – Total tax rate (% of profit)
db_ricost	Doing Business	Resolving insolvency — Cost (% of estate)
db_riout	Doing Business	Resolving insolvency — Outcome (0 as piecemeal sale and 1 as going concern)
db_rirec	Doing Business	Resolving insolvency-recovery rate (cents on the dollar)

continued on page 178

Indicator	Source	Description
db_ritime	Doing Business	Resolving insolvency-Time (years)
db_rpcopv	Doing Business	Registering Property-Cost (% of property value)
db_rpproc	Doing Business	Registering Property-Procedures (number)
db_rptime	Doing Business	Registering Property-Time (days)
db_sbipc	Doing Business	Starting a Business-Cost (% of income per capita)
db_sbpimc	Doing Business	Starting a Business-Paid-in Min. Capital (% of income per capita)
db_sbproc	Doing Business	Starting a Business-Procedures (number)
db_sbtime	Doing Business	Starting a Busines-Time (days)
db_tabcost	Doing Business	Trading Acr. Boarders-cost to export (US$ per container)
db_tabexpdoc	Doing Business	Trading Acr. Boarders-Documents to export (number)
db_tabexptime	Doing Business	Trading Acr. Boarders-Time to export (days)
db_tabimpcost	Doing Business	Trading Acr. Boarders- Cost to import (US$ per container)
db_tabimpdoc	Doing Business	Trading Acr. Boarders-Documents to import (number)
db_tabimptime	Doing Business	Trading Acr. Boarders-Time to import (days)
dbdaysexport	Doing Business	DB export time (customs + term. Handling)
dbdaysimport	Doing Business	DB import time (customs + time term. Handling)
dbexpdocprep	Doing Business	DB export time document preparation
dbimpdocprep	Doing Business	DB import time document preparation
lpi_customs	Logistics Perform. Index	Customs index (1=worst to 5=best)

Indicator	Source	Description
lpi_score	Logistics Perform. Index	LPI Score (1=worst to 5=best)
wef_1p01	World Econ. Forum GCI	Property rights
wef_1p09	World Econ. Forum GCI	Burden of government regulation
wef_6p01	World Econ. Forum GCI	Intensity of local competition
wef_6p02	World Econ. Forum GCI	Extent of market dominance
wef_6p03	World Econ. Forum GCI	Effectiveness of anti-monopoly policy
wef_6p09	World Econ. Forum GCI	Prevalance of trade barriers
wef_6p10	World Econ. Forum GCI	Trade tariffs, % duty
wef_6p11	World Econ. Forum GCI	Prevalence of foreign ownership
wef_6p12	World Econ. Forum GCI	Business impact of rules on FDI
wef_6p13	World Econ. Forum GCI	Burden of customs procedures

Appendix D
Literature Review on the Impact of Regulatory Reforms

Several studies have linked economic growth with various measures of institutional development (Acemoglu, Johnson, and Robinson 2001; Keefer and Knack 1997; Knack and Keefer 1995; Mauro 1995).[1] Many of these studies include measures of the burden of regulation among their measures of institutional development (Knack and Keefer 1995). However, some components of institutional development, such as corruption, the rule of law, the risk of expropriation, and contract enforceability, have only an indirect link with regulation (Knack and Keefer 1995; Keefer and Knack 1997; Langbein and Knack 2010).[2] Moreover, several important sector- and firm-level studies have found a strong link between property rights and investment using firm-level data. Claessens and Laeven (2003) find that firms allocated resources grow faster in countries where the protection of property rights is stronger. The effect of strengthening property rights is as large as the effect of improving access to finance. Using data from Poland, Romania, Russia, Slovakia, and Ukraine, Johnson, McMillan, and Woodruff (2002) find that insecure property rights discouraged firms from reinvesting profits in these countries. Cull and Xu (2005) find similar results for China, noting that secure property rights are a significant predictor of firm reinvestment in China as well.

Other studies suggest that there might be a correlation between regulation and growth. Countries with a high burden of regulation appear to have grown more slowly in the period before regulation is measured (Djankov, McLeish, and Ramalho 2006; Hanush 2012). Yet causality is much harder to prove. Eifert (2009) finds that improvements in the Doing Business indicators do not appear to affect subsequent investment and only one—enforcing contracts—affects growth across countries.

At the same time some impact can be detected in a smaller subset of countries. In particular, business registration and contract enforcement appear to affect investment in poor countries and countries with relatively good institutions. Labor regulations might also affect economic and employment growth (Besley and Burgess 2004). Some studies have attributed China's rapid growth in part to its relatively flexible labor regulations (Dong and Xu 2008, 2009). Similarly, Ahsan and Pages (2009) find that firms grow more slowly in Indian states with stricter employment protection laws than they do in other states. Labor regulation was especially harmful in states with strict dispute resolution legislation. Labor regulations have also been seen to increase labor cost relative to capital. As a result, firms are likely to adopt labor-saving technologies when labor regulation is burdensome. Consistent with this, Amin (2009) shows that retail firms in India adopted computers more quickly in Indian states where labor regulation was less flexible.

Some observers have suggested that regulation tends to be a greater burden on small firms (Altenburg and van Drachenfels 2006). The empirical evidence for labor regulation, however, does not support this assertion. Several studies have found that large firms appear to be more concerned about labor regulation than small firms (Clarke 2014; Gelb and others 2006; Pierre and Scarpetta 2006; Ahsan and Pages 2009; Abidoye, Orazem, and Vodopivec 2009). This could further affect firm growth by discouraging firms from expanding.

Finally, Djankov and others (2010) and Sentance (2013) find that administrative burdens related to paying taxes did not have impact on investments, whereas the tax rate did. Lawless (2013) finds that burdensome tax administration reduces the likelihood of foreign direct investment (FDI), although he noted that if FDI does occur, tax complexity does not appear to affect its level. Other studies find that higher corporate taxes are associated with lower GDP per capita growth across countries (Lee and Gordon 2005), as well labor productivity in Europe (Dall'Olio and others 2013) and total factor productivity, except in small and young firms with low levels of profitability (Arnold and Schwellnus 2008).

Many studies have suggested that regulation and corruption are intimately linked, although the direction of causality is not clear. Some studies suggested that firms might see regulation as less problematic when they can pay bribes to get around them (Leff 1964; Meon and Sekkat 2005; Meon and Weill 2009; Kaufmann and Wei 1999). This, however, is not the case with other studies that show a positive correlation between the burden of regulation and corruption at the country level (Langbein and Knack 2010; Djankov and others 2002), leading some authors to argue that corrupt regimes might create burdensome regulations on purpose so they can collect bribes (Shleifer and Vishny 1993).

Some papers have used instrumental variables to argue that corruption encourages excessive regulation (Faria and others 2013). Although the burden of regulation might be correlated with corruption, it is not the only aspect of regulation that is important. The predictability of regulation might also be important. Hallward-Driemeier, Khun-Josh, and Pritchett (2010) show that firms are more likely to say that policy implementation is more predictable in countries where corruption is lower.

Some studies concluded that reducing registration requirements might increase business formation. Two studies, in particular, used Mexico's System of Fast Opening of Firms program, which reduced the time to register a business from 30 to 2 days, to assess how it affected business registration (Bruhn 2013; Kaplan, Piedra, and Seira 2011).[3] Because the program was introduced at different times in different provinces, the two studies exploited this in a quasi-experimental setting. That is, they compared changes in registration rates in provinces that did and did not adopt the program and between firms that did and did not qualify for the program. Both studies found that the program affected registration rates significantly. Bruhn (2013) estimated that the reform increased the number of registered businesses by 5 percent. Kaplan, Piedra, and Seira (2011) estimated that new start-ups increased by about 5 percent per month in eligible industries. Similar results were obtained in other studies in Colombia (Cárdenas and Rozo 2009) and Portugal (Branstetter and others 2010), which found that new registration increased by 5.2 percent and 21.7 percent, respectively. Aghion and Marinescu (2008) estimated that licensing reforms in India encouraged formation by increasing the number of factories by 6 percent, and Chari (2011) showed that total factor productivity improved by around 15 percent.

However, these increases in registration might be temporary, depending on other factors of the business environment. For example, Kaplan, Piedra, and Seira (2011) showed that the increase in registration in Mexico was concentrated in the first 15 months after implementation, with a subsequent decline. Similar results were shown in Peru (IEG 2011), where registration went up significantly after the reform but by the third year tapered off. In other cases, a simplification of registration procedures might lead to a decreased entry. Bruhn and McKenzie (2013) showed that a business start-up simplification program in Brazil led to a reduction in the number of firms registering during the first two months of implementation,, followed by no impact in subsequent months. This was probably a result of the reform consolidating registration at the municipal, state, and federal level, something that firms might have not liked.

Chari (2011) showed that different effects on formation depended on labor regulations. Output increased more in states where labor regulations were more pro-employer. In contrast, limited effect was detected by Alcazar, Andrade, and Jaramillo (2011) in Peru, where by using a randomized control trial the authors showed that licensing reform had little effect on sales, profit, investment, or employment. This result is consistent with Economisti Associati (2011) in Burkina Faso, Liberia, Rwanda, and Sierra Leone.

At the same time, some studies point out that a critical mass of reforms might be needed to be able to see an impact on business formation. The increase in entry is associated with a significant drop in time to register, suggesting that more modest improvements (for example, in countries with procedures that are already relatively streamlined) might have a more modest effect. Consistent with this, using cross-country data from the Doing Business report and World Bank Entrepreneurship snapshots, Klapper and Love (2014) found that reductions of less than 40 percent in the cost and time required to start a business did not have a significant impact on new firm creation. Kaplan, Piedra, and Seira (2011) reached a similar conclusion: that bigger programs of reform could have a greater impact.

Empirical tests of the expectation that reducing the time and cost of registration might affect formalization have found mixed results. The Doing Business report provides anecdotal evidence that relaxing entry restrictions might encourage registration. For example, the World Bank (2008, p. 13) notes that "[after] Madagascar reduced it minimum capital requirement by more than 80 percent in 2006, the rate of new registrations jumped from 13 percent to 26 percent." The report also notes that after it introduced a one-stop shop to help firms register, "Croatia saw company formation in Zagreb and Split increase by more than 300 percent over 3 years."

Klapper, Amit, and Guillen (2010) note that the ratio of corporations to population increased by more than 30 percent, after electronic registries were introduced in Azerbaijan, Guatemala, Jordan, Oman, Slovenia, and Sri Lanka. Finally, Kaplan, Piedra, and Seira (2011) also showed that entry after reforms was mainly done by informal enterprises. However, Bruhn (2008, 2013) showed that in Mexico there was limited indication that formalization took place. Moreover, Bruhn found that the effect was not a result of existing informal enterprises becoming formal but of employed persons at formal firms starting their own businesses. De Giorgi and Rahman (2013) conducted a randomized control trial in Bangladesh and were unable to show significant registration by informal firms. Cost of registration and information on the process were not the main issues for informal firms.

Formalization might also be favored by tax registration. McKenzie and Sakho (2010) showed that officials in Bolivia were able to expand the tax base, thanks to the issuance of tax receipts, which enabled firms to increase their profitability after formalization. This was the case for very small firms (two to five employees). Similar results were obtained by Medvedev and Oveido (2013) in Ecuador. In Vietnam, firms that formalized though tax registration were shown to increase investment and performance, in part because they replaced causal labor with formal employment (Rand and Torm 2012). Finally, in Sri Lanka only a small share of firms that formalized showed an increase in profitability, and formalization had no effect on access to finance (de Mel, McKenzie, and Woodruff 2012). Additional evidence points to the fact that large informal firms have limited incentives to formalize their tax status, since this did not have any benefit in terms of access to finance and firms have learned how to benefit from formalization without registering (McKenzie and Sakho 2010). Increased enforcement might have a larger impact than tax reform for particular types of firms. Large firms are visited more often by tax inspectors if formal than informal (77 percent of times compared to 25 percent, respectively).

In three African countries firms did not register for tax because they knew they would not be inspected (Economisti Association 2011). Similarly, a randomized control trial in Brazil showed that having an inspector visit a neighboring firm had little impact on formalization. At the same time, having an inspector visit the firm had a significant impact on the probability of registration.

Notes

[1] Indeed, Sala-i-Martin (1997) concludes that one measure of institutional development, the rule of law, is one of 22 variables out of the 62 that he tested that appeared to be robust according to his definition and variety of extreme-bound-analysis. Levine and Renelt (1992) did not include any measures of institutional development in their extreme-bound analysis.

[2] See Kaufmann, Kraay, and Mastruzzi (2009) for a description of the Worldwide Governance Indicators and Kaufmann, Kraay, and Mastruzzi (2010) for a response to Langbein and Knack's (2010) critique.

[3] Consistent with this, Klapper, Laeven, and Rajan (2006) find that entry regulations affect firm formation in Europe and that the effect is particularly large in sectors such as retail that generally have high entry rates. For a comprehensive review, see also IFC (2013).

References

Abidoye, B., P. F. Orazem, and M. Vodopivec. 2009. "Firing Costs and Firm Size: A Study of Sri Lanka's Severance Pay System." World Bank SPD Discussion Paper 0916, Washington, DC.

Acemoglu, D., S. Johnson, and J. A. Robinson. 2001. "The Colonial Origins of Comparative Development: An Empirical Investigation." *American Economic Review* 91, 1369–1401.

Aghion, P., and Marinescu. 2008. "Cyclical Budgetary Policy and Economic Growth: What Do We Learn from OECD Panel Data?" *NBER Macroeconomics Annual* 2007 Volume 22.

Ahsan, A., and C. Pages. 2009. "Are All Labor Regulations Equal? Evidence from Indian Manufacturing." *Journal of Comparative Economics* 37: 62–75.

Alcázar, L., R. Andrade, and M. Jaramillo. 2011. "Panel/Tracer Study on the Impact of Business Facilitation Processes on Enterprises and Identification of Priorities for Future Business Enabling Environment Projects in Lima, Peru." Report 6, Mimeo, Grupo para Analysis de Desarollo, Lima, Peru.

Altenburg, T., and C. van Drachenfels. 2006. "The 'New Minimalist Approach' to Private-Sector Development: A Critical Assessment." *Development Policy Review* 24: 387–411.

Amin, M. 2009. "Are Labor Regulations Driving Computer Usage in India's Retail Stores?" *Economics Letters* 102: 45–8.

Arnold, J., and C. Schwellnus. 2008. "Do Corporate Taxes Reduce Productivity and Investment at the Firm Level? Cross-Country Evidence from the Amadeus Dataset." CEPII research center Working Papers 2008-19, Paris, France.

Besley, T., and R. Burgess. 2004. "Can Labor Regulation Hinder Economic Performance? Evidence from India." *The Quarterly Journal of Economics* 119 (1).

Branstetter, L., and others. 2010. "Do Entry Regulations Deter Enterpreneurship And Job Creation? Evidence From Recent Refroms In Portugal." National Bureau of Economic Research Working Paper 16473, Cambridge, MA.

Bruhn, M. 2008. "License to Sell: The Effect of Business Registration Reform on Entrepreneurial Activity in Mexico." Policy Research Working Paper 4538, World Bank, Washington, DC.

———. 2013. "A Tale of Two Species: Revisting the Effect of Registration Reform on Informal Business Owners in Mexico." *Journal of Development Economics* 103: 275–83.

Bruhn, M., and D. McKenzie. 2013. "Entry Regulation and Formalization of Microenterprises in Developing Countries." World Bank Policy Research Working Paper 6507, Washington, DC.

Cárdenas, M., and S. Rozo. 2009. "Informalidad empresarial en Colombia: problemas y soluciones." *Revista Desarrollo y Sociedad,* Universidad de Los Andes-Cede, Colombia.

Chari, A. V. 2011. "Identifying the Aggregate Productivity Effects of Entry and Size Restrictions: An Empirical Analysis of License Reform in India." *American Economic Review: Economic Policy* 3 (2): 66–96.

Claessens, S., and L. Laeven. 2003. "Financial Development, Property Rights and Growth." *Journal of Finance* 58: 2401–36.

Clarke, G. R. G. 2014. "Firm Characteristics, Bribes, and the Burden of Regulation in Developing Countries." *Journal of Academy of Business and Economics.*

Cull, R., and L. C. Xu. 2005. "Contract Enforcement, Ownership and Finance: Determinants of investment in China." *Journal of Financial Economics* 77: 117–46.

Dall'Olio and others. 2013. "Productivity Growth in Europe." World Bank Policy Research Working Paper 6425, Washington, DC.

De Giorgi, G., and A. Rahman. 2013. "SME Registration Evidence from a Randomized Controlled Trial in Bangladesh." World Bank Policy Research Working Paper Series 6382, Washington, DC.

de Mel, S., D. McKenzie, and C. Woodruff. 2012. "The Demand for, and Consequences of, Formalization among Informal Firms in Sri Lanka." World Bank Policy Research Working Paper 5991, Impact Evaluation Series 52, Washington, DC.

Djankov, S., T. Ganser, C. McLeish, R. Ramalho, and A. Shleifer. 2010. "The Effect of Corporate Taxes on Investment and Entrepreneurship." *American Economic Journal: Macroeconomics* 2: 51–64.

Djankov, S., R. La Porta, F. Lopez-de-Silanes, and A. Shleifer. 2002. "The Regulation of Entry." *Quarterly Journal of Economics* 117: 1–37.

Djankov, S., C. McLeish, and R. Ramalho. 2006. "Regulation and Growth." *Economics Letters* 92: 395–401.

Dong, X. Y., and L. C. Xu. 2008. "The Impact of China's Milllennium Labor Restructuring Program on Firm Performance and Employee Earnings." *Economics of Transition* 16: 223–45.

———. 2009. "Labor restructuring in China: Toward a functioning labor market." *Journal of Comparative Economics* 37, 47–61.

Economisti Associati. 2011. *Investment Climate in Africa Program: Four Country Impact Assessment, Liberia Country Report.* Bologna: Economisti Associati.

Eifert, B. 2009. "Do Regulatory Reforms Stimulate Investment and Growth? Evidence from the Doing Business Data, 2003–07." Center for Global Development Working Paper 159, Washington, DC.

Faria, H. J., H. M. Monetesinos-Yufa, D. R. Morales, B. C. G. Aviles, and O. Brito-Bigott. 2013. "Does Corruption Cause Unencumbered Business Regulations? An IV Approach." *Applied Economics* 45: 65–83.

Gelb, A., V. Ramachandran, M.K. Shah, and G. Turner. 2006. "What Matters to African Firms? The Relevance of Perceptions Data." World Bank, Washington, DC.

Hallward-Driemeier, M., G. Khun-Josh, and L. Pritchett. 2010. "Deals Versus Rules:Policy Implementarion, Uncertainty, and Why Firms Hate It." World Bank Policy Research Working Paper 5321, Washington, DC.

Hanusch, M. 2012. "The Doing Business Indicators, Economic Growth and Regulatory Reform." World Bank Policy Research Working Paper 6176, Washington, DC.

IEG (Independent Evaluation Group). 2011. *Peru: Country Program Evaluation for the World Bank Group, 2003–09.* Washington, DC: World Bank.

IFC (International Finance Corporation). 2013. *Systematic Review of SME Banking and Business Regulation (draft).* Washington, DC: World Bank.

Johnson, S., J. McMillan, and C. Woodruff. 2002. "Property Rights and Finance." *American Economic Review* 92: 1335–56.

Kaplan, D. S., E. Piedra, and E. Seira. 2011. "Entry Regulation and Business Start-Ups: Evidence from Mexico." *Journal of Public Economics* 95: 1501–15.

Kaufmann, D., A. Kraay, and M. Mastruzzi. 2009. "Governance Matters VIII: Governance Indicators for 1996–2008." World Bank Policy Research Working Paper 4978, Washington, DC.

——— . 2010. "Response to: The Worldwide Governance Indicators: Six, One, or None." World Bank, Washington, DC.

Kaufmann, D., and S. J. Wei. 1999. "Does Grease Money Speed Up the Wheels of Commerce?" World Bank Policy Research Working Paper 2254, Washington DC.

Keefer, P., and S. Knack. 1997. "Why Don't Poor Countries Catch Up? A Cross-National Test of an Institutional Explanation." *Economic Inquiry* 35, 590–602.

Klapper, L. F., R. Amit, and M. F. Guillen. 2010. "Entrepreneurship and Firm Formation Across Countries." In *International Differences in Entrepreneurship*, eds. J. Lerner, A. Schoar, 129–58. Chicago: University of Chicago Press.

Klapper, L. F., L. Laeven, and R. Rajan. 2006. "Entry Regulation as a Barrier to Entrepreneurship." *Journal of Financial Economics* 82: 591–629.

Klapper, L. F., and I. Love. 2014. "The Impact of Business Environment Reforms in New Firm Registration." World Bank, Washington, DC.

Knack, S., and P. Keefer. 1995. "Institutions and Economic Performance: Cross-Country Tests Using Alternative Institutional Measures." *Economics and Politics* 7, 207–27.

Langbein, L., and S. Knack. 2010. "The Worldwide Governance Indicators: Six, One, or None?" *Journal of Development Studies* 46: 350–70.

Lawless, M. 2013. "Do Complicated Tax Systems Prevent Foreign Direct Investment?" *Economica* 80: 1–22.

Lee, Y., and R. H. Gordon. 2005. "Tax Structure and Economic Growth." *Journal of Public Economics* 89: 1027–43.

Leff, N. 1964. "Economic Development through Bureaucratic Corruption." *American Behavioral Scientist* 8: 6–14.

Levine, R., and D. Renelt. 1992. "A Sensitivity Analysis of Cross-Country Growth Regressions." *American Economic Review* 82: 942–63.

Mauro, P. 1995. "Corruption and Growth." *Quarterly Journal of Economics* 110: 681–712.

McKenzie, D., and Y. S. Sakho. 2010. "Does It Pay Firms to Register for Taxes? The Impact of Formality on Firm Productivity." *Journal of Development Economics* 91: 15–24.

Medvedev, D., and A. Oviedo. 2013. "Informality and Profitability: Evidence from a New Firm Survey in Ecuador." World Bank Policy Research Working Paper 6431, Washington, DC.

Meon, P. G., and K. Sekkat. 2005. "Does Corruption Grease or Sand the wheels of growth?" *Public Choice* 122: 69–97.

Meon, P. G., and I. Weill. 2009. "Is Corruption an Efficient Grease?" *World Development* 38: 244–59.

Pierre, G., and S. Scarpetta. 2006. "Employment Protection: Do Firms' Perception Match with Legislation?" *Economics Letters* 90: 328–34.

Rand, J., and N. Torm. 2012. "The Benefits of Formalization: Evidence from Vietnamese Manufacturing SMEs." *World Development* 40 (5).

Sala-i-Martin, X. 1997. "I Just Ran Two Million Regressions." *American Economic Review* 87: 178–83.

Sentance, A. 2013. "An Economic Analysis. Taxation, Economic Growth and Investment." In *Paying Taxes 2013. The Global Picture,* eds. A Lopez Claros, A. Packman, 23–8. Washington: PwC and World Bank Group.

Shleifer, A., and R. W. Vishny. 1993. "Corruption." *Quarterly Journal of Economics* 108: 599–617.

World Bank. 2008. *Doing Business 2009.* Washington: World Bank.

Appendix E
World Bank Group Projects with Investment Climate Support

TABLE E.1 IFC Projects

Country/Project	Project Name	Specified Stakeholders/intended Beneficiaries
Armenia	Regulatory simplification – Doing Business Reform	National government; subnational government; financial intermediaries; other intermediaries; large companies; SMEs
Bangladesh 1	BICF public private dialogue and stakeholder engagement component	National government; subnational government; other intermediaries; large companies; SMEs; the public
Bangladesh 2	BICF institutional capacity building	National government; other intermediaries; large companies; SMEs; the public
Bangladesh 3[a]	Bangladesh Investment Climate Fund – Regulatory Reform, Phase 2	National government; sub-national government; other intermediaries; large companies; SMEs; the public
Egypt, Arab Rep.[a]	Alexandria Business Association – Private Business Observatory	Large companies; SMEs
Honduras	National plan for municipal simplification	National government; sub-national government; large companies; SMEs
Indonesia[a]	National One-stop Shop Guidelines	National government; sub-national government; large companies; SMEs
Kenya 1	Improving regulatory performance and capacities	National government; subnational government; large companies; SMEs

continued on page 190

Country/Project	Project Name	Specified Stakeholders/intended Beneficiaries
Kenya 2	National Hospital Insurance Fund — Strategic Review and Market Assessment	SMEs; the public
Kenya 3	Monitoring and Evaluation of the Government of Kenya's Business Licensing Reform	Large companies; SMEs; licensing authorities.
Liberia	PSD post-conflict program: phase 2	National government; large companies
Mali	Investment climate reform program: phase 2	National government; sub-national government; large companies; SMEs
Montenegro[a]	Subnational competitiveness	National government; sub-national government; large companies; SMEs
São Tomé and Príncipe	Licensing reform program	National government; SMEs
Sierra Leone	Tax simplification rollout	Large companies; SMEs
Sudan 1[a]	Administrative Barriers Reform Programme	National government; financial intermediaries; other intermediaries;
Sudan 2[a]	Removing Barriers to Investment in Southern Sudan	National government; other intermediaries; large companies; SMEs
Ukraine	PEP business enabling environment: phase 3	Other intermediaries; large companies; SMEs
Vietnam	BEE-VN business tax simplification	National government; large companies

SOURCES: IFC products - Advisory Services PDS Approval forms; Kenya 3- Jacobs and Associates (2012) Update Report.
NOTE: BEE-VN = Business Enabling Environment - Vietnam; BICF = Bangladesh Investment Climate Facility; PEP = Private Enterprise Partnership; PSD = private sector development; SME = small and medium-size enterprise.
a. Countries selected by the World Bank Group as among the clearest, setting out the methods and assumptions underpinning regulatory reform assessments.

Country/Project	Project name	Stakeholders/intended Beneficiaries
Bangladesh	Telecommunications Technical Assistance Project	General public, especially rural population, by increasing availability, affordability and quality of telecommunication services, and by contributing to sustainable economic growth; information technology industry and other businesses through lower costs and the greater variety of value added services.
Central Bank of West African States	BCEAO Regional Payment Systems Project	Government, regional financial institutions, firms, bank clients (businesses and individuals), non-bank clients
Moldova	Energy 2 Project	Businesses supplying electricity; residential consumers, including vulnerable social groups such as the poor and those in rural locations; public agencies operating the buildings receiving improved heating (schools and hospitals) and buildings users experiencing improvements in comfort, well-being and health; environmental benefits, estimated substantial reductions in the annual emissions of harmful gases and dust
Thailand	Additional Financing — Highways Management Project	Users of the national highways and trunk roads, through improved safety rates, lower vehicle operating costs and shorter travel times; businesses, including small and medium-size enterprises, engaged in delivery and management of road infrastructure and services; business and nonbusiness stakeholders located in remote parts of the country; government departments, through lower costs and improved process efficiency; indirectly, taxpayers who fund government.

continued on page 192

Country/Project	Project name	Stakeholders/intended beneficiaries
Ukraine	State Tax Service Modernization Project (APL #1)	General public benefits from fiscal and macro-economic stability. Taxpayers benefit from reduced compliance costs, misadministration and corruption. Honest taxpayers benefit from greater client orientation and reduction in tax burden arising from noncompliance. Honest tax officers benefit from an improvement in the internal tax service integrity and more effective tools to conduct tax administration. Outcome anticipated being more sustainable economic growth benefiting the whole population of Ukraine.
Yemen, Rep.	Port Cities Development Program	Residents, businesses and civic groups of Aden and other participating port cities, as well as larger investors, with focus on improved business services and infrastructure, renovation of municipal buildings, opportunities for public-private sector partnerships, and generation of new revenue streams for the Aden Governorate.

SOURCE: World Bank database.
NOTE: APL = Adaptable Program Loan; BCEAO = Banque Centrale des Etats de L'Afrique de l"Ouest.

Appendix F
Staff Survey Questionnaire

1. **Please select the Department you are currently mapped to:**
   — CIC
   — IFC Regional Investment Climate team/Regional AS Unit
   — FPD Financial and Private Sector Development
   — HDN Human Development Network
   — PREM Poverty Reduction and Economic Management Network
   — SDN Sustainable Development Network
   — Other (please specify)

2. **If you are mapped to a region, please select the region:**
   — Africa
   — East Asia and Pacific
   — Europe and Central Asia
   — Latin America and the Caribbean
   — Middle East and North Africa
   — South Asia
   — None

3. **Where are you based?**
   — Headquarters
   — Field Office

4. **What is your grade level?**
   — GA–GD
   — GE
   — GF
   — GG
   — GH+
   — ETC/JPA
   — STC/STT
   — Other (please specify)

5. **How many years have you worked in the World Bank Group?** _____ Years

6. **Over the last three years, how many advisory services and/or lending projects with investment climate activity/component have you been a part of (as lead or as a team member)?**
   — 0
   — 1
   — 2
   — 3
   — 4
   — 5+
   — N/A – I am predominantly working in an enabling support role (M&E, Finance, donor coordination and so forth)

7. Of those projects, how many have included some collaboration between World Bank and IFC?

— 0   — 3
— 1   — 4
— 2   — 5

8. What was the nature of the collaboration? [SELECT ALL THAT APPLY]
— Sharing information about the project with Bank/IFC colleagues
— Peer reviewing and/or providing comments on the project documents
— Going on missions for the project
— Designing the projects (that is, concept, Project Appraisal Document, Project Data Sheet Technical Assistance and Advisory Services
— Implementing the projects
— Other (please specify)

9. In your personal experience, have the differences between IFC and World Bank business models (for example, project size, project duration, pricing policy, response to client, project governance) fostered or discouraged?

— Fostered   — It has not mattered
— Discouraged   — Don't know
— Both (at times fostered and at times discouraged)

10. In your personal experience, have the factors listed below fostered or discouraged collaboration between IFC and World Bank on projects with Investment Climate activity/component? (Leave blank if not applicable)

Factors	Foster	Discourage	BOTH (In Some Cases Fostered, in Others Discouraged Collaboration)	Don't Know
Strategies/priorities of the two institutions				
IFC Advisory Services accountability matrix (processes and staff accountability during project cycle)/ World Bank organizational structure				

Factors	Foster	Discourage	BOTH (In Some Cases Fostered, in Others Discouraged Collaboration)	Don't Know
Program/project overlap (that is, both working in the same space/ providing similar services to clients)				
Same client (that is, both agencies working directly with government)				
Degree of familiarity with each other's operations (for example, project cycle, product lines, HR systems, funding)				
Formal incentive structure (for example, cross support measured, recognition of collaboration by project operational systems)				
Signals/directions from management				
Proximity to colleagues from the other institution (for example, both institutions located in the same building in the field)				
Personal networks				
Staff personalities				
Previous experience working with World Bank/IFC				
Pricing policy				
Project funding				

continued on page 196

Factors	Foster	Discourage	BOTH (In Some Cases Fostered, in Others Discouraged Collaboration)	Don't Know
Complementarity of instruments (combining rapid technical assistance and long-term lending)				
Staff presence in the field				
Other (please specify)				

11. In your personal experience, do these factors foster or discourage collaboration between center (HQ) and regions within each institution?
Note: For World Bank staff: "center (HQ) and regions" refers to network and Bank regions For IFC staffs: "center (HQ) and region" refers to investment climate Global Staff and the investment climate regional staff.

Factors	Foster	Discourage	BOTH (in Some Cases Fostered, in Others Discouraged Collaboration)	Don't Know
IFC Advisory Services accountability matrix (processes and staff accountability during project cycle)/ World Bank organizational structure				
Degree of familiarity with each other's operations (for example, project cycle, product lines, human resources systems, funding)				
Formal incentive structure (for example, cross support measured, recognition of collaboration by project operational systems)				
Signals/directions from management				
Personal networks				

Factors	Foster	Discourage	BOTH (in Some Cases fostered, in Others Discouraged Collaboration	Don't Know
Staff personalities				
Previous experience working with World Bank/IFC				
Project funding				
Expertise in the anchor (global teams, headquarters)				
Staff awareness of the roles of headquarters and regions				
Other (please specify)				

12. **Over the last three years, which of the following areas have you worked in? [SELECT ALL THAT APPLY]**
— Bankruptcy
— Debt Resolution and Insolvency
— Commercial and Company Laws (for example, Business Licensing/Permits, Business Registration, Inspections)
— Competition Policy
— Courts and Proceedings
— Intellectual Property and other Goods Protection
— Investment Policy/Promotion
— Labor
— Building and Construction
— Land Regulations
— Property Law
— Taxation
— Trade and Logistics
— Industry/Sector Specific Policies
— Other (please specify)

13. **In your view, which World Bank Group Investment Climate areas have been the most impactful for clients? [SELECT ALL THAT APPLY]**
— Bankruptcy
— Debt Resolution and Insolvency
— Commercial and Company Laws (for example, Business Licensing/Permits, Business Registration, Inspections)
— Competition Policy
— Courts and Proceedings

- Intellectual Property and other Goods Protection
- Investment Policy/Promotion
- Labor
- Building and Construction
- Land Regulations
- Property Law
- Taxation
- Trade and Logistics
- Industry/Sector Specific Policies
- Other (please specify)

14. What type of impact did they have? [SELECT ALL THAT APPLY]
- Change in time to comply
- Change in cost to businesses
- Change in number of steps
- Change in number of firms registered
- Change in domestic investments
- Change in foreign investment
- Change in employment
- Change in productivity
- Change in exports and/or imports
- Change in commercial judicial efficiency
- Change in institutional efficiency
- Other (please specify)

15. In your view, are there any areas where the World Bank Group should develop more expertise or capacity to respond to client demand? [SELECT ALL THAT APPLY]
- Bankruptcy
- Debt Resolution and Insolvency
- Commercial and Company Laws (for example, Accounting and Auditing, Business Licensing/Permits, Business Registration, Inspections, Contract Laws)
- Competition Policy
- Consumer Protection
- Courts and Proceedings
- Environmental Law
- Industry/Sector Specific Laws
- Intellectual Property and other Goods Protection (for example, Privacy Laws, Copyrights/Patents/Trademarks, Unfair Business Practices Act)

- Investment Policy/Promotion
- Labor (for example,, Employment Law, Labor Protection, Apprenticeships and Training, Labor Safety and Health)
- Building and Construction
- Land Regulations
- Property Law
- Taxation
- Trade and Logistics
- Other (please specify)

16. **If you wish to be included in the random drawing for a Starbucks gift card, please write your full name and email below.**

    Full Name

    Email

Bibliography

Acemoglu, D., and J. D. Angrist. 2001. "Consequences of Employment Protection? The Case of the Americans with Disabilities Act." *Journal of Political Economy* 109: 915–57.

Aghion, P., Yann Algan, Pierre Cahuc, and Andrei Shliefer. 2009. "Regulation and Distrust" NBER Working Paper 14648, National Bureau of Economic Research, Inc., Cambridge, MA.

Alemani, E., C. Klein, I. Koske, C. Vitale, and I. Wanner. 2013. "New Indicators of Competition Law and Policy in 2013 for OECD and Non-OECD countries." OECD Economics Department Working Paper 1104, Paris.

Almeida, R., and P. Carneiro. 2009. "Enforcement of Labor Regulation and Firm Size." *Journal of Comparative Economics* 37: 28–46.

Ambec, S., M. A. Cohen, S. Elgie, and P. Lanoie. 2013. "The Porter Hypothesis at 20: Can Environmental Regulation Enhance Innovation and Competitiveness?" *Review of Environmental Economics and Policy* 7 (1): 2–22.

Arnold, J., G. Nicoletti, and S. Scarpetta. 2008. "Regulation, Allocative Efficiency and Productivity in OECD Countries." OECD Economics Department Working Papers 616, Paris.

Arrunada, B. 2007. "Pitfalls to Avoid when Measuring Instiions: Is Doing Business Damaging Business?" *Journal of Comparative Economics* 35: 729–47.

Arvis, J. F., M. A. Mustra, L. Ojala, B. Sheppard, and D. Saslavsky. 2012. "Connecting to Compete 2012: Trade Logistics in the Global Economy." World Bank, Washington, DC.

Bakvis, P. 2006. "How the World Bank and IMF Use the Doing Business Report to Promote Labor Market Dergulation in Developing Countries." ICTFU/Global Unions, Washington, DC.

Batra, G., D. Kaufmann, and A. H. W. Stone. 2002. "Investment Climate Around the World: Voices of the Firms from the World Business Environment Survey." World Bank, Washington, DC.

Beck, T., A. Demirguc-Kunt, and R. Levine. 2001. "Legal Theories of Financial Development." *Oxford Review of Economic Policy* 17: 483–501.

Bertrand, M., S. Djankov, R. Hanna, and S. Mullainathan. 2007. "Obtaining a Driver's License in India: An Experimental Approach to Studying Corruption." *Quarterly Journal of Economics* 122: 1639–76.

Bertrand, M., and S. Mullainathan. 2001. "Do People Mean What They Say ? Implications for Subjective Survey Data." *American Economic Review: Papers and Proceedings* 91: 67–72.

Botero, J., Djankov S., La Porta R., Lopez-de-Silanes F., and Shleifer A. 2004. "The regulation of labor." *Quarterly Journal of Economics* 119, 1339–1382.

Bray, J. 2005. "International Companies and Post-Conflict Reconstruction." World Bank, Washington, DC.

———. 2010. *Foreign Direct Investment in Conflict-Affected Contexts.* International Alert, London, UK.

Buehn, A., and F. Schneider. 2012. "Corruption and the Shadow Economy: Like Oil and Vinegar, Like Water and Fire." *International Tax and Public Finance* 19: 172–94.

Clarke, G. R. G., and Y. Kim. 2011. "Why Do Microenterprises Remain Informal?" Texas A&M International University, Laredo, TX.

de Andrade, G. H., M. Bruhn, and D. Mckenzie. 2013. "A Helping Hand or the Long Arm of the Law? Experimental Evidence on What Governments Can Do to Formalize Firms." World Bank Policy Research Working Paper 6435, Washington, DC.

de Soto, H. 1988. *The Other Path*. New York: Basic Books.

DFID (Department for International Development). 2011. *The Engine of Development: The Private Sector and Prosperity for Poor People*. London: DFID.

Djankov, S. 2008. "A Response to 'Is Doing Business Damaging Business?'" World Bank, Washington, DC.

Djankov, S., and R. Ramalho. 2009. "Employment Laws in Developing Countries." *Journal of Comparative Economics* 37 (1): 3–13.

Dreher, A., and F. Schneider. 2010. "Corruption and the Shadow Economy: An Empirical Analysis." *Public Choice* 144: 215–38.

Feintuck, M. 2010. "Regulatory Rationales Beyond the Economic: In Search of the Public Interest." In *The Oxford Handbook of Regulation*, eds. R. Baldwin, M. Cave, and M. Lodge. Oxford: Oxford University Press.

Filmer, D., and L. Fox. 2014. "Youth Employment in Sub-Saharan Africa." World Bank, Washington, DC.

Fischer, P. 2006. *Rent-Seeking, Institutions and Reforms in Africa: Theory and Empirical. Evidence for Tanzania*. New York: Springer.

Government of Georgia. 2003. Economic Development and Poverty Reduction Program.

Government of Kenya. 2008. Kenya Vision 2030. Online at http://www.vision2030.go.ke/.

———. 2011. Regulatory Reform Strategy June 2011-June 2014. Available at http://www.vision2030.go.ke/.

Government of Rwanda. 2000. RwandaVision 2020. Available at http://www.minecofin.gov.rw/fileadmin /General/Vision_2020/Vision-2020.pdf.

Government of the United Kingdom. 2014. *Measuring national well-being*. Available at: http://www.ons.gov. uk/ons/guide-method/user-guidance/well-being/ index.html.

Government of Yemen. 2000. Yemen's Strategic Vision 2025.

Hallward-Driemeier, M. 2009. "Who Survives? The Impact of Corruption, Competition, and Property Rights Across Firms." World Bank Policy Research Working Paper 5084, Washington, DC.

Hausman, R., D. Rodrik, and A. Velasco. 2006. "Growth Diagnostics." In *The Washington Consensus Reconsidered: Towards a New Global Governance*, eds. N. Sierra and J. E. Stiglitz, 324–354. New York, Oxford: Oxford University Press.

Herrendorf, B., and A. Teixeira. 2011. "Barriers to Entry and Development." *International Economic Review* 52: 573–602.

Holton, R. J. 1992. *Economy and Society*. London: Routledge.

IEG (Independent Evaluation Group). 2006. *Improving Investment Climates: An Evaluation of World Bank Group Assistance*. Washington, DC: World Bank.

———. 2008. *Doing Business: An Independent Evaluation*. Washington, DC: World Bank.

———. 2011. *Cambodia: World Bank Country-Level Engagement on Governance and Anticorruption*. Washington, DC: World Bank.

———. 2012. *Implementation Completion Report Review (ICRR)—Mali: Poverty Reduction Support Credit3*. Washington, DC: World Bank.

———. 2013a. *Private Sector Growth And Social Protection DPG*. Implementation Completion and Results Report Review. Washington, DC: World Bank.

———. 2013b. *Independent Panel Review of the Doing Business Report*. Washington, DC: World Bank.

———. 2013c. *World Bank Group Assistance to Low-Income Fragile and Conflict-Affected States*. Washington, DC: World Bank.

Jacobs, Cordova and Associates. 2012. *Kenya 3 Update Report*. Washington, DC: Jacobs, Cordova and Associates.

Kaplan, D. S., and V. Pathania. 2010. "What Influences Firms' Perceptions?" *Journal of Comparative Economics* 38: 419–31.

Kaufmann, D., A. Kraay, and M. Mastruzzi. 2010. "The Worldwide Governance Indicators: Methodology and Analytical Issues." World Bank Policy Research Working Paper 5430, Washington DC.

Knack, S. 2006. "Measuring Corruption: A Critique of Indicators in Eastern Europe and Central Asia." *Journal of Public Policy* 27: 255–91.

KPMG. 2013. *Risky Business: Promoting Private Sector Development in Post-Conflict States: Lessons from the Africa Enterprise Challenge Fund*. Development in Practice: International Development Advisory Services Impact Paper 12. Amstelveen: KPMG.

La Porta, R., Lopez-de-Silanes F., and Shleifer A. 2008. "The economic consequences of legal origins." *Journal of Economic Literature* 46, 285.

La Porta R., F. Lopez-de-Silanes, A. Shleifer, and R. W. Vishny. 1997. "Legal Determinants of External Finance." *Journal of Finance* 52: 1131–50.

———. 1998. "Law and Finance." *Journal of Political Economy* 106: 1113–55.

Lederman, D., M. Olarreaga, and L. Payton. 2010. "Export Promotion Agencies: Do They Work?" *Journal of Development Economics* 91: 257–65.

Levi-Faur, D. (ed.) 2012. *The Oxford Handbook of Governance*. Oxford and New York: Oxford University Press.

Levine, R. 1997a. "Financial Development and Economic Growth: Views and Agenda." *Journal of Economic Literature* 35: 688–726.

———. 1997b. "The Legal Environment, Banks, and Long-Run Growth." *Journal of Money, Credit and Banking* 30: 596–613.

———. 1999. "Law, Finance and Economic Growth." *Journal of Financial Intermediation* 8: 8–35.

Lin J. Y., and C. Monga. 2010. "Growth Identification and Facilitation." World Bank Policy Reasearch Working Paper 5313, Washington, DC.

McKenzie, D. 2009. "Impact Assessments in Finance and Private Sector Development: What Have We Learned and What Should We Learn?" *World Bank Research Observer* 25: 209–33.

Miller, T., A. B. Kim, and K. R. Holmes. 2014. *2014 Index of Economic Freedom*. Washington, DC: The Heritage Foundation.

Nicoletti, G., and S. Scarpetta. 2003. "Regulation, Productivity and Growth: OECD Evidence." *Economic Policy* 18: 9–51.

Nicoletti, G., S. Scarpetta, and O. Boylaud. 2000. "Summary Indicators of Product Market Regulation and an Extension to Employment Protection Legislation." OECD Economics Department Working Paper 266, Paris.

OECD (Organisation for Economic Co-Operation and Development). 2011. *Better Life Initiative*. Paris: OECD. Available at http://www.oecd.org/statistics/betterlifeinitiativemeasuringwell-beingandprogress.htm.

Parker, J. C. 2008. "A Synthesis of Practical Lessons from Value Chain Projects in Conflict Affected Environments." Agency for International Development Working Paper, Washington, DC.

Pawson R., and N. Tilley. 1997. *Realistic Evaluation*. London: Sage.

Poverty Reduction and Equity Group and OPCFC. 2011. *Approaches to Employment Generation in Fragile and Conflict-Affected Countries*. Washington, DC: World Bank Group.

Pritchett, L., M. Woolcock, and M. Andrews. 2010. "Capability Traps? The Mechanisms of Persistent Implementation Failure." Center for Global Development Working Paper 234, Washington, DC.

Razafindrakoto, M., and F. Roubaud. 2010. "Are International Databases on Corruption Reliable? A Comparison of Expert Opinion Surveys and Household Surveys in Sub-Saharan Africa." *World Development* 38: 1057–69.

Recanatini, F., S. Wallsten, and L. C. Xu. 2000. "Surveying Surveys and Questioning Questions: Learning from World Bank Experience." World Bank Policy Research Working Paper 2307, Washington, DC.

Rodrik, D. 2004. *A Practical Approach to Formulating Growth Strategies*. Cambridge, MA: Harvard University Press.

———. 2008. "Normalizing Industrial Policy." World Bank Growth Commission Working Papers Series 5, Washington, DC.

Sader, F. 2003. "Do 'One-Stop' Shops Work?" World Bank FIAS Paper, Washington, DC.

Schwab, K. 2013. *The Global Competitiveness Report, 2013-14.* Geneva: World Economic Forum.

Schwartz, J., S. Hahn, I. Bannon. 2004. "The Private Sector's Role in the Provision of Infrastructure in Post-Conflict Countries: Patterns and Policy Options." World Bank Working Paper, Washington, DC.

Seib, G. 2013. "In Crisis, Opportunity for Obama." *Wall Street Journal.*

Stiglitz, J.E. and N. Serra (eds.). 2006. *The Washington Consensus Reconsidered: Towards a New Global Governance.* Oxford: Oxford University Press.

Transparency International. 2003. *Transparency International Corruption Perceptions Index 2003.* Berlin: Transparency International.

Wolfl, A., I. Wanner, O. Rohn, and G. Nicoletti. 2010. "Product Market Regulation: Extending the Analysis beyond OECD Countries." OECD Economics Department Working Paper 799, Paris.

World Bank. 2003a. *Country Assistance Strategy for the Kingdom of Nepal for FY03–07.* Washington, DC: World Bank.

———. 2003b. *Productivity and Investment Climate Survey Implementation Manual.* Washington, DC: World Bank.

———. 2005a. *Country Assistance Strategy for the Kingdom of Cambodia for FY05–08.* Washington, DC: World Bank.

———. 2005b. *Country Partenrship Strategy for Georgia for FY06–09.* Washington, DC: World Bank.

———. 2005c. *World Development Report.* Washington, DC: World Bank.

———. 2006. *Country Assistance Strategyfor the Hashemite Kingdom of Jordan for FY06–09.* Washington, DC: World Bank.

———. 2007a. *Country Assistance Strategy for the Socialist Republic of Vietnam for FY07–11.* Washington, DC: World Bank.

———. 2007b. *Investment Climate Analysis.* Washington, DC: World Bank.

———. 2007c. *Vietnam Development Results.* Washington, DC: World Bank.

———. 2008. *Country Assistance Strategy for Rwanda for FY09–12.* Washington, DC: World Bank.

———. 2009a. *Country Assistance Strategy for the Republic of Philippines FY10–12.* Washington, DC: World Bank.

———. 2009b. *Doing Business 2010: Reforming Through Difficult Times.* Washington, DC: World Bank.

———. 2009c. *Interim Strategy Note for the Guinea Bissau for FY09–10.* Washington, DC: World Bank.

———. 2010a. *Country policy and institutional assessments.* Washington, DC: World Bank.

———. 2010b. "Project Completion Report for the Sudan Administrative Barriers Reform Program." World Bank, Washington, DC.

———. 2011a. *Environment Sector Strategy Strategy for FY12–15.* Washington, DC: World Bank.

———. 2011b. *Fostering Women's Economic Empowerment Through Special Economic Zones: Comparative Analysis of Eight Countries and Implications for Government, Zone Authorities and Businesses.* Washington, DC: World Bank.

———. 2011c. *Managing for Impact. FIAS Strategy for FY12–16.* Washington, DC: World Bank.

———. 2012a. *Agriculture and Rural Development Strategy for FY12–15.* Washington, DC: World Bank.

———. 2012b. *Country Assistance Strategy for the Hashemite Kingdom of Jordan for FY12–15.* Washington, DC: World Bank.

———. 2012c. *Enterprise Surveys: Indicator Descriptions.* Washington, DC: World Bank.

———. 2012d. *ICT for Greater Development Impact: World Bank Group Strategy for Information and*

Communication Technology 2012-2015. Washington, DC: World Bank.

———. 2012e. *Infrastructure Strategy for FY12–15*. Washington, DC: World Bank.

———. 2012f. *Toward a Green, Clean, and Resilient World for All: A World Bank Group Environment Strategy 2012–2022*. Washington, DC: World Bank.

———. 2013a. *Energy Strategy*. Washington, DC: World Bank.

———. 2013b. Kyrgyz Republic, Agribusiness and Marketing Project. Implementation Completion and Results Report. http://www-wds.worldbank.org/external/default/WDSContentServer/WDSP/IB/2013/07/23/000333037_20130723114701/Rendered/PDF/ICR23940ICR0Ky000PUBLIC00Box377382B.pdf.

———. 2013c. *PSD Policy Notes: Enhancing Private Sector Competitiveness in Rwanda. Increasing Private Investment and Competitiveness*. Washington, DC: World Bank.

———. 2013d. *A Stronger, Connected Solutions World Bank Group*. Washington, DC: World Bank.

———. 2013e. *Toward a Sustainable Energy Future for All: Directions for the World Bank Group's Energy Sector*. Washington, DC: World Bank.

———. 2014a. *Enhancing Private Sector Competitiveness in Rwanda. Increasing Private Investment in Rwanda: Options for R eforms with Greater Impact*. Washington, DC: World Bank.

———. 2014b. *Reports on the Observance of Standards and Codes*. Washington, DC: World Bank.

WEF (World Economic Forum). 2013. *Global Competitiveness Report 2013-1014*. New York: WEF.

Zoellick, R. 2008. "Fragile States: Securing Development. Survival." *Global Politics and Strategy* 50 (6).

www.ingramcontent.com/pod-product-compliance
Lightning Source LLC
Chambersburg PA
CBHW080849300326
41935CB00040B/1606